Row - Peterson Arithmetic

BOOK FOUR

By

HARRY GROVE WHEAT

GERALDINE KAUFFMAN

HARL R. DOUGLASS

Illustrated by Mary Royt

ROW, PETERSON AND COMPANY

EVANSTON, ILLINOIS   WHITE PLAINS, NEW YORK

CONTENTS

1. Starting a New Grade 4
2. Easy Multiplications and Divisions . 20
3. Working with Tens 42
4. Our Money 60
5. Carrying 72
6. Reading and Solving Problems . . 96
7. New Multiplications and Divisions . . 108
8. Measures 124
9. The Eights and Nines 138
10. Solving Problems 154

Copyright, 1952, by Row, Peterson and Company
International and Imperial Copyright secured. All rights reserved for all countries, including the right of translation. Printed in the U.S.A. 3962

11. The Uneven Divisions	.	.	.	168
12. Carrying in Division	.	.	.	178
13. Working with Hundreds	.	.	.	192
14. More about Carrying	.	.	.	208
15. Carrying Back	.	.	.	226
16. Working with Thousands	.	.	.	244
17. Multiplying by Tens	.	.	.	268
18. More about Measures	.	.	.	280
19. Two-Step Problems	.	.	.	292
20. Getting Ready for Next Year	.	.	.	306
Index	.	.	.	317

Chapter 1
Starting a New Grade

The School Picnic

Every year soon after school starts, the pupils of Pine School have a picnic in the country. They go on Saturday and spend all day in the woods. They play games, wade in the creek, and gather nuts. Of course, eating the lunch is a part of the fun.

It takes a lot of planning to get ready for the picnic. Here are some of the questions the pupils must answer to make their plans:

How many children from each room are going?

How many children in all will go?

How many busses will be needed to take them to the country?

What time must they tell the bus driver to be ready to pick them up?

To answer the last question, they must decide what time they want to get to the picnic grounds. Then they must find out how far it is to the woods and how long it will take them to go that far.

They will need to decide what they want to eat. Then they must find out how much of each thing to buy and what it will cost. They will need to decide how much milk they should take and find out how much it will cost.

How many sandwiches should they take? How much bread will they need to make the sandwiches?

How much will everything cost? How much will each pupil's share be?

Will the pupils use arithmetic to make their plans?

Do *you* need arithmetic?

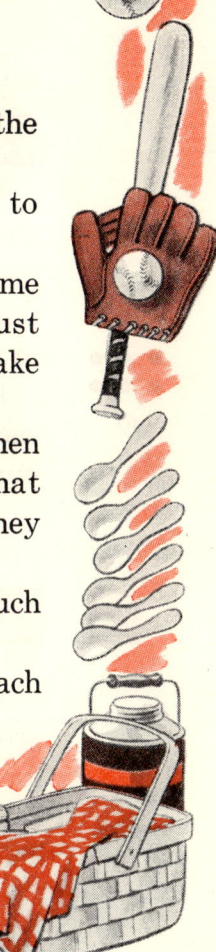

Our Number System

The arithmetic we learn in school is a way to think about the **numbers** of things. To help us think this way about the numbers of things, we have and use number **names** and number **figures**.

Groups to Nine

We think of each number from one to nine as a **single** group, and we use a **single** name and a **single** figure to tell how many are in each group. We call them **one-place** numbers because each number is written with **one figure**.

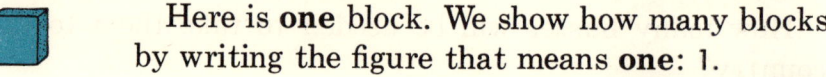
Here is **one** block. We show how many blocks by writing the figure that means **one**: 1.

Here are **five** blocks. We think of the five blocks as one group, and we use a **single** word (five) and a **single** figure (5) to tell how many blocks are in the group. Five is a one-place number.

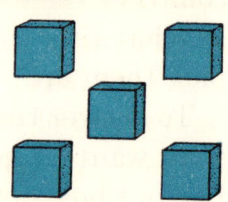

six
6

Draw dots to show each number from one to nine. Under each picture write the word and the figure that tell the number you have shown.

Ten—A Special Group

10

We also think of ten as a single group, and we give the group a single name—**ten**. But we have no single figure for ten. To write ten, we use two figures, 1 and 0: 10. We write 1 in ten's place and 0 in one's place to put and hold the 1 in ten's place.

Draw a group of ten dots. Now write the figures for ten.

The Teen Numbers

Eleven, twelve, thirteen, fourteen, fifteen, sixteen, seventeen, eighteen, and nineteen are called **teen** numbers. Do you know why?

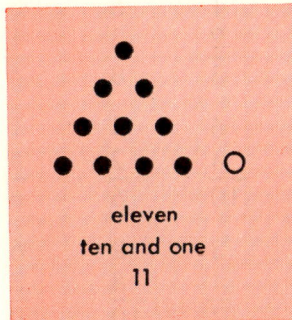
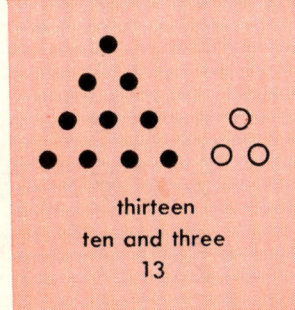
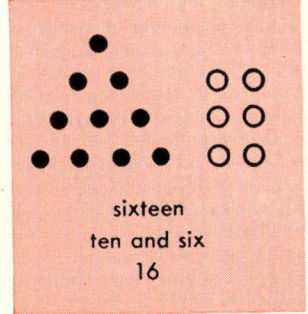

Each teen number is one ten and so many more. We think of **eleven** as 1 group of ten and 1. We think of **twelve** as a group of ten and two.

Draw a dot picture of each teen number.

For each teen number we have and use a **double** name. **Thirteen** may not sound like a double name, but it really is. It means "three and ten," or "ten and three." So we think of thirteen as two groups—ten and three. To write our idea of thirteen, we use two figures, 1 and 3. We write 1 in ten's place and 3 in one's place: 13. Thirteen and all other teen numbers are **two-place** numbers.

We think of a teen number not as a single group but as two groups—a ten and so many more. We give each teen number a double name, and we use two figures to write it.

Under each picture of the teen numbers that you drew, write the word and the figures that tell the number.

What do you think when you hear "fourteen"?
What do you think when you see 17?

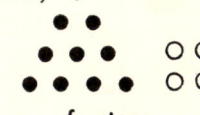

The Eighty-one Additions [Self-test]

There are 81 additions. Study each addition.
Then cover the answers. Say the answers as quickly as you can, but do not guess.

2	1	5	4	2	2	1	5	3
1	4	2	3	2	3	2	3	1
3	5	7	7	4	5	3	8	4

1	2	3	6	2	1	6	4	1
3	4	2	1	5	1	4	2	5
4	6	5	7	7	2	10	6	6

2	3	4	2	1	9	3	2	6
6	3	1	7	6	1	4	8	3
8	6	5	9	7	10	7	10	9

1	6	3	4	5	8	5	7	3
7	2	5	4	1	2	4	1	6
8	8	8	8	6	10	9	8	9

3	1	5	7	4	1	7	4	8
7	8	5	2	5	9	3	6	1
10	9	10	9	9	10	10	10	9

8	6	8	7	9	8	6	8	4
6	9	8	4	7	3	7	4	9
14	15	16	11	16	11	13	12	13

9	7	9	8	6	6	5	9	6
3	6	9	5	6	8	9	2	5
12	13	18	13	12	14	14	11	11

4	8	7	5	5	8	2	9	5
8	9	5	8	7	7	9	5	6
12	17	12	13	12	15	11	14	11

7	3	9	4	7	7	3	9	9
7	8	6	7	9	8	9	8	4
14	11	15	11	16	15	12	17	13

Follow the leader

8

Finding the Answer

Jack did not know the answer to $\begin{smallmatrix}7\\6\end{smallmatrix}$. He did not guess. He used dots to find the answer.

He thought:
 "Seven and three are ten.
 Three from six is three.
 Ten and three are thirteen.
 So seven and six are thirteen."

$$\begin{array}{r}7\\6\\\hline 13\end{array}$$

Then he said over and over, "Seven and six are thirteen."

Jane said:
 "I can think the answer without dots.
 Eight and two are ten.
 Two from seven is five.
 Ten and five are fifteen.
 So eight and seven are fifteen."

$$\begin{array}{r}8\\7\\\hline 15\end{array}$$

Say the answers. If you do not know an answer, do not guess. Find the answer. Then say that addition over and over.

7	5	9	9	7	6	4	9	6
4	7	6	2	6	8	7	3	6
9	8	4	6	8	9	8	7	8
9	6	8	9	8	7	3	7	5
6	4	8	6	8	3	8	5	7
7	9	4	5	9	8	7	8	5
5	2	7	9	5	7	3	9	9
9	9	9	5	6	8	9	4	8

The Eighty-one Subtractions [Self-test]

There are 81 subtractions. Study each subtraction.
Then cover the answers. Say the answers as quickly as you can, but do not guess.

Climb the ladder

11 − 6
9 − 5
15 − 7
13 − 8
8 − 5
16 − 7
13 − 9

2 −1 = 1	8 −4 = 4	7 −5 = 2	4 −3 = 1	10 −9 = 1	7 −1 = 6	9 −6 = 3	10 −5 = 5	3 −2 = 1
5 −3 = 2	3 −1 = 2	10 −2 = 8	9 −4 = 5	6 −5 = 1	10 −8 = 2	8 −1 = 7	4 −2 = 2	10 −3 = 7
7 −4 = 3	10 −4 = 6	4 −1 = 3	9 −2 = 7	6 −3 = 3	5 −2 = 3	8 −5 = 3	9 −1 = 8	7 −6 = 1
8 −2 = 6	7 −3 = 4	6 −4 = 2	5 −1 = 4	6 −2 = 4	10 −6 = 4	8 −7 = 1	9 −3 = 6	10 −9 = 1
5 −4 = 1	9 −5 = 4	8 −6 = 2	7 −2 = 5	6 −1 = 5	8 −3 = 5	9 −7 = 2	9 −8 = 1	10 −7 = 3
14 −8 = 6	15 −6 = 9	16 −8 = 8	11 −7 = 4	16 −9 = 7	13 −6 = 7	11 −8 = 3	14 −5 = 9	13 −4 = 9
12 −9 = 3	13 −7 = 6	18 −9 = 9	13 −8 = 5	12 −6 = 6	17 −8 = 9	12 −8 = 4	11 −9 = 2	11 −6 = 5
12 −4 = 8	14 −6 = 8	12 −7 = 5	11 −2 = 9	12 −5 = 7	15 −8 = 7	13 −5 = 8	14 −9 = 5	11 −5 = 6
14 −7 = 7	11 −3 = 8	15 −9 = 6	11 −4 = 7	13 −9 = 4	15 −7 = 8	12 −3 = 9	17 −9 = 8	16 −7 = 9

Finding the Answer

Joe does not know the answer to $\frac{15}{-8}$. He does not guess. He uses dots to find the answer.

He thinks:

"Eight from ten is two.
Two and five are seven.
Eight from fifteen is seven."

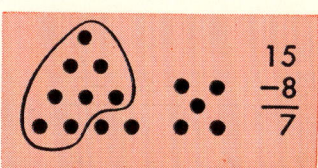

Alice thinks the answer without dots.
She thinks:

"Seven from ten is three.
Three and three are six.
Seven from thirteen is six."

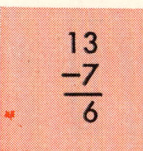

Think the answers. Use the dots if you need them.

 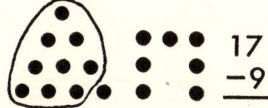 

Say the answers. If you do not know an answer, do not guess. Find the answer. Then say that subtraction over and over.

14	12	15	11	12	14	15	16	14
−8	−9	−9	−2	−6	−7	−6	−8	−5

13	16	13	11	12	11	15	17	14
−7	−9	−6	−7	−5	−4	−7	−9	−9

11	13	18	12	14	13	12	16	11
−3	−4	−9	−4	−6	−9	−3	−7	−8

13	13	15	17	12	11	12	11	11
−8	−5	−8	−8	−7	−6	−8	−5	−9

Ways to Help Yourself

It will help you remember the additions and subtractions if you practice saying together those that use the same numbers.

4 +3	3 +4	7 −4	7 −3	4 +5	5 +4	9 −5	9 −4	4 +2	2 +4	6 −4	6 −2
2 +6	6 +2	8 −2	8 −6	8 +2	2 +8	10 −2	10 −8	7 +3	3 +7	10 −3	10 −7
3 +2	2 +3	5 −2	5 −3	2 +5	5 +2	7 −2	7 −5	5 +3	3 +5	8 −5	8 −3
3 +6	6 +3	9 −6	9 −3	2 +7	7 +2	9 −7	9 −2	4 +6	6 +4	10 −6	10 −4
8 +3	3 +8	11 −8	11 −3	7 +6	6 +7	13 −7	13 −6	7 +4	4 +7	11 −7	11 −4
8 +4	4 +8	12 −8	12 −4	8 +7	7 +8	15 −8	15 −7	7 +5	5 +7	12 −7	12 −5
8 +5	5 +8	13 −8	13 −5	6 +8	8 +6	14 −8	14 −6	9 +2	2 +9	11 −9	11 −2
9 +4	4 +9	13 −9	13 −4	9 +3	3 +9	12 −9	12 −3	6 +5	5 +6	11 −5	11 −6
9 +5	5 +9	14 −9	14 −5	9 +6	6 +9	15 −9	15 −6	7 +9	9 +7	16 −7	16 −9
6 +6	12 −6	7 +7	14 −7	5 +5	10 −5	4 +4	8 −4	8 +8	16 −8	9 +9	18 −9

Number Cards

Make a number card for each addition that seems hard for you to remember. On one side write the addition question. On the other side make a dot picture of the addition question.

Look at the front of the card and say the answer. If you do not know the answer, do not guess. Look at the back of the card and find the answer. Look at the front of the card again and say the addition over and over.

Make a number card for each subtraction that seems hard for you to remember. On one side of the card write the subtraction question. On the other side make a dot picture of the subtraction.

Look at the front of the card and say the answer. If you do not know the answer, do not guess. Look at the back of the card and find the answer. Look at the front of the card again and say the subtraction over and over.

Study each addition and subtraction that you do not know. Practice until you do not need to use the cards.

Say the answers:

9	4	7	8	5	15	11	17	14	15	16	18
+8	+7	+8	+8	+8	−9	−4	−9	−8	−6	−7	−9

Addition Problems

When we add, we think numbers together.

Read each problem carefully. Then tell why we must add to answer the question that is asked. Does the question help us to see that we must add to answer it?

1. Mary picked 8 roses. Then she picked 9 more roses. How many roses did she pick **in all**?

2. Jane made 5 sandwiches, and Helen made 6 sandwiches. How many sandwiches did **both** girls make?

3. Jim paid 9¢ for a top and 5¢ for a rubber ball. How much did he spend for both?

4. Jack had 6 brown rabbits. Uncle Joe gave him 6 white rabbits. How many rabbits did Jack have **then**?

5. Dick bought two bags of marbles. There were 8 marbles in one bag and 6 in the other. How many marbles were in the **two bags**?

6. Jane bought a spool of thread for 8¢ and a package of pins for 5¢. What was the **total** cost of the things she bought?

7. Joe sold 4 boxes of strawberries to Mrs. Jones and 8 boxes to Mrs. West. How many boxes of strawberries did he sell **altogether**?

8. Ann had 9 books. She got 3 new books for her birthday. Then how many books did she have?

9. Jim saw 7 airplanes flying in a group. Then he saw 5 more airplanes in another group. How many airplanes did he see in both groups?

Now start over. Read each problem again. Then find the answer to the question in the problem.

Subtraction Problems

Read each problem carefully. What does the question ask? Now tell why we subtract to answer the question. Does the question help us to see that we must subtract to answer it?

1. Betty has 12 cookies. If she eats 3 of them, how many will she have **left**?

2. Jack had 12 rabbits. He sold 4 of them. Then how many did he have?

3. Ten cars were needed to take the children on a picnic. When Jack got to the meeting place, only 3 cars were there. How many cars had already gone?

4. Joe wants to have the tail of his kite 10 feet long. He has made 6 feet of it. How many more feet of tail does he need to make for his kite?

5. Jack jumped 5 feet. Jerry jumped 4 feet. How much farther did Jack jump?

golf clubs

6. Jack's father had 9 golf clubs in the bag. There are only 5 clubs there now. How many clubs are missing?

7. Mary is 9 years old, and her brother is 17. What is the **difference** in their ages?

8. Dick had 15 rabbits. One morning he found the door of the cage open, and only 7 rabbits were in the cage. How many rabbits were **gone**?

9. Jane wants to put 9 buttons on her dress. She has 4 buttons of the kind and size that she wants. How many more buttons of that kind and size does she need?

Now find the answer to each question.

Adding Columns

Jim had a watermelon stand by the side of the road. He kept a record of the number of melons that he sold. On Saturday Jim sold 4 watermelons to some people who were going on a picnic, 3 to Mr. Bell, 2 to the driver of a truck, and 3 to Mrs. James. How many watermelons did Jim sell that day?

```
 4
 3
 2
 3
---
12
```

First, we write the numbers in a column. Then we begin at the top and add down. We think, "4 and 3 are 7, and 2 are 9, and 3 are 12."
Jim sold 12 watermelons that day.

Copy and add:

	(a)	(b)	(c)	(d)	(e)	(f)	(g)	(h)	(i)	(j)
1.	6	5	2	2	3	1	3	4	2	5
	2	3	3	7	5	6	4	5	4	3
	5	6	6	4	8	7	8	7	9	9
2.	3	1	1	2	3	4	5	6	2	3
	3	2	3	2	2	1	1	2	4	4
	3	5	4	2	2	4	2	1	1	1
	6	9	4	8	5	3	2	8	9	8
3.	2	2	2	3	1	6	2	3	2	5
	1	3	1	1	3	1	1	2	4	2
	6	4	2	3	2	2	4	2	3	2
	4	4	7	3	6	5	8	8	7	8
4.	1	4	3	4	3	2	2	4	2	4
	3	2	2	3	4	5	3	3	3	3
	5	2	4	2	2	2	4	2	4	1
	8	6	4	6	9	7	9	5	6	9

Buying Things for School

1. Dick bought a pencil for 2¢, an eraser for 5¢, and a ruler for 9¢. How much did he spend at the store?

2. Jack paid 7¢ for a tablet, 2¢ for a pencil, and 8¢ for a pencil sharpener. How much did he pay for the things that he bought?

3. Jane needs a pen, a card of thumbtacks, and a ruler. They cost 3¢, 4¢, and 9¢. How much money does she need to pay for them?

4. Tom bought a bottle of paste, a pen, and a tablet. Find the total cost of the things that he bought.

5. Alice wants to buy some thumbtacks, an eraser, and a bottle of paste. How much will these things cost?

6. Helen bought an eraser, a card of thumbtacks, and a pencil sharpener. How much should she pay for them?

7. Susan needs a pen, a pencil, and a tablet. How much will these things cost?

Susan has a dime. Has she enough money to pay for them? How much more money does she need?

8. Joe has a nickel and a dime. Can he buy a tablet and a pencil sharpener?

The Scoreboard

Tim and Tom sold programs at the entrance to the ball park. It was late, and the game between the Indians and Braves had already started when they got to their seats.

"What's the score?" Tim asked.

"What inning is it?" Tom wanted to know. "Let's look at the scoreboard and see."

Inning	1	2	3	4	5	6	7	8	9	Runs
Indians		1								
Braves				2						

Can you tell the score? Can you tell the inning? Why can't you?

The scoreboard really looked like this:

Inning	1	2	3	4	5	6	7	8	9	Runs
Indians	0	1	0	0	0					
Braves	0	0	0	2	0					

The figures 1 and 2 tell the score. The Indians have 1 run, and the Braves have 2 runs. Are the zeros needed to help tell the score?

The zeros help to tell the innings that have been played. The zeros do this by filling up spaces, or by **holding places**, when no scores are made.

The zero is a useful figure. Its use is to **hold a place**. Zero is a **place holder**. It means "not any."

18

Ringtoss

In this game each player has four turns. If a ring misses all the pegs, it counts **zero**. The 0 shows that the player had his turn but did not make a score.

Joe has thrown his four rings. Jack wrote each score in a column and 0 when no score was made. Jack wrote the 0 to show that Joe had a turn. He did not need to write 0 to show that Joe made no score. Why?

Then Jack added to find Joe's total score. He thought, "2 and 1 are 3, and 5 are 8." Why did he skip 0?

$$\begin{array}{r} 2 \\ 1 \\ 0 \\ 5 \\ \hline 8 \end{array}$$

Find the total score of each player:

Sue	Bob	Jim	Jerry	Jane	Tom	Betty	Alice
0	4	5	2	1	3	0	5
2	0	3	4	2	2	3	2
0	1	3	3	5	0	5	0
3	2	0	5	4	0	3	5

Chapter 2
Easy Multiplications and Divisions

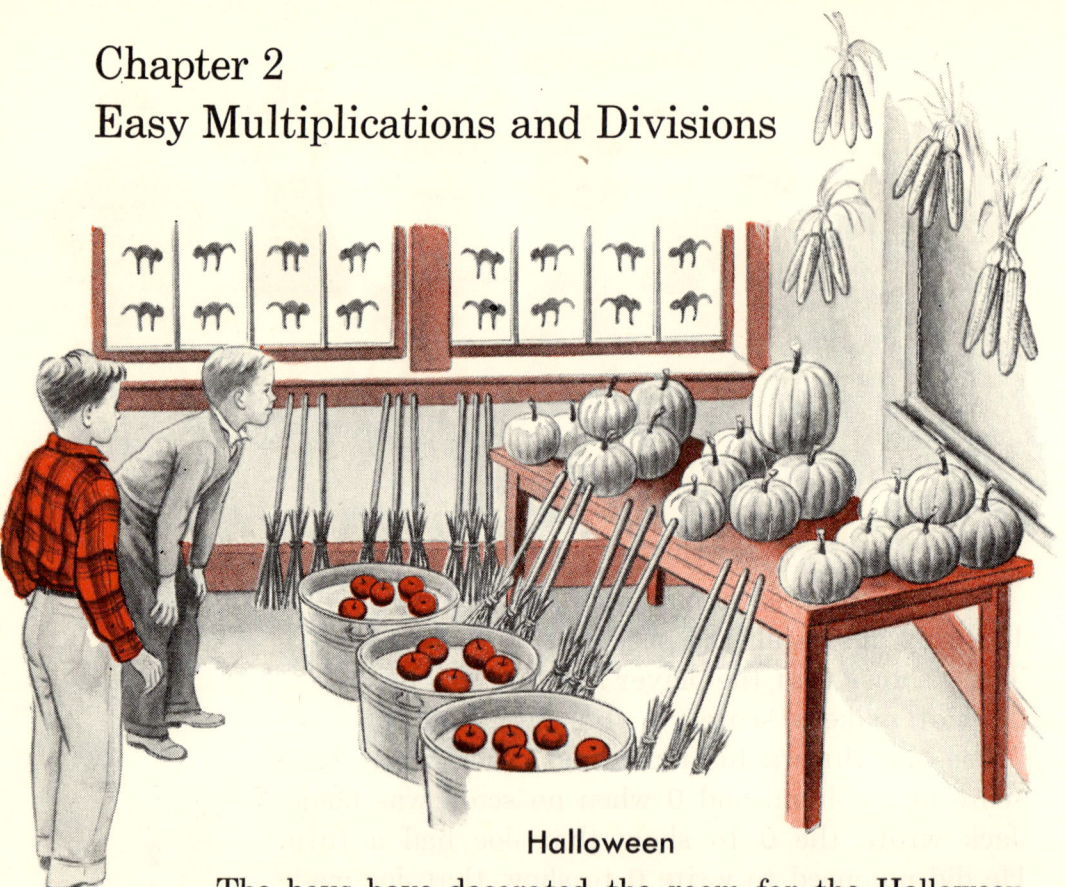

Halloween

The boys have decorated the room for the Halloween party. They want to surprise the girls. They decorated the room with ears of corn, apples, black cats, pumpkins, and brooms to show multiplications.

Jack looked at the ears of corn, and said, "Two fours are eight. Three fours are twelve. Four fours are sixteen."

Look at the brooms and answer these questions:

Three threes are how many? How many are two threes? How many are four threes? five threes? six threes?

Look at the pumpkins. Three sixes are how many? What other multiplications do the pictures show?

Our Number System

Twenty means "two tens." We always think of twenty as two groups of ten. We show twenty by writing 2 in ten's place and 0 in one's place. The 0 keeps the 2 in ten's place.

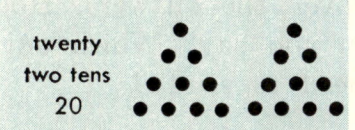
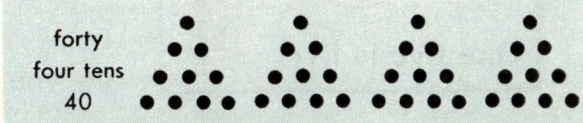

Draw dots to show twenty, fifty, sixty, eighty, ninety. Now write the word and the figures for each number.

Twenty-one is a double name. The name tells how many tens and how many ones. As you know, twenty-one means "two tens and one." So we always think of it as two tens and one, and we always use two figures to write it: 21. We write the 2 in ten's place and the 1 in one's place.

Draw a dot picture to show what each of these number names means: thirty-seven; fifty-two; ninety-nine. Write the figures that show the number in each picture.

Read each sentence saying the right word for each blank:
1. Fifty-three means _five_ tens and _three_ ones.
2. Forty-four means ___ tens and ___ ones.
3. Eighty-two means ___ tens and ___ ones.
4. Seventy means ___ tens.
5. Seventy-eight means ___ tens and ___ ones.

One five is five. $\begin{array}{r}5\\ \times 1\\ \hline 5\end{array}$

The Multiplications [Self-test]

There are 81 multiplications. Last year we learned 65 of them. This year we will learn the rest. Study the multiplications below.

Now cover the answers. How many can you say? Which ones do you need to study?

Pop the balloons

$\begin{array}{r}5\\ \times 8\\ \hline\end{array}$
$\begin{array}{r}4\\ \times 6\\ \hline\end{array}$
$\begin{array}{r}5\\ \times 7\\ \hline\end{array}$
$\begin{array}{r}3\\ \times 9\\ \hline\end{array}$
$\begin{array}{r}9\\ \times 4\\ \hline\end{array}$

1 ×1 1	3 ×2 6	5 ×2 10	7 ×1 7	2 ×1 2	4 ×2 8	6 ×2 12	2 ×8 16	5 ×5 25
5 ×8 40	3 ×3 9	1 ×2 2	3 ×6 18	4 ×3 12	2 ×9 18	6 ×5 30	3 ×1 3	4 ×8 32
3 ×9 27	4 ×1 4	4 ×4 16	5 ×3 15	6 ×1 6	6 ×3 18	1 ×3 3	7 ×2 14	2 ×2 4
5 ×9 45	8 ×5 40	7 ×3 21	1 ×6 6	2 ×4 8	3 ×5 15	4 ×5 20	8 ×4 32	5 ×7 35
2 ×5 10	4 ×6 24	5 ×4 20	1 ×5 5	9 ×2 18	3 ×8 24	7 ×4 28	1 ×9 9	6 ×4 24
4 ×7 28	8 ×2 16	1 ×7 7	9 ×1 9	2 ×6 12	9 ×3 27	8 ×1 8	5 ×6 30	3 ×7 21
1 ×8 8	2 ×3 6	2 ×7 14	3 ×4 12	8 ×3 24	9 ×4 36	4 ×9 36	1 ×4 4	7 ×5 35

Finding the Answer

Jim did not know the answer to $\begin{array}{r}8\\ \times 4\\ \hline\end{array}$. He made a dot picture of **four eights**.

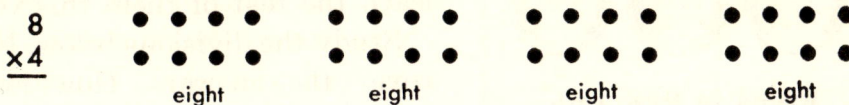

Then he found the answer. He drew lines to mark off groups of ten. He found that 4 eights are 3 tens and 2.

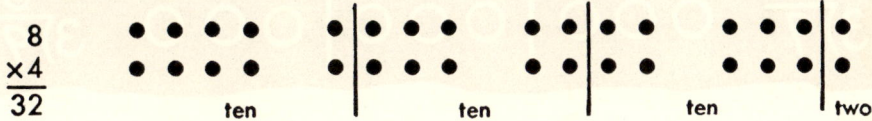

Say the answers. If you do not know an answer, find it. Then say that multiplication over and over.

5 ×5	5 ×8	3 ×6	4 ×8	3 ×9	2 ×8	4 ×4	4 ×3	2 ×9
6 ×3	5 ×9	7 ×2	5 ×3	8 ×5	7 ×3	6 ×5	8 ×4	2 ×5
4 ×6	3 ×5	3 ×8	7 ×4	4 ×5	5 ×4	4 ×7	8 ×2	6 ×4
5 ×7	9 ×3	5 ×6	3 ×7	3 ×4	9 ×4	7 ×5	2 ×6	4 ×9

Make number cards and use them to study the multiplications that you did not know.

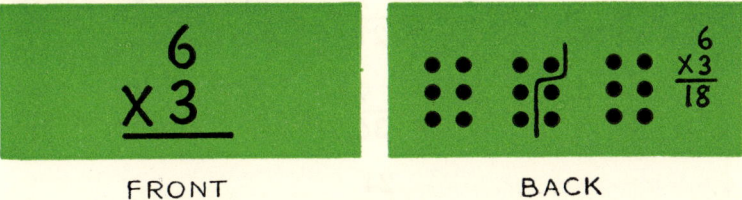

FRONT   BACK

$5\overline{)5}^{\,1}$

Fives in five, one.

The Divisions [Self-test]

There are 81 divisions that go with the 81 multiplications. We have studied 65 of them. We will learn the rest of them this year.

Study the divisions below. Now cover the answers. How many can you say?

$3\overline{)9}$ ooo | ooo | ooo $3\overline{)9}^{\,3}$

Open the locks

$9\overline{)36}$ $4\overline{)28}$ $8\overline{)32}$ $7\overline{)28}$

$2\overline{)4}^{\,2}$	$2\overline{)10}^{\,5}$	$5\overline{)30}^{\,6}$	$3\overline{)9}^{\,3}$	$4\overline{)12}^{\,3}$	$2\overline{)18}^{\,9}$	$2\overline{)2}^{\,1}$	$4\overline{)8}^{\,2}$
$1\overline{)1}^{\,1}$	$4\overline{)20}^{\,5}$	$3\overline{)3}^{\,1}$	$3\overline{)12}^{\,4}$	$5\overline{)10}^{\,2}$	$6\overline{)30}^{\,5}$	$2\overline{)6}^{\,3}$	$3\overline{)6}^{\,2}$
$6\overline{)6}^{\,1}$	$2\overline{)12}^{\,6}$	$4\overline{)4}^{\,1}$	$6\overline{)12}^{\,2}$	$5\overline{)35}^{\,7}$	$3\overline{)15}^{\,5}$	$1\overline{)4}^{\,4}$	$2\overline{)8}^{\,4}$
$5\overline{)5}^{\,1}$	$5\overline{)25}^{\,5}$	$1\overline{)3}^{\,3}$	$8\overline{)16}^{\,2}$	$5\overline{)45}^{\,9}$	$4\overline{)16}^{\,4}$	$9\overline{)9}^{\,1}$	$1\overline{)8}^{\,8}$
$1\overline{)7}^{\,7}$	$7\overline{)14}^{\,2}$	$1\overline{)9}^{\,9}$	$4\overline{)24}^{\,6}$	$3\overline{)18}^{\,6}$	$5\overline{)15}^{\,3}$	$7\overline{)7}^{\,1}$	$1\overline{)6}^{\,6}$
$1\overline{)2}^{\,2}$	$9\overline{)36}^{\,4}$	$8\overline{)8}^{\,1}$	$5\overline{)40}^{\,8}$	$2\overline{)16}^{\,8}$	$6\overline{)18}^{\,3}$	$2\overline{)14}^{\,7}$	$8\overline{)24}^{\,3}$
$7\overline{)35}^{\,5}$	$4\overline{)28}^{\,7}$	$5\overline{)20}^{\,4}$	$3\overline{)21}^{\,7}$	$8\overline{)40}^{\,5}$	$4\overline{)32}^{\,8}$	$7\overline{)21}^{\,3}$	$9\overline{)45}^{\,5}$
$3\overline{)24}^{\,8}$	$6\overline{)24}^{\,4}$	$9\overline{)18}^{\,2}$	$4\overline{)36}^{\,9}$	$3\overline{)27}^{\,9}$	$8\overline{)32}^{\,4}$	$7\overline{)28}^{\,4}$	$9\overline{)27}^{\,3}$

Finding the Answer

Were there any divisions that you did not know? If so, you should learn them **now**. Suppose you did not know 9)36. The figures ask, "How many nines are in thirty-six?" Make a dot picture of 3 tens and 6, or 36.

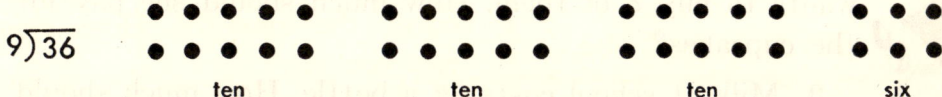

Then draw lines to mark off groups of nine. There are four groups of nine; so there are four nines in thirty-six.

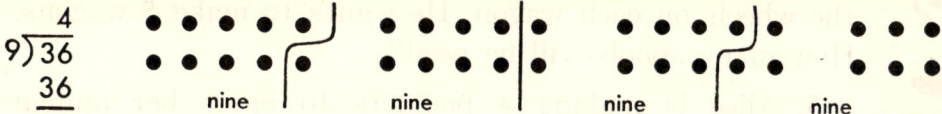

Now say the division over and over so that you will remember it. Make number cards and use them to study the divisions that you did not know.

Say the answers:

5)20 6)24 9)45 8)32 7)28 6)18 4)20 5)30

4)28 5)25 6)30 3)18 3)27 5)35 5)45 8)40

7)21 4)32 7)35 4)36 5)40 3)21 9)27 4)24

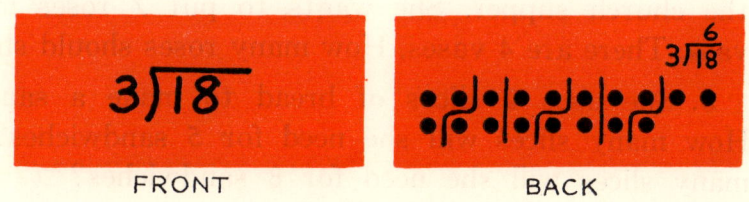

FRONT   BACK

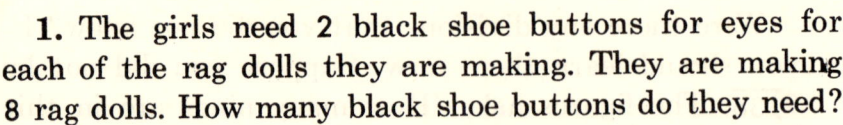

Multiplication Problems

1. The girls need 2 black shoe buttons for eyes for each of the rag dolls they are making. They are making 8 rag dolls. How many black shoe buttons do they need?

2. Cupcakes are 4¢ each at Mr. Bob's store. Mary wants to buy 6 of them. How much should she pay for the cupcakes?

3. Milk at school costs 3¢ a bottle. How much should a pupil pay for milk for a school week of 5 days if he buys a bottle each day?

4. Jack is making toy wagons. He uses 4 spools for the wheels on each wagon. He wants to make 5 wagons. How many spools will he need?

5. Alice is making 4 booklets to paste her animal pictures in. She is cutting out letters to put the word ANIMALS on the cover of each booklet. So she must cut out 7 letters for each booklet. How many letters will she cut out in all?

6. Jane uses 9 eggs to make an angel food cake. How many eggs will she need for 5 angel food cakes? How many eggs will she need for 3 cakes?

7. Bill has 6 letters to mail. He must buy a 3-cent stamp for each letter. How much will the stamps cost?

8. Ann is going to fix the flowers on the tables for the church supper. She wants to put 7 roses in each vase. There are 4 vases. How many roses should she get?

9. Sue uses 2 slices of bread to make a sandwich. How many slices will she need for 5 sandwiches? How many slices will she need for 8 sandwiches?

Division Problems

1. At the bakery doughnuts are marked 3 for 12 cents. How much does one doughnut cost?

doughnuts

2. Henry's garden is long enough to put 7 tomato plants in a row. He has 28 plants. How many rows of tomato plants will there be?

3. Jane got 6 apples for Mary, Sue, and herself. How many apples were there for each girl?

4. Helen has 12 tulip bulbs. She has 4 pots to plant them in. How many bulbs can she put in each pot if she puts the same number in each?

bulbs

5. Five children can sit at Jack's table. He has 10 pieces of paper. How many pieces has he for each child?

6. Ann has 20 silver stars and 4 booklets. She wants to paste the same number of stars on the cover of each booklet. How many stars should she put on each cover?

7. Bill, Jim, and Tom bought a bag of marbles together and divided them equally. There were 27 marbles in the bag. How many marbles should each boy get?

8. Ann picked 21 flowers. She put the same number of flowers in each of 7 vases. How many flowers did she put in each vase?

vase

9. Jim bought a box of pencils for 16 cents. There were 8 pencils in the box. How much did each pencil cost?

10. Betty has 24 cents. She wants to buy oranges that cost 4 cents each. How many oranges can she buy?

11. Tom put a rubber band around each group of 4 pencils. He had 36 pencils. How many rubber bands did he need?

The 2's in Multiplication and Division

Here are the multiplications and divisions for twos. We want to be sure that we know all of them.

$$\begin{array}{r}2\\ \times 1\\ \hline 2\end{array} \quad \begin{array}{r}2\\ \times 5\\ \hline 10\end{array} \quad \begin{array}{r}2\\ \times 4\\ \hline 8\end{array} \quad \begin{array}{r}2\\ \times 6\\ \hline 12\end{array} \quad \begin{array}{r}2\\ \times 3\\ \hline 6\end{array} \quad \begin{array}{r}2\\ \times 9\\ \hline 18\end{array} \quad \begin{array}{r}2\\ \times 2\\ \hline 4\end{array} \quad \begin{array}{r}2\\ \times 8\\ \hline 16\end{array} \quad \begin{array}{r}2\\ \times 7\\ \hline 14\end{array}$$

$$2\overline{)4}\quad 2\overline{)10}\quad 2\overline{)14}\quad 2\overline{)16}\quad 2\overline{)6}\quad 2\overline{)8}\quad 2\overline{)18}\quad 2\overline{)2}\quad 2\overline{)12}$$

Look at the toy soldiers. Then answer each question:

$\begin{array}{r}2\\ \times 6\\ \hline \end{array}$ $2\overline{)12}$ $\begin{array}{r}2\\ \times 5\\ \hline \end{array}$ $2\overline{)10}$

$\begin{array}{r}2\\ \times 4\\ \hline \end{array}$ $2\overline{)8}$ $\begin{array}{r}2\\ \times 3\\ \hline \end{array}$ $2\overline{)6}$

$\begin{array}{r}2\\ \times 7\\ \hline \end{array}$ $2\overline{)14}$ $\begin{array}{r}2\\ \times 2\\ \hline \end{array}$ $2\overline{)4}$

$\begin{array}{r}2\\ \times 9\\ \hline \end{array}$ $2\overline{)18}$ $\begin{array}{r}2\\ \times 8\\ \hline \end{array}$ $2\overline{)16}$

The 3's in Multiplication and Division

Here are the multiplications and divisions for threes.

$$\begin{array}{r}3\\ \times 2\\ \hline 6\end{array} \quad \begin{array}{r}3\\ \times 6\\ \hline 18\end{array} \quad \begin{array}{r}3\\ \times 4\\ \hline 12\end{array} \quad \begin{array}{r}3\\ \times 3\\ \hline 9\end{array} \quad \begin{array}{r}3\\ \times 7\\ \hline 21\end{array} \quad \begin{array}{r}3\\ \times 1\\ \hline 3\end{array} \quad \begin{array}{r}3\\ \times 8\\ \hline 24\end{array} \quad \begin{array}{r}3\\ \times 5\\ \hline 15\end{array} \quad \begin{array}{r}3\\ \times 9\\ \hline 27\end{array}$$

$$3\overline{)18}^{\,6} \quad 3\overline{)6}^{\,2} \quad 3\overline{)15}^{\,5} \quad 3\overline{)21}^{\,7} \quad 3\overline{)9}^{\,3} \quad 3\overline{)27}^{\,9} \quad 3\overline{)12}^{\,4} \quad 3\overline{)3}^{\,1} \quad 3\overline{)24}^{\,8}$$

Look at the pictures. Then say the answers:

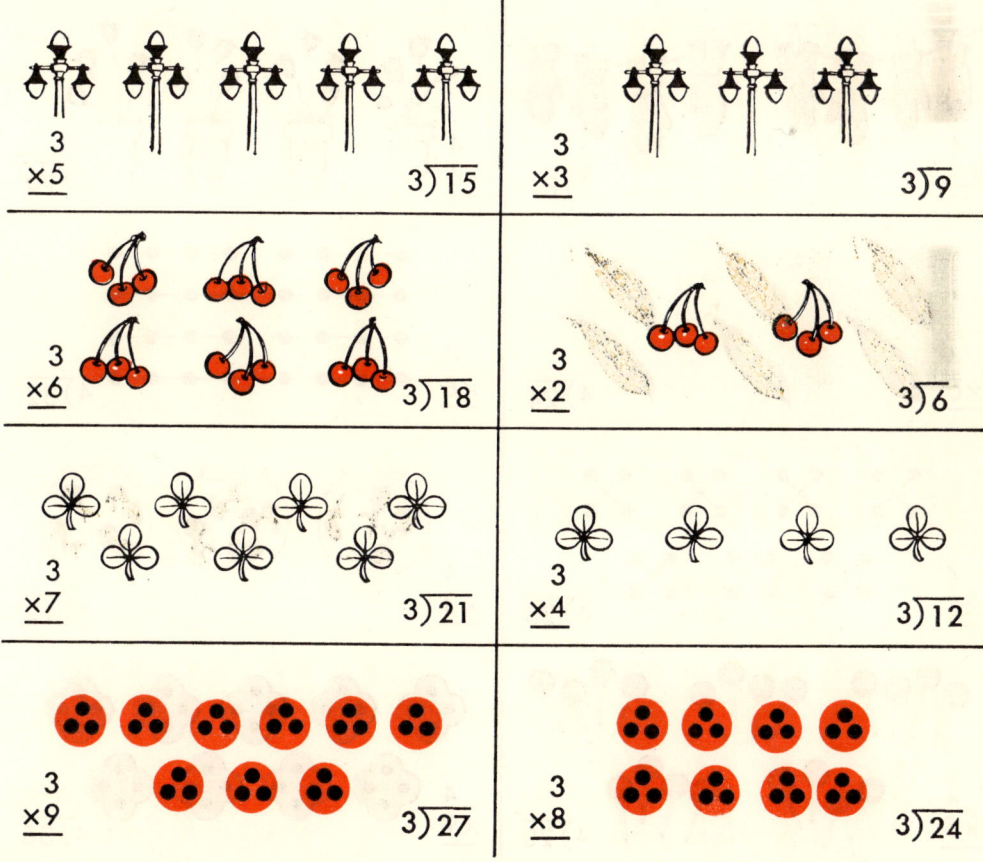

The 4's in Multiplication and Division

Here are the multiplications and divisions for fours.

| $\begin{array}{r}4\\\times 3\\\hline 12\end{array}$ | $\begin{array}{r}4\\\times 5\\\hline 20\end{array}$ | $\begin{array}{r}4\\\times 7\\\hline 28\end{array}$ | $\begin{array}{r}4\\\times 4\\\hline 16\end{array}$ | $\begin{array}{r}4\\\times 2\\\hline 8\end{array}$ | $\begin{array}{r}4\\\times 6\\\hline 24\end{array}$ | $\begin{array}{r}4\\\times 9\\\hline 36\end{array}$ | $\begin{array}{r}4\\\times 1\\\hline 4\end{array}$ | $\begin{array}{r}4\\\times 8\\\hline 32\end{array}$ |

$4\overline{)20}\ 5 \quad 4\overline{)36}\ 9 \quad 4\overline{)4}\ 1 \quad 4\overline{)12}\ 3 \quad 4\overline{)28}\ 7 \quad 4\overline{)8}\ 2 \quad 4\overline{)16}\ 4 \quad 4\overline{)24}\ 6 \quad 4\overline{)32}\ 8$

Look at the pictures. Then say the answers:

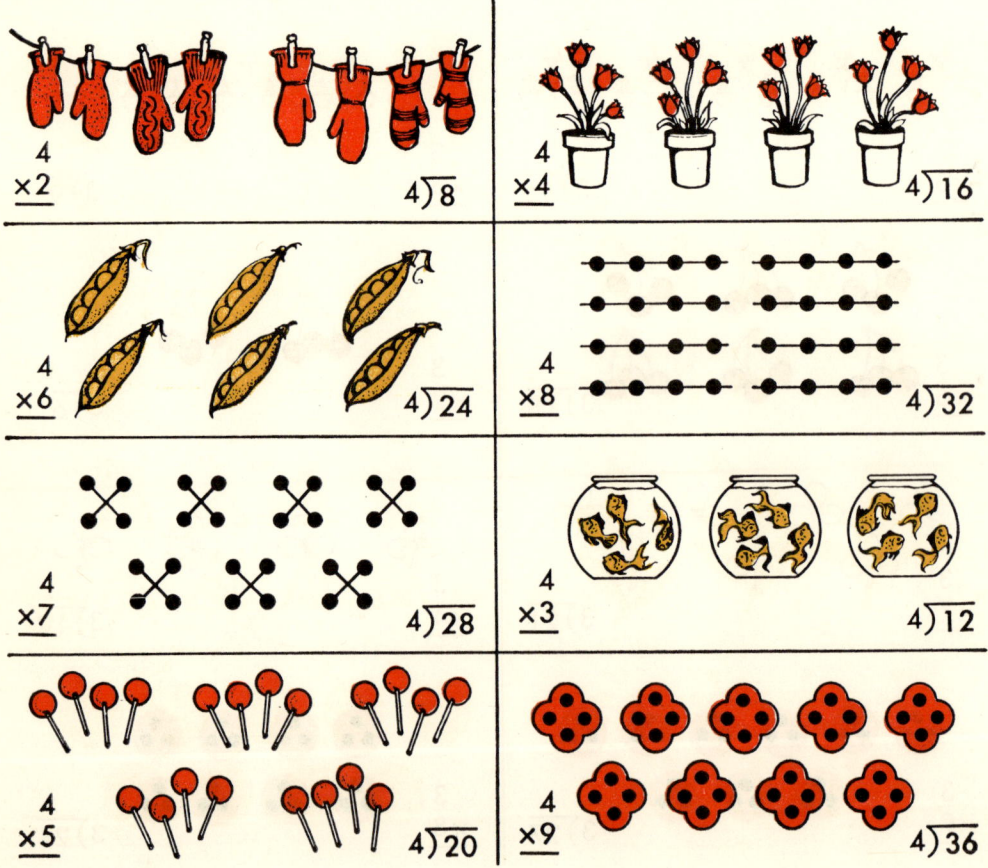

30

The 5's in Multiplication and Division

Here are the multiplications and divisions for fives.

| $\begin{array}{r}5\\ \times 1\\ \hline 5\end{array}$ | $\begin{array}{r}5\\ \times 8\\ \hline 40\end{array}$ | $\begin{array}{r}5\\ \times 6\\ \hline 30\end{array}$ | $\begin{array}{r}5\\ \times 4\\ \hline 20\end{array}$ | $\begin{array}{r}5\\ \times 2\\ \hline 10\end{array}$ | $\begin{array}{r}5\\ \times 5\\ \hline 25\end{array}$ | $\begin{array}{r}5\\ \times 7\\ \hline 35\end{array}$ | $\begin{array}{r}5\\ \times 3\\ \hline 15\end{array}$ | $\begin{array}{r}5\\ \times 9\\ \hline 45\end{array}$ |

$5\overline{)25}=5 \quad 5\overline{)10}=2 \quad 5\overline{)30}=6 \quad 5\overline{)45}=9 \quad 5\overline{)5}=1 \quad 5\overline{)15}=3 \quad 5\overline{)35}=7 \quad 5\overline{)40}=8 \quad 5\overline{)20}=4$

Look at the pictures. Then answer each question:

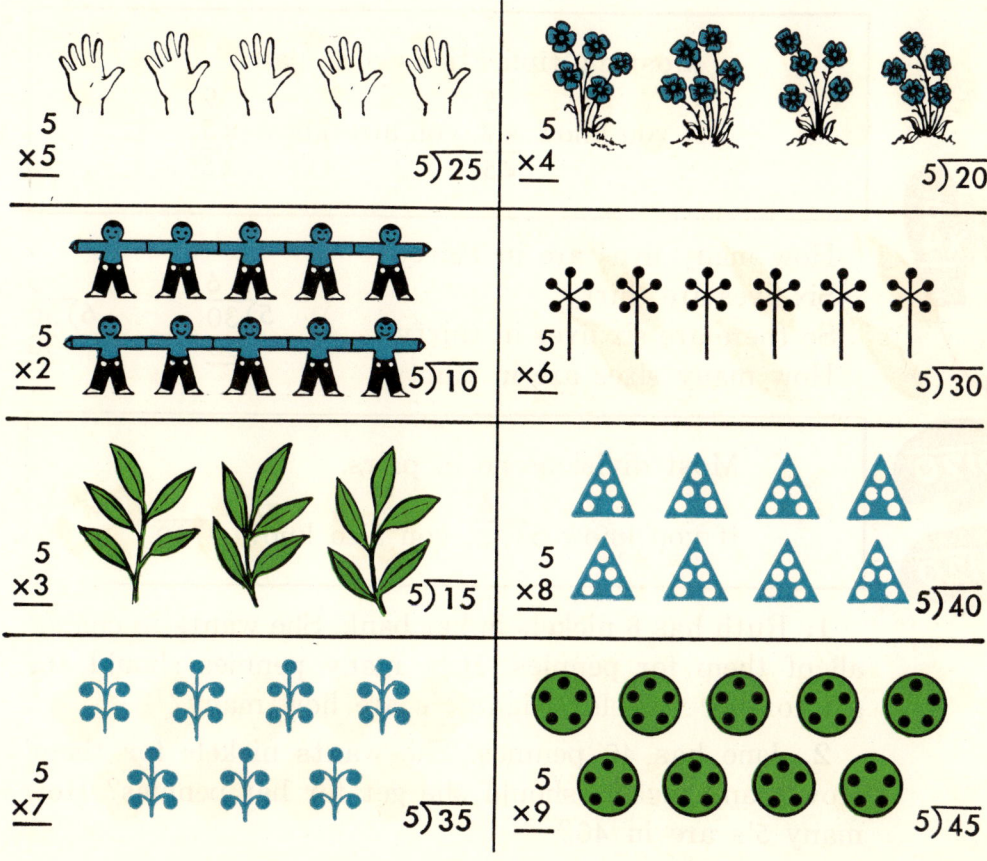

Multiplication and Division Pairs

How many are 6 fives? $\begin{array}{r}5\\ \times 6\\ \hline\end{array}$ $\begin{array}{r}6\\ \times 5\\ \hline\end{array}$

How many are 5 sixes?

Are the products the same when the numbers change places?

Tell the products that are not given:

$\begin{array}{r}5\\ \times 7\\ \hline 35\end{array}$ $\begin{array}{r}7\\ \times 5\\ \hline\end{array}$ $\begin{array}{r}5\\ \times 8\\ \hline 40\end{array}$ $\begin{array}{r}8\\ \times 5\\ \hline\end{array}$ $\begin{array}{r}5\\ \times 9\\ \hline 45\end{array}$ $\begin{array}{r}9\\ \times 5\\ \hline\end{array}$

Most multiplications go in pairs.

If you know $\begin{array}{r}5\\ \times 9\\ \hline 45\end{array}$, you also know $\begin{array}{r}9\\ \times 5\\ \hline 45\end{array}$.

How many fives are in thirty?
Six fives are thirty.
So there are six fives in thirty.
How many sixes are in thirty?

$\begin{array}{r}6\\ 5\overline{)30}\\ 30\end{array}$ $\begin{array}{r}5\\ 6\overline{)30}\\ 30\end{array}$

Most divisions go in pairs.

If you know $5\overline{)30}^{\,6}$, you also know $6\overline{)30}^{\,5}$.

---

1. Ruth has 8 nickels in her bank. She wants to change all of them for pennies. How many pennies should she get for her nickels? Eight 5's are how many?

2. Jane has 40 pennies. She wants nickels for them. How many nickels should she get for her pennies? How many 5's are in 40?

Ways to Help Yourself

It will help you remember the multiplications and the divisions if you practice saying together those that use the same numbers.

4 ×9 = 36	9 ×4 = 36	4)36 = 9	9)36 = 4	4 ×2 = 8	2 ×4 = 8	2)8 = 4	4)8 = 2
5 ×3 = 15	3 ×5 = 15	5)15	3)15	4 ×5 = 20	5 ×4 = 20	4)20	5)20
2 ×8 = 16	8 ×2 = 16	2)16	8)16	6 ×2 = 12	2 ×6 = 12	6)12	2)12
9 ×3 = 27	3 ×9 = 27	9)27	3)27	7 ×2 = 14	2 ×7 = 14	7)14	2)14
2 ×3 = 6	3 ×2 = 6	2)6	3)6	6 ×3 = 18	3 ×6 = 18	6)18	3)18
3 ×8 = 24	8 ×3 = 24	3)24	8)24	5 ×2 = 10	2 ×5 = 10	2)10	5)10
7 ×3 = 21	3 ×7 = 21	3)21	7)21	9 ×2 = 18	2 ×9 = 18	2)18	9)18
4 ×6 = 24	6 ×4 = 24	4)24	6)24	7 ×4 = 28	4 ×7 = 28	4)28	7)28
5 ×6 = 30	6 ×5 = 30	5)30	6)30	4 ×3 = 12	3 ×4 = 12	4)12	3)12
5 ×7 = 35	7 ×5 = 35	5)35	7)35	5 ×8 = 40	8 ×5 = 40	5)40	8)40
5 ×9 = 45	9 ×5 = 45	5)45	9)45	4 ×8 = 32	8 ×4 = 32	4)32	8)32
3 ×3 = 9	3)9	4 ×4 = 16	4)16	5 ×5 = 25	5)25	2 ×2 = 4	2)4

The Whole Story of Two Numbers

One day Pat's teacher wrote the whole story of two numbers on the board.

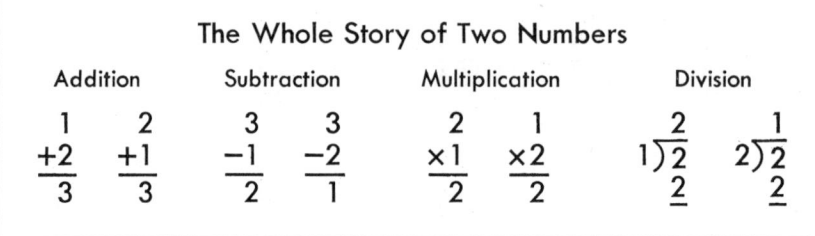

"I understand that," said Pat. "Give us the story of two numbers bigger than 1 and 2."

So the teacher wrote the whole story of 4 and 5.

Addition		Subtraction		Multiplication		Division	
4 +5 ― 9	5 +4 ― 9	9 −5 ― 4	9 −4 ― 5	4 ×5 ― 20	5 ×4 ― 20	5 4)20 20	4 5)20 20

Finish writing these stories:

| 3
+7
― | 7
+3
― | 10
−7
― | 10
−3
― | 3
×7
― | 7
×3
― | 3)21 | 7)21 |
| 4
+9
― | 9
+4
― | 13
−4
― | 13
−9
― | 4
×9
― | 9
×4
― | 4)36 | 9)36 |

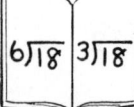

Write the whole story of:

5 and 2	3 and 9	3 and 8	5 and 5
2 and 6	4 and 5	4 and 6	7 and 5
2 and 9	5 and 6	4 and 4	5 and 8
3 and 5	4 and 8	4 and 7	5 and 9
9 and 4	7 and 2	3 and 3	4 and 2

Sometimes a problem tells us how many things there are in one group. Then it asks us to find how many things are in 2 or more groups of the same kind.

When we know how many there are in one group, we multiply to find how many there are in two or more groups of the same kind.

Solving Problems

1. Ann saves 5¢ a week. How much will she save in 8 weeks?

2. Fred learns to spell 4 new words each day. How many words does he learn to spell in 5 days?

3. Jim feeds his pony 5 ears of corn each day. How many ears of corn does Jim feed him in a week?

4. How many players are on a baseball team? There are how many players on two teams?

5. How many players are on a basketball team? How many players are on two teams?

6. Bob needs 4 wheels for each wagon he is making. How many wheels will he need for 4 wagons?

7. Dick needs 3 wheels for each airplane he is making. How many wheels will he need for 6 airplanes?

8. Three groups of girls were playing hopscotch. There were 5 girls in each group. How many girls were playing hopscotch?

hopscotch

Making Things

1. Jack is making darts. To make a dart, he drives a nail through a cork and sticks three feathers in the cork.

Jack has **18** feathers. It takes **3** feathers to make one dart. How many darts can he make with the feathers?

Think: Jack needs **3** feathers to make one dart. So he can make as many darts from **18** feathers as there are 3's in 18. How many 3's are in 18?

2. Jim is building a house with boards. He has **18** boards. He hauls **6** boards in his wagon at a time. How many trips must he make to haul the boards? How many 6's are in 18?

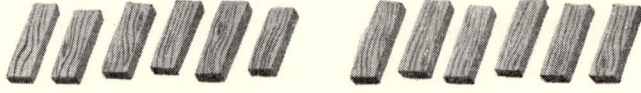

3. Jane is making animals for the zoo. She can make a giraffe with **4** pipe cleaners. If there are **24** pipe cleaners in a package, how many giraffes can she make from one package? How many 4's are in 24?

4. Bobby has **24** spools. He builds houses for the animals. If he uses **6** spools for 1 house, how many houses can he build with the 24 spools? How many 6's are in 24?

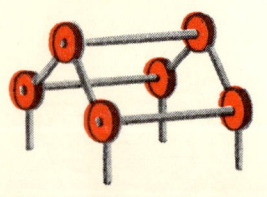

5. Tom is making cages for the monkeys. If he uses **8** spools for one cage, how many cages can he make from **24** spools? How many 8's are in 24?

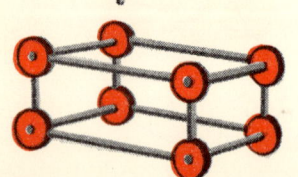

Problems

Read each problem carefully. **Think** what it tells you. **Think** what it asks you to find. Then **decide** whether you must add, subtract, multiply, or divide.

1. Helen can make 4 everyday napkins from a flour sack. She has 9 flour sacks. How many napkins can she make?

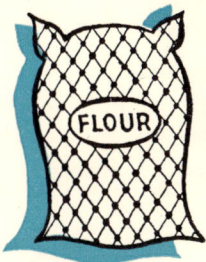 

2. Jane uses 9 eggs to make a cake. She has only 5 eggs. How many more eggs does she need to make the cake?

3. Bill wants to buy 3 tablets. They cost 8 cents each. How much money will he need to pay for them?

4. Mary picked 21 tomatoes. She put them in 3 boxes to take to 3 neighbors. If she put the same number of tomatoes in each box, how many will there be for each neighbor?

5. Jane picked 4 boxes of cherries. Jack said that he would pick 5 times as many as Jane did. How many boxes of cherries should Jack pick?

6. Alice wants to mail 8 letters. She must put a 3-cent stamp on each letter. How much will the stamps cost her?

7. How many air-mail stamps at 6¢ each can you buy with twenty-four cents?

8. Susan picked 24 daisies. How many bunches can she make if she puts 8 daisies in each bunch?

9. Mrs. Jackson sent 18 socks to the laundry. How many pairs of socks did she send?

10. Mrs. Brown plans to use boxes that hold 8 doughnuts. How many boxes will she need for 32 doughnuts?

Parts of Things

1. Take a sheet of paper and fold it from top to bottom into two equal parts.

2. Now take another sheet of paper and fold it from corner to corner into two equal parts.

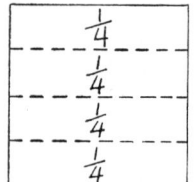

> One of the 2 equal parts is called **one half**.
> One half means one of the two equal parts.
> We write one half like this: $\frac{1}{2}$.

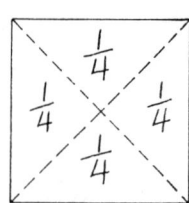

3. Now fold a piece of paper into 4 equal parts.
When anything is divided into 4 equal parts, one of the parts is called **one fourth**.

We write one fourth like this: $\frac{1}{4}$.

4. Alice, Jane, and Betty had a brick of ice cream. They divided it into three equal parts. What part did each girl get? What is one of 3 equal parts called?

We write **one third** like this: $\frac{1}{3}$.

5. Susan used a paper plate to show the class the meaning of **one sixth**.

First, she cut the plate into three equal parts. Each part is one third of the whole plate.

Then she cut each third into 2 equal parts. She had 6 pieces the same size. Each piece is one sixth of the whole plate. We write one sixth like this: $\frac{1}{6}$.

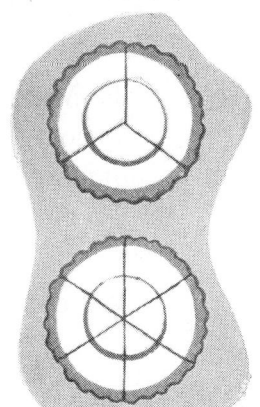

6. Alice cut a ribbon into 5 equal pieces.

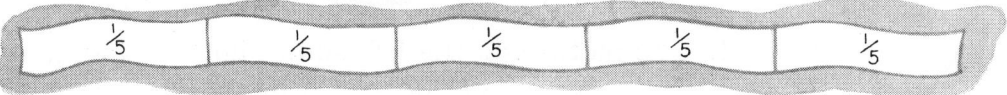

What is one of the 5 equal parts called? How do we write **one fifth**?

The apple pie is cut into *four* equal parts. Each part is *one fourth* of the pie.

The lemon pie is cut into ___ equal parts. Each part is ___ _____ of the pie.

The pumpkin pie is cut into ___ equal parts. Each part is ___ _____ of the pie.

The cherry pie is cut into ___ equal parts. Each part is ___ _____ of the pie.

What things on this page are divided into fourths?
What things on this page are divided into fifths?
What things on this page are divided into sixths?

Parts of a Group

1. Mary baked 16 cookies. She wants to put them in two boxes with the same number in each box. How many cookies should she put in each box?

Mary wants to divide the cookies into two equal groups. She wants to put one half of the cookies in each box.

We divide a number by 2 to find one half of it.

   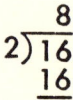

½ of 16 is 8.

 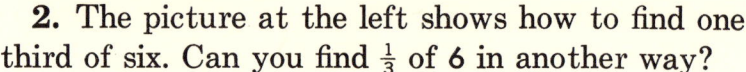

 **2.** The picture at the left shows how to find one third of six. Can you find ⅓ of 6 in another way?

3. Ann baked 24 cookies. She wants to put them in three boxes, and she wants to put the same number in each box. How many cookies should Ann put in each box?

We divide a number by 3 to find one third of it.

⅓ of 24 is 8.

4. Sue baked 24 cookies. She put them in 4 boxes with the same number in each box. How many cookies did she put in each box? How many are ¼ of 24 cookies?

We divide a number by 4 to find one fourth of it.

¼ of 24 is 6.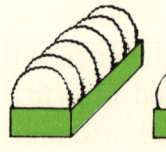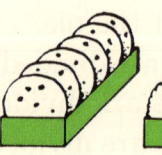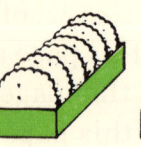

5. Betty baked 30 cookies. She wants to put the same number of cookies in each of the 5 boxes that she has. How many cookies should she put in each box?

How do we find one fifth of a number? What is $\frac{1}{5}$ of 30?

$\frac{1}{5}$ of 30 is 6

$$5\overline{)30} \;\; \begin{array}{r} 6 \\ \underline{30} \end{array}$$

6. Five boys decided to buy a baseball that cost 45 cents. They shared the cost equally. How much was each boy's share?

What part of the cost should each boy pay?

7. Mary bought 1 dozen colored lights to put on the Christmas tree. How many colored lights did she buy?

How many lights are there in $\frac{1}{2}$ dozen?
How many lights are there in $\frac{1}{4}$ dozen?

8. Miss West sent 6 boys to get 18 chairs from the storeroom. The boys carried all the chairs in one trip. How many chairs did each boy carry?

What is $\frac{1}{6}$ of 18?

9. Say the answers:

$\frac{1}{2}$ of 4 =	$\frac{1}{3}$ of 6 =	$\frac{1}{4}$ of 8 =	$\frac{1}{2}$ of 6 =
$\frac{1}{2}$ of 12 =	$\frac{1}{3}$ of 12 =	$\frac{1}{4}$ of 12 =	$\frac{1}{5}$ of 15 =
$\frac{1}{2}$ of 10 =	$\frac{1}{3}$ of 15 =	$\frac{1}{4}$ of 16 =	$\frac{1}{5}$ of 20 =
$\frac{1}{6}$ of 18 =	$\frac{1}{6}$ of 24 =	$\frac{1}{6}$ of 30 =	$\frac{1}{5}$ of 40 =
$\frac{1}{2}$ of 18 =	$\frac{1}{4}$ of 36 =	$\frac{1}{3}$ of 24 =	$\frac{1}{4}$ of 28 =

Chapter 3
Working with Tens

How Many Tens?

How many pennies does Jim have? There are ten pennies in each row, and there are ten rows. How many tens are there?

How many bundles of sticks are there? How many sticks are in each bundle? How many tens are there?

Ten tens have a special name: **hundred**. Ten tens are one hundred. We show one hundred by writing 1 in hundred's place. To put 1 in hundred's place, we write 0 in one's place and 0 in ten's place. The 00 in 100 put the 1 in hundred's place.

Since we use 3 figures to write 100, we call it a **three-place** number. The figure for hundred is always written in the third place at the left.

Writing Numbers

Before our number names and number figures came into use, people counted with an **abacus**. At first the abacus was just a board covered with dust. What number is shown on each abacus?

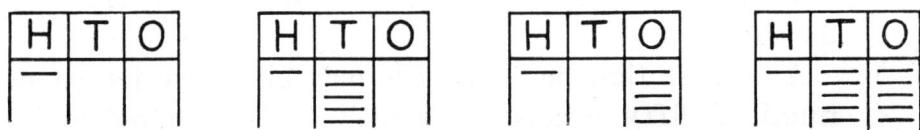

Later people learned to write numbers with figures.

Here is the way we write them: 100; 150; 105; 155.

Zero has not always had the same shape or name, but it has always had the same use. Zero meant "empty" and was used as the sign for the empty column. Today we still use 0 to fill empty places when we write such numbers as:

    10   50   100   150   110   101   105

Our figure 1 stands for one. It also stands for 1 ten when we write 1 in ten's place: 10. How do we get the 1 in ten's place? The 1 also stands for 10 tens, or one hundred, when we write the 1 in hundred's place: 100. How do we get the 1 in hundred's place?

The figure 1 tells **one**.

The figures 11 tell 1 ten and 1, or **eleven**.

The figures 111 tell 1 hundred, 1 ten, and 1, or **one hundred eleven**.

The same figure written in different places tells different numbers.

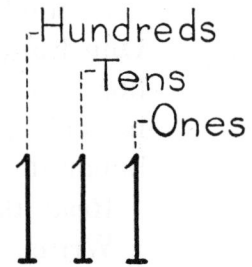

Ones   Reading and Writing Numbers

A figure may be used in any place in a number. If the figure is in one's place, it tells how many **ones**. If it is in ten's place, it tells how many **tens**. What does it tell if it is in hundred's place?

What does the 5 in 65 show? What does the 5 in 54 show?

A number that has hundreds may also have tens. **One hundred fifty** means "15 tens," or "1 hundred and 5 tens." To write one hundred fifty, we write 1 in hundred's place, 5 in ten's place, and 0 in one's place. We write it: 150. The 0 in one's place puts and keeps the 5 in ten's place and the 1 in hundred's place.

Read these numbers: 110   130   160   150   190

Write these numbers: one hundred twenty; one hundred forty; one hundred eighty; one hundred seventy.

A number that has hundreds may also have tens and ones. **One hundred forty-six** means "14 tens and 6 ones," or "1 hundred, 4 tens, and 6 ones." We write it: 146. We write 1 in hundred's place, 4 in ten's place, and 6 in one's place.

Read these numbers: 135   158   192   174   128   199

Write these numbers: one hundred twenty-seven; one hundred sixty-two; one hundred eighty-eight.

A number may have hundreds and ones but no tens. **One hundred eight** means "10 tens and 8 ones," or "1 hundred, no tens, and 8 ones." We write it: 108. The 0 in ten's place keeps the 8 in one's place and the 1 in hundred's place. The 0 fills the empty space.

Read these numbers: 105   109   107   108   106

Write: one hundred four; one hundred one.

The School Picnic

1. At the picnic there were 64 pupils from the lower grades and 95 pupils from the upper grades. How many more pupils were there from the upper grades than from the lower grades?

2. The pupils rode to the picnic in the school busses. There were 40 pupils in one bus, 42 in another, 41 in the third bus, and 36 in the fourth bus. How many pupils rode in the four busses?

3. There were 21 pupils from the first grade, 20 from the second, and 23 from the third grade. How many pupils were there from the three grades?

4. There were 38 children playing prisoner's base. After a while 15 of them went to wade in the pool. How many children were left to play prisoner's base?

5. There were 76 boys and 83 girls at the picnic. How many pupils were there in all?

To work these problems, we have to know how to add and subtract tens.

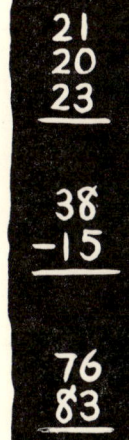

Adding Tens

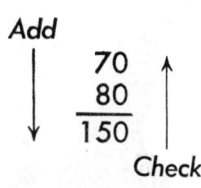

See 0. There are no ones to add. We write 0 in one's place so that our ten's answer will be in ten's place. Then we add the tens: 7 and 8 are 15. 15 tens are 1 hundred and 5 tens. We write 1 in hundred's place and 5 in ten's place.

Explain how these examples were worked:

```
 60    50    73    88    40    86    63    95
 40    90    65    60    76    20    41    11
---   ---   ---   ---   ---   ---   ---   ---
100   140   138   148   116   106   104   106
```

We add tens the way we add ones.	8 5 — 13	80 50 — 130	84 55 — 139

The answer to an addition example is called the **sum**. We add up to check. The sum should be the same either way we add.

Find the sums and check:

	(a)	(b)	(c)	(d)	(e)	(f)	(g)	(h)	(i)	(j)
1.	90 20	80 70	60 70	80 50	90 30	80 40	70 70	90 70	50 50	20 80
2.	60 95	74 50	86 80	80 38	90 61	43 90	39 80	50 67	32 70	54 55
3.	40 76	45 80	71 66	77 30	33 96	64 45	62 55	98 40	91 50	44 94
4.	10 90	93 95	70 42	45 63	60 63	96 83	52 77	50 89	21 90	25 84

Reading and Solving Problems

1. When school started in September, the school nurse weighed the children. Tom weighed 92 pounds. Today when Tom was weighed, he said, "I am 7 pounds heavier than I was in September." How much does Tom weigh now?

In many problems something happens. Here are the things that happened in this problem:

(a) The school nurse weighed Tom and the other children. *(b)* Tom was weighed again today. *(c)* He has gained weight.

Read each problem. Forget about the numbers, but be able to tell in your own words what happens.

2. Tom helped Miss West put covers on the new books. He put covers on 33 books, and Miss West put covers on 15 books. How many books did they put covers on?

3. Tom put the books in the bookcase for Miss West. He put 50 books on one shelf and 58 books on another shelf. How many books did he put on the two shelves?

4. Jim and Joe have a newsstand. One day Jim sold 64 papers, and Joe sold 42. How many papers did the boys sell that day?

5. The class is studying about ways of travel. The girls brought 56 travel pictures to school, and the boys brought 63. How many travel pictures did they bring?

6. Mary went to town to shop. She spent 26¢ in one store and 73¢ in another store. How much did she spend in the stores?

Now read each problem again. This time find the answer to the question that the problem asks.

Adding Columns

1. When Mary was in the hospital, she received 15 letters, 42 cards, and 12 packages. How many pieces of mail did she get in all?

```
 15
 42
 12
 ──
 69
```

First, add the ones: 5 and 2 are 7, and 2 are 9.
Write 9 in one's place in the answer.
Then add the tens: 1 and 4 are 5, and 1 are 6.
Write 6 in ten's place in the answer.
Mary got 69 pieces of mail.

2. Tom wants to make a kite. He bought paper for 10¢, string for 20¢, and paste for 10¢. How much did these things cost him?

```
 10¢
 20¢
 10¢
 ───
 40¢
```

There are **no ones** to add.
So we write 0 in one's place in the answer.
Then we add the tens; 1 and 2 are 3, and 1 are 4.
The paper, string, and paste cost Tom 40¢.

3. Jim has a half dollar, a quarter, and 2 dimes. How much money does he have?

```
 50¢
 25¢
 20¢
 ───
 95¢
```

There are only 5 ones.
So we write 5 in one's place in the answer.
Then we add the tens; 5 and 2 are 7, and 2 are 9.
Jim has 95¢.

4. Joe went to the stockyards with his father. There were pigs in three pens. Joe counted 64 pigs in the first pen, 31 in the second pen, and 63 in the third pen. How many pigs did he count?

```
  64
  31
  63
 ───
 158
```

First, add the ones.
Then add the tens: 6 and 3 are 9, and 6 are 15.
Write 5 in ten's place and 1 in hundred's place.
Joe counted 158 pigs.

5. How much did Jack save in each three months?

January	5¢	April	60¢	July	48¢
February	80¢	May	10¢	August	40¢
March	14¢	June	76¢	September	70¢

6. The girls used 30 pieces of red paper, 31 pieces of green paper, and 58 pieces of yellow paper to make paper hats for Halloween. How many pieces of colored paper did they use?

Add the columns **down**. Add **up** to check.

	(a)	(b)	(c)	(d)	(e)	(f)	(g)	(h)
7.	12	66	30	24	20	10	10	34
	56	32	50	35	43	12	30	64
	91	71	28	60	62	52	79	51
8.	31	30	66	22	20	10	15	11
	37	67	10	40	70	70	40	12
	70	90	40	41	30	80	83	90
9.	10	44	85	83	23	90	54	21
	82	30	4	16	60	44	30	20
	87	35	30	20	46	3	50	68
10.	53	90	54	42	14	31	30	22
	3	12	25	52	3	8	20	60
	53	7	60	52	92	70	70	67
11.	16	11	33	41	20	37	48	23
	10	20	6	31	27	11	30	62
	83	88	90	81	82	91	90	94
12.	20	50	93	54	32	52	31	42
	34	40	52	21	67	31	37	53
	95	90	4	84	70	86	91	84

Subtracting Tens

```
 160
 -80
 ———
  80
```

There are no ones to subtract; so we write 0 in one's place in the answer. Then we subtract the tens: 8 from 16 is 8. We write 8 in ten's place in the answer.

How do we check our answer when we subtract?

Explain these subtraction examples and their checks:

110	70	106	42	175	95	164	80
−70	+40	−42	+64	−95	+80	−80	+84
40	110	64	106	80	175	84	164

We subtract tens the way we subtract ones.

```
 9      90
 5      50
 —      ——
 4      40
```

Subtract and check each answer:

	(a)	(b)	(c)	(d)	(e)	(f)	(g)	(h)
1.	100 60	170 90	120 60	140 90	110 40	110 80	100 80	130 80
2.	132 61	106 52	135 94	115 65	117 94	118 32	108 13	129 83
3.	112 72	125 70	116 56	137 73	189 99	177 87	156 93	106 20
4.	148 78	107 90	149 86	103 73	129 97	122 40	151 80	128 54
5.	168 85	169 95	159 74	104 44	148 66	133 50	111 21	109 38
6.	129 32	164 70	157 65	138 40	177 82	156 84	145 61	149 50

Reading and Solving Problems

1. Jack bought a box of marbles. There were 100 marbles in the box. He sold 60 of the marbles to Jim and kept the rest. How many marbles did Jack keep for himself?

In many problems something happens. Here are the things that happened in this problem:

(a) Jack bought a box of marbles. *(b)* He sold some of them to Jim. *(c)* He kept the rest of the marbles.

A problem always tells you more than one fact. Here are the facts that this problem tells:

(a) Jack bought 100 marbles. *(b)* He sold 60 of them to Jim.

Read each problem. Tell what happens in it. What two facts does the problem tell?

2. One day Jack took 15 of his marbles to school. He lost 8 of them playing "keeps." How many marbles did he have then?

3. Bob has a book of 148 pages to read. After reading 56 pages during the library period, he still has a lot of pages to read. How many pages has he yet to read?

4. Ruth earns 80¢ a week. She puts 50¢ in the school bank each week and spends the rest. How much does she spend each week?

5. The class needs 150 programs for its visitors. The boys made 60 programs, and the girls made the rest. How many programs did the girls make?

6. The program was to last 45 minutes. The children gave a play that took 20 minutes. How many minutes were left for the rest of the program?

Now solve each problem.

favors

Do We Add or Subtract? [Test]

Read each problem carefully so that you will know: (a) what happened, (b) what two facts it tells, and (c) what question it asks. From these you should know whether to add or to subtract to answer the question.

1. Mary wants to have 45 favors for her party. She has made 12 of them. How many more favors does she need to make?

2. Mary paid 25¢ for the paper and 70¢ for the ribbon to make the favors. How much did the favors cost?

3. Mary had 10 yards of ribbon. She used 6 yards of it. How many yards of ribbon did she have left?

ordered

4. Mary ordered 45 pints of milk. She asked for 10 pints of chocolate milk and the rest regular milk. How many pints of regular milk did she order?

5. Mary's father bought ice-cream cups for the party. There were 36 cups in one box and 12 in another box. How many ice-cream cups did he get?

6. Helen helped Mary make cards for a game. Helen made 24 blue cards, and Mary made 32 red cards. How many cards did the two girls make?

7. Forty-two children came to the party. Twenty of them were girls. How many boys came to the party?

8. Mary needs 45 chairs in all for her party. She has 24 chairs. How many more chairs does she need?

9. The children came to the party at 2:30 o'clock and left at 5:30 o'clock. How long did they stay?

Our Number System

Jerry went to the store to buy some paper for his father. He saw 5 packages of paper on the table.

Jerry asked, "How many sheets of paper are in each package?"

"One hundred," answered the clerk.

How many sheets of paper are in the five packages? We can count them by hundreds: **one hundred, two hundred, three hundred, four hundred, five hundred.** We write: 500.

Our figure 5 stands for five. It also stands for five tens when we write 5 in ten's place. The 5 may stand for fifty tens, or five hundreds when we write 5 in hundred's place.

We say:	We write:
Two hundred	200
Two hundred twenty	220
Two hundred forty-five	245
Two hundred five	205

Read these numbers:
300   370   375   307   305   503   350   750   902

Write these numbers:
Four hundred sixty   Three hundred ten   Six hundred
Two hundred eighty   Four hundred six   Nine hundred

432 means ___ hundreds ___ tens and ___ ones.
200 means ___ hundreds.
320 means ___ hundreds ___ tens.
309 means ___ hundreds ___ ones.

Multiplying Tens

We multiply tens the way we multiply ones.	4 ×3 ――― 12	40 ×3 ――― 120
We write the ten's answer in ten's place.		

1. Mrs. Green bought 4 dozen eggs. How many eggs did she buy?

<table>
<tr><td>

12
×4

12
×4
―――
48

</td><td>

We know there are 12 eggs in a dozen. To answer the question, we multiply 12 by 4.

First, we multiply the ones. We write 8 in one's place. Then we multiply the tens. We write the ten's answer in ten's place.

Mrs. Green bought 48 eggs.

</td></tr>
</table>

2. Mrs. Allen took 4 boxes of cookies to the bake sale. She put 40 cookies in each box. How many cookies did she take to the bake sale?

<table>
<tr><td>

40
×4
―――
0

40
×4
―――
160

</td><td>

We write 0 in one's place. Why?

Now we are ready to multiply the tens. When we multiply 4 by 4, we get 16 tens. 16 tens are 1 hundred and 6 tens; so we write 1 in hundred's place and 6 in ten's place.

Mrs. Allen took 160 cookies to the sale.

</td></tr>
</table>

3. Betty bought 2 tablets. There were 50 pieces of paper in each tablet. How many pieces of paper were there in the 2 tablets? How many pieces of paper would there be in 3 tablets?

4. Explain the multiplications below:

32	20	62	40	20	54	52	23¢	71
3	4	4	7	5	2	4	2	5
96	80	248	280	100	108	208	46¢	355

Multiply:

	(a)	(b)	(c)	(d)	(e)	(f)	(g)	(h)
5.	24 2	43 3	32 3	60 4	21 8	50 2	41 5	31¢ 2
6.	51 4	40 5	71 2	40 8	71 3	40 7	82 3	23¢ 3
7.	72 4	92 2	20 7	82 4	41 9	63 3	90 4	42¢ 2
8.	41 6	30 7	83 2	91 3	60 2	40 4	31 8	12¢ 4

9. Ann paid 3¢ **a card** for buttons. She got 3 cards. How much did the buttons cost?

10. Mary bought 2 books that cost 44¢ each. How much should she pay for them?

11. Jack bought 4 toy airplanes. He paid a dime for each airplane. How much did the airplanes cost?

12. The boys in Jack's class at school need rubber bands for the airplanes they are making. Jack bought 3 packages of rubber bands. There were 50 rubber bands in each package. How many rubber bands did he get?

13. Edward has a stamp book. He has 4 of the pages filled. There are 32 stamps on each page. How many stamps does he have in his stamp book?

Dividing Tens

1. Uncle Jim gave Ann, Sue, and Betty a box of pennies, which they were to divide **equally**. There were 90 pennies in the box. How many pennies should each girl get?

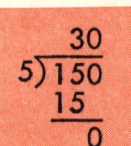

We divide 90 by 3 to find how many pennies each girl should get as her equal share. We divide tens the way we divide ones, but we write the ten's answer in ten's place. How many threes are in nine? Write 3 in ten's place in the answer.

There are no ones to divide; so we write 0 in our answer to put the 3 in ten's place.

Each girl should get 30 pennies.

2. Ann is putting her 150 bird pictures in 5 piles. If she puts the same number of pictures in each pile, how many pictures will be in each pile?

```
    30
5)150
   15
    0
```

We think of 150 as 15 tens. So we divide 15 tens by 5. How many fives are in fifteen?

Where do we write the 3 in the answer?

How do we make the 3 show 3 tens?

3. Finish working each example.

Remember: We are dividing tens; so our answer will be tens and must be written in ten's place.

```
  1         4         2         2         5         4         3
4)40     2)80      3)60     8)160     2)100    4)160    9)270
  4        8                   16         10
  0        0
```

Copy and divide:

	(a)	(b)	(c)	(d)	(e)	(f)	(g)
4.	5)50	7)280	5)400	8)240	8)320	9)360	5)200
5.	2)180	3)180	4)240	7)140	4)280	1)200	3)210

Dividing Tens and Ones

1. Tom, Joe, and Jim found 69 sea shells. They divided the shells so that each of them got the same number. How many shells did each boy get?

3)69   We divide 69 by 3 to find how many shells each boy got.

First, divide the tens.

How many threes are in six?

```
  2
3)69
  6
```

Write 2 in ten's place in the answer.
Multiply: Two threes are six.
Write 6 under the 6 in 69, and draw a line.
We have divided the tens.

```
  2
3)69
  6
  9
```

Next, divide the ones.
We bring down the 9.
We write 9 below the line.
Now we are ready to divide the ones.
How many threes are in nine?

```
  23
3)69
  6
  9
  9
```

Write 3 in one's place in the answer.
Multiply: Three threes are nine.
Write 9 under 9, and draw a line.
We have divided the tens and ones.
Each boy should get 23 shells.

2. Tom has 128 snapshots. He can put 4 on each page of his book. How many pages of his book will he use?

Think: 128 is 12 tens and 8 ones.

First, divide the tens and write the answer in ten's place. Then divide the ones and write the answer in one's place.

```
   32        Check
4)128          32
  12           4
   8         128
   8
```

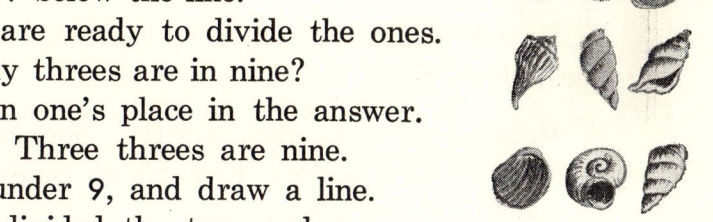

bookcase

Our Problems

1. There are 248 books in our room. The boys want to put them in the bookcase, and they want to put the same number of books on each shelf. There are 4 shelves in the bookcase. How many books should they put on each shelf?

2. Fred goes to the gym class. He exercises 20 minutes each day. How many minutes does he exercise in a school week of 5 days?

3. Susan said, "Fred exercises 100 minutes each school week of 5 days. So he exercises 20 minutes each day."

Is Susan right? How did she find the answer?

exercise

4. Tom missed 12 of the 48 words in a spelling test. How many words did he spell right?

5. Jim spelled correctly 36 of the 48 words in a spelling test. How many words did he miss?

6. Alice lives in the country. She rides 8 miles each day in the school bus. How many miles does she ride in a month of 20 school days?

7. Alice rides in one of the big busses. The bus has 40 seats, and 2 children can ride in each seat. How many children can ride the bus at a time if no one stands?

8. It takes the bus 20 minutes to go from Alice's house to school. The clock shows the time that she left home. What time did she get to school?

9. There were 77 children in the bus, and 35 of them were boys. How many girls were there?

Practice | Test

Copy and divide:

	(a)	(b)	(c)	(d)	(e)	(f)	(g)
1.	3)96	2)84	3)219	4)328	5)205	3)276	9)279
2.	3)249	4)368	4)284	3)189	9)189	7)217	2)102
3.	2)124	4)164	4)208	5)155	5)105	3)126	3)153

Find:

	(a)	(b)	(c)	(d)	(e)
4.	$\frac{1}{2}$ of 166	$\frac{1}{4}$ of 320	$\frac{1}{4}$ of 328	$\frac{1}{3}$ of 189	$\frac{1}{5}$ of 100
5.	$\frac{1}{3}$ of 270	$\frac{1}{4}$ of 360	$\frac{1}{3}$ of 210	$\frac{1}{4}$ of 200	$\frac{1}{6}$ of 240
6.	$\frac{1}{3}$ of 216	$\frac{1}{4}$ of 240	$\frac{1}{2}$ of 188	$\frac{1}{3}$ of 249	$\frac{1}{6}$ of 180

Copy and add:

	(a)	(b)	(c)	(d)	(e)	(f)	(g)	(h)	(i)
7.	65 82	42 93	80 94	71 80	50 90	80 80	64 43	98 10	73 56
8.	15 32 42	32 12 25	83 10 76	40 34 35	57 42 20	60 30 60	73 14 50	54 23 80	41 54 73

Copy and subtract:

	(a)	(b)	(c)	(d)	(e)	(f)	(g)	(h)	(i)
9.	120 80	173 93	118 68	141 70	109 50	168 84	136 55	127 72	159 84

Copy and multiply:

	(a)	(b)	(c)	(d)	(e)	(f)	(g)	(h)	(i)
10.	32 3	41 2	22 4	13 3	24 2	20 3	30 2	52 4	21 6
11.	31 9	31 5	40 8	20 7	93 3	82 4	84 2	73 3	50 4

Chapter 4
Our Money

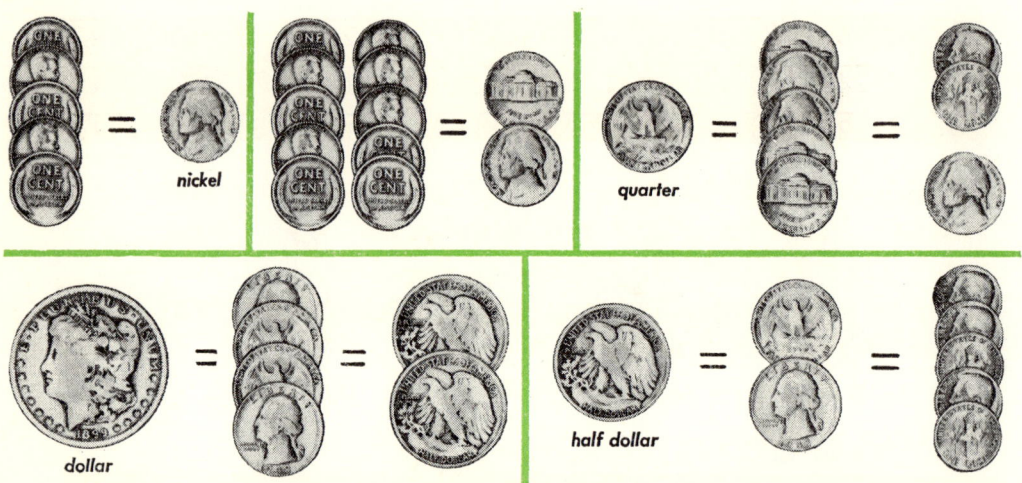

Our Coins

1. How many pennies have the same **value** as a nickel?
How many pennies have the same value as a dime?
How many pennies have the same value as a quarter?
How many pennies have the same value as a half dollar?
How many pennies have the same value as a dollar?

2. How many nickels have the same value as a dime?
How many nickels have the same value as a quarter?
How many nickels have the same value as a dollar?

3. How many dimes have the same value as a dollar?
How many dimes have the same value as a half dollar?

4. How many quarters have the same value as a dollar?

5. What one coin has the same value as a quarter, one nickel, and two dimes?

Counting Change

1. Jim bought a box of crayons for 8¢. He gave the clerk a quarter. How should the clerk count the change?

The clerk began with the price of the crayons. He said, "Eight." Then he gave Jim 2 pennies and said, "Nine, ten." Then he gave Jim a nickel and said, "Fifteen." Then he gave Jim a dime and said, "Twenty-five." Why did he begin with 8 and stop with 25?

2. Jack bought crayons for 8¢. Count the change he got from a dollar.

3. Count the change from a quarter for each amount:
12¢   23¢   15¢   4¢   18¢   9¢   13¢   5¢

4. Count the change from a half dollar for each amount:
27¢   19¢   41¢   23¢   9¢   15¢   45¢   33¢

5. Count the change from one dollar for each amount:
65¢   10¢   26¢   89¢   20¢   36¢   74¢   44¢

6. Jack bought some socks for 26¢. He gave the clerk a half dollar. This is the way the clerk counted Jack's change: 26¢—27, 28, 29, 30, 40, 50. What coins did Jack get in change?

Writing Dollars and Cents

We use three signs to write dollars and cents:

1. The sign $ means dollar or dollars. We always write it **before** the figures that tell the number of dollars.

$1 $10 $100 $5 $50 $500 $65

2. The sign ¢ means cent or cents. It is always written **after** the figures that tell the number of cents. If the amount of money is in cents and the number of cents is less than 100, that is, less than one dollar, we may write the amount with the sign ¢ after the number.

1¢   10¢   50¢   75¢   86¢   90¢   99¢

3. The point (.) is used to show cents. We never use the point without using the $ sign also. The sign ¢ and the point are never used together.

$.50 $.65 $.77 $.10 $.99 $.25 $.83

When we have less than ten cents, we write a zero between the point and the cent's figure. The 0 keeps the cent's figure in its proper place.

$.01 $.03 $.07 $.08 $.09 $.04 $.05

When we write the dollar sign to show dollars, or dollars and cents, we put the point between the dollars and cents. The point is used to separate the figures that tell the number of dollars from those that tell the number of cents. Cents take two places to the right of the point.

The sign $ and the sign ¢ are never used together.

To show in writing:	We write:
One dollar	$1.00
Five dollars	$5.00
One dollar and twenty-five cents	$1.25
Five dollars and ten cents	$5.10
Ten dollars and five cents	$10.05

Write these amounts of money, using the dollar sign and the point:

Three dollars and twenty-five cents	Four dollars
One dollar and sixty-two cents	Sixty cents
Seventy-eight cents	Seven cents
Seven dollars and forty cents	Ten cents
One dollar and eleven cents	One cent

Some of these money numbers are not written correctly. Find each mistake. Then write that amount of money as it should be written.

60¢	$2.35	.60¢	$5.00	$.75	$.40
.8	$1.5	$6.30¢	6$	¢25	$.04

Miss Bell asked the pupils to write nine cents on the board. Here are the ways it was written. Which are wrong? Why?

Mary	Jane	Sue	Ann	Helen
9¢	.09	$.9	$.90	$.09

Jack	Bill	Tom	Dick	Joe
$9.00	.09¢	$9.00¢	$9	.9¢

Reading Amounts of Money

We read $5: *Five dollars.*
We read $5.00: *Five dollars.*
We read $2.35: *Two dollars and thirty-five cents.*
When we have dollars and cents, we read the point **and**.
We read $48: *Forty-eight dollars.*
We read $.75: *Seventy-five cents.*
We read $.09: *Nine cents.*
We read $6.01: *Six dollars and one cent.*

Read the following amounts of money:

| $4 | $4.00 | $.40 | $.04 | 60¢ | $.60 |
| 9¢ | $3.25 | $750 | $7.50 | $2.02 | $.09 |

1. How much does the bicycle cost? the bicycle bell?

2. How much does the airplane cost?

3. Read the price of each thing that you see in the toy store.

Adding Cents

1. Carl bought a pair of shoestrings for 10¢, a pair of socks for 62¢, and a shoebrush for 25¢. How much did he pay for them?

A	**B**	**C**
10	10¢	$.10
62	62¢	.62
25	25¢	.25
97 cents	97¢	$.97

The sum is less than one dollar; so each way is correct.

2. Helen paid 63 cents for her history notebook and 95 cents for her geography workbook. How much did she pay for both books?

A	**B**	**C**
63	63¢	$ .63
95	95¢	.95
158 cents	158¢	$1.58

The answer is 158 cents, but we write 158 cents as $1.58. So we should use Form C. We always use the dollar sign ($) and the point (.) for amounts of one dollar or more. When we use Form A or Form B, we must rewrite our answer. When we use Form C, our answer is in the right form when we write it. Before we add, we usually do not know whether the sum will be one dollar or more. So if we write the numbers with the dollar sign and the point, the answer will always be in the right form.

Write these numbers in the best form and add:
3. Sixty-four cents, fifteen cents, forty cents
4. Eight cents, eighty cents, ninety-one cents
5. Twenty-five cents, fifty-two cents, ninety cents
6. Seventy cents, four cents, and seventy-five cents

Adding Cents

1. Bob made some money selling vegetables from his garden. One Saturday he sold 30 cents worth of tomatoes, some sweet potatoes for 45 cents, and 40 cents worth of celery. How much did he get for these vegetables?

2. If you have 85 cents, can you buy a bat for 50 cents and a kite for a quarter?

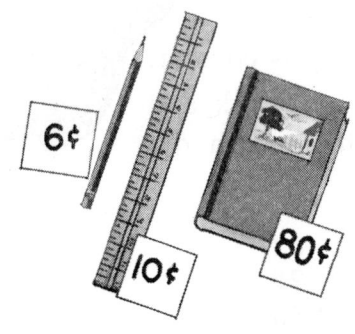

3. How much money must Ella save to buy a doll for 70¢ and a toy rocking chair for 55¢?

4. If you have a nickel, a dime, and a half dollar, how much money do you have in all?

5. Jane said, "These things will cost ninety-six cents." Is she right?

6. James put a quarter, a half dollar, and a dime in his bank. How many cents did he put in the bank?

7. How would you find the cost of several different things if you knew the price of each?

Copy and add:

	(a)	(b)	(c)	(d)	(e)	(f)
8.	$ .53	$ .28	$ .60	$ .32	$ .42	$ .64
	.46	.30	.30	.50	.43	.32
	.70	.60	.90	.84	.94	.83
9.	$ .40	$ .45	$ .15	$ .33	$ .50	$ .64
	.54	.50	.50	.34	.43	.24
	.75	.32	.80	.42	.75	.81
10.	$ .15	$ .42	$ .22	$ .90	$ .55	$ .65
	.84	.60	.97	.25	.94	.44

Subtracting Cents

1. Kate had 98 cents when she went to the store. She spent 75 cents. How much money did she have left?

A	98	**B**	98¢	**C**	$ .98
	−75		−75¢		−.75
	23 cents		23¢		$ .23

Using either Form A, B, or C, we get the right answer.

2. Jane had one dollar and twenty-five cents before she spent 75 cents for flowers. How much did she have left?

We subtract cents the way we subtract other amounts. When we subtract cents from a dollar or more, we should use the dollar sign and the point.

$1.25
 .75
$ .50

3. Jack has 80 cents. How much more money does he need to buy a scooter that costs $1.65?

Copy these amounts in the best form and add:

	(a)	(b)	(c)	(d)	(e)	(f)	(g)
4.	24¢	36¢	40¢	32¢	75¢	60¢	40¢
	63¢	20¢	25¢	60¢	21¢	30¢	50¢
	12¢	52¢	32¢	40¢	83¢	60¢	99¢
5.	50¢	78¢	42¢	90¢	6¢	91¢	84¢
	40¢	20¢	55¢	30¢	10¢	8¢	90¢
	50¢	41¢	11¢	8¢	90¢	70¢	5¢

Copy and subtract:

	(a)	(b)	(c)	(d)	(e)	(f)
6.	$ .75	$ .98	$ .98	$1.75	$1.62	$1.10
	.60	.75	.48	.95	.80	.90
7.	$1.48	$1.50	$1.75	$1.68	$1.37	$1.86
	.73	.90	.82	.85	.55	.55

Problems

scarf

1. Betty had $1.32 when she went downtown to shop for a new scarf. She bought one for 82¢. How much money did she have left after she paid for it?

2. Mary had 85 cents. She bought some fruit for 25¢. How much money had she left?

3. Jack is saving his money so he can buy a horn for his bicycle. The horn costs $1.58. Jack has already saved 85 cents. How much does he have yet to save?

4. Jack has 60 cents. When he gets a dollar, he puts his savings in the city bank. How much more money does he need before he can put a dollar in the bank?

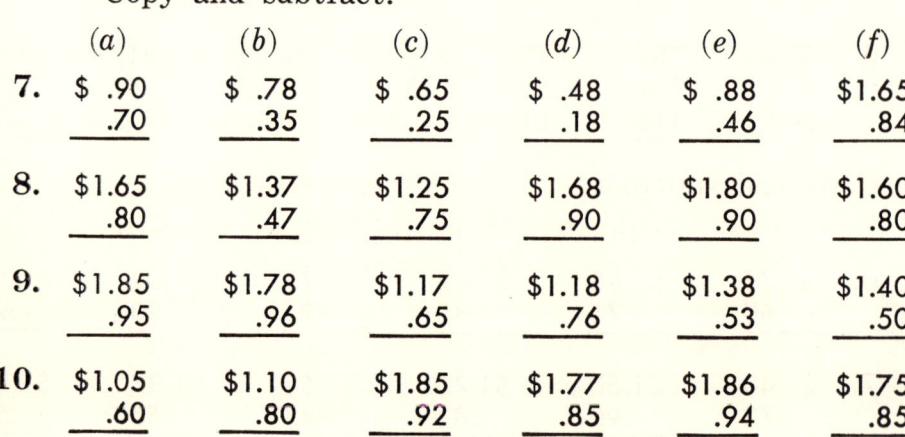
roast

5. Mrs. Brown spent $1.25 at the store for meat. She spent 55¢ for hamburger and the rest for a roast. How much did the roast cost?

6. If you know the price of an article and do not have enough money to buy it, how can you find how much more you need?

Copy and subtract:

	(a)	(b)	(c)	(d)	(e)	(f)

7.	$ .90
	  .70
		$ .78
		  .35
			$ .65
			  .25
				$ .48
				  .18
					$ .88
					  .46
						$1.65
						  .84

8.	$1.65
	  .80
		$1.37
		  .47
			$1.25
			  .75
				$1.68
				  .90
					$1.80
					  .90
						$1.60
						  .80

9.	$1.85
	  .95
		$1.78
		  .96
			$1.17
			  .65
				$1.18
				  .76
					$1.38
					  .53
						$1.40
						  .50

10.	$1.05
	  .60
		$1.10
		  .80
			$1.85
			  .92
				$1.77
				  .85
					$1.86
					  .94
						$1.75
						  .85

Multiplying Cents

It is best to use the dollar sign and the point when we multiply cents.

```
    23¢         23 cents        $.23
    ×3          ×3              ×3
    ───         ─────────       ─────
    69¢         69 cents        $.69
```

One way does not seem better than the others. What happens when we multiply 62¢ by 3?

```
    62¢         62 cents        $ .62
    ×3          ×3              ×3
    ───         ─────────       ─────
   186¢        186 cents        $1.86
```

When we have enough cents to make a dollar or more, we should write the amount as dollars, or dollars and cents. So 186¢, or 186 cents, should be written again, using the dollar sign and the point: $1.86.

Copy and multiply. Be sure you write cents in cent's place and dollars in dollar's place.

	(a)	(b)	(c)	(d)	(e)	(f)
1.	$ .62 ×4	$ .70 ×4	$ .51 ×6	$ .30 ×5	$ .72 ×3	$ .63 ×3
2.	$ .22 ×4	$ .82 ×4	$ .90 ×2	$ .50 ×5	$ .05 ×4	$ .60 ×5

3. Write these numbers in the best form and multiply:
   a. Multiply 81 cents by 4. Multiply 92 cents by 3.
   b. Multiply seventy-two cents by 4.
   c. Multiply fifty-three cents by 3.
   d. Multiply 8 cents by 4.
   e. Multiply 70 cents by 5.
   f. Multiply ninety cents by 3.

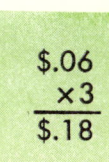

```
$.06
×3
─────
$.18
```

Problems

1. What must Jane pay for 6 cans of corn at 31¢ each?

2. Frank earned 40¢ on each of 6 days of last week. How much did he earn that week?

3. If a pound of sugar costs 21¢, how much money will you need to buy 8 pounds?

4. Raspberries were offered for sale at 20¢ a pint. Jack said, "There are two pints in a quart. So a quart of raspberries will cost **2 times** 20¢, or 40¢."
Was Jack right?

5. If you know the cost of one dozen eggs, how can you find the cost of 6 dozen eggs?

6. Frank said that he needed 28 cents to buy 2 loaves of bread at 14¢ a loaf. Was he right?

7. Was Henry right when he said that at 4¢ each, a dozen oranges would cost about a half dollar? Exactly how much would they cost?

8. How much should Walter pay for 3 football tickets at 50 cents each?

9. Was Tom right when he said that 3 movie tickets at 42 cents each would cost $1.26?

10. Ralph picked 8 quarts of sweet cherries and sold them for 30 cents a quart. How much money did he get for the cherries?

11. Bob bought 8 dozen oranges at 40¢ a dozen. How much did he pay for the oranges?

12. Jack bought 4 rolls of film for his new camera. If the films were 40¢ a roll, how much did they cost him?

Dividing Dollars and Cents

It is always best to use the dollar sign and the point when we divide dollars, or dollars and cents.

1. Mrs. Wilson paid $2.08 for 4 dozen eggs. What was the price of the eggs by the dozen?

```
      $.52
   4)$2.08
      2 0
        8
        8
```

Tell how to find the cost of one dozen eggs if you know the cost of several dozen.

2. Nuts cost 46 cents a pound. Mary said that ½ pound would cost 23 cents. Was she right?

3. Helen needs $2.80 to buy a new sweater for Jack. She wants to give it to him on his birthday, which is exactly 4 weeks from now. How much must Helen save each week to have enough money to pay for the sweater?

4. Susan said, "I have $2.00 to spend for lunches this week. I have to buy my lunch on 5 days. So I can spend $.50 for lunch each day."

5)$2.00

Was Susan right? Prove it.

5. Jack went to Oregon. He sent 4 boxes of cherries to friends back home. Altogether the cherries cost $3.68. How much did each box of cherries cost?

6. Tom spent ¼ of his $1.60 for a ticket to the show. How much did the ticket cost?

Copy and divide:

	(a)	(b)	(c)	(d)	(e)	(f)
7.	4)$1.68	4)$2.48	4)$3.60	3)$2.19	6)$1.80	3)$2.49
8.	2)$1.86	3)$1.59	3)$1.26	3)$2.76	4)$1.28	2)$1.48
9.	2)$1.66	3)$1.53	6)$1.86	4)$2.84	5)$2.00	4)$2.04

Chapter 5
Carrying

Thinking

1. Simon is painting the floor of his room. Has his thinking been good or bad?

2. Of course, we do not expect Fido to do much thinking. If he can think at all, has his thinking been good or bad?

3. Jim and Tom have built a doghouse for Fido. They built it inside their playhouse. Now, when they have the doghouse finished, they find that it is too big to go through the door. Has their thinking been good or bad?

4. Jim needs 4 pieces of board each 2 feet long. Jim is trying to saw the 4 pieces from a board that is 7 feet long. Can he do it?

Thinking about Carrying

"How many girls will there be at the Camp Fire Girls' Camp?" asked Susan.

"I heard that there will be 25 Wood Gatherers and 27 Fire Makers," answered Edith. "I will add the numbers: *Five and seven are twelve. Two and two are four.* There will be 412 girls at camp."

"Your answer must be wrong," said Susan. "I am sure our camp will not hold even a hundred girls."

Then Susan added the numbers. She got 52.

Did Edith make a mistake in adding? Or did she make a mistake in thinking about carrying?

Do you understand how Jane **carried** 1 ten?

Counters

Here is a counter in the kind of store that you see every day. You know how the counter is used. But do you know how it got its name?

Here is a counter in another store. It is the kind of store and counter that an old storekeeper used about five hundred years ago. What is the storekeeper doing? How do you think the counter in a store got its name?

Long ago people did not know how to add as we do now. They added by counting wooden discs on a **counter**. Suppose a customer had bought something for 25¢ and something else for 27¢.

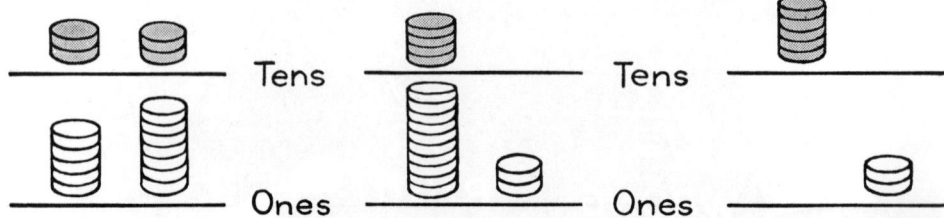

The storekeeper put 2 discs on the ten's line and 5 discs on the one's line to stand for 25, and he put 2 discs on the ten's line and 7 discs on the one's line to stand for 27. Then he piled the discs together. He put the one's discs together first. Then he put the ten's discs together. He had 12 ones. He knew that 12 is 1 ten and 2 ones. So he took 10 discs from the one's pile and put 1 disc with the tens. He had 5 tens and 2 ones, or 52. He knew that the customer owed 52 cents.

Adding by Endings

7 2 ― 9	We know that 7 and 2 are 9. So we know that 17 and 2 are 19, and we also know that 27 and 2 are 29.	17 27 2 2 ―― ―― 19 29

Say the answers:

17	13	12	11	14	13	11	10	14	10
1	3	5	6	3	5	2	7	4	5

12	11	13	12	13	10	13	12	13	11
3	8	2	1	6	8	1	2	4	5

14	10	11	10	12	12	14	11	15	16
1	2	1	6	4	6	5	3	1	3

11	12	14	16	15	16	17	15	15	11
4	7	2	1	2	2	2	3	4	7

6 8 ―― 14	Sometimes when we add, the sum of the ones is ten or more than ten. 6 and 8 are 14, and 10 are 24.	16 8 ―― 24

Say the answers:

11	12	14	18	13	12	14	13	19	16
9	8	9	7	7	9	7	9	3	4

13	14	18	18	15	14	16	16	19	16
8	6	8	5	5	8	6	5	1	9

17	18	19	17	19	19	19	17	19	16
7	6	8	3	5	6	2	4	9	7

17	15	15	17	15	19	18	15	17	18
8	7	6	5	8	4	2	9	9	9

Carrying a Ten

1. Tom and Jim want to put their savings together to buy a football that costs 90 cents. Tom has 36 cents, and Jim has 46 cents. How much money have the boys together? Have they enough money to buy the football?

$$\begin{array}{r} \overset{1}{3}6¢ \\ 46¢ \\ \hline 82¢ \end{array}$$

First we add the ones: Six and six are twelve. Twelve (12) is 1 ten and 2. So we write the 2 in one's place and carry the 1 (ten) to the ten's column.

Now we add the tens. We add the 1 ten that we carried with the other tens: One and three are four, and four are eight. We write 8 in ten's place in the answer.

Together Tom and Jim have 82 cents, but that is not enough money to buy the 90-cent football.

2. Jack is going to Springfield with his father.

"How far is it from here to Springfield?" asked Jack.

"From Ridgeville to Clinton is 68 miles, and from there to Springfield is 45 miles," answered his father. "Now you tell me how far it is."

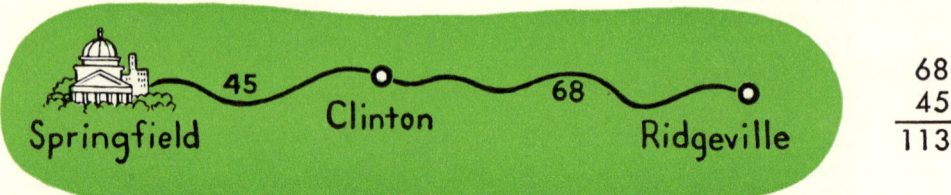

$$\begin{array}{r} 68 \\ 45 \\ \hline 113 \end{array}$$

3. Tell how these numbers were added:

26	95	47	98	75	68	48¢	39¢	39
18	75	56	22	25	47	42¢	25¢	14
44	170	103	120	100	115	90¢	64¢	53

We Study Science

The children in the Science Club put their collections of rocks, leaves, fruits, nuts, flowers, and animals in the hall for the other children to see.

1. Helen brought 24 pictures of fruit and 16 pictures of nuts. How many pictures were in her collection?

2. Jack brought 48 pictures of wild animals and 14 pictures of tame animals. How many animal pictures did he bring?

3. Susan brought 46 pictures of wild flowers and 26 pictures of garden flowers. How many pictures of flowers did she bring?

4. Jack brought 16 shells, and Sam brought 27. How many shells did the two boys bring?

5. Betty brought 2 big cardboards with leaves pasted on them. There were 26 leaves on one cardboard and 45 leaves on the other. How many leaves were in her collection?

6. Joe and Jim brought rocks. Joe brought 24 kinds of rocks, and Jim brought 18 kinds of rocks. How many different kinds of rock did the boys bring?

Copy and add:

	(a)	(b)	(c)	(d)	(e)	(f)	(g)	(h)
7.	68	94	78	67	56	58	97	78
	95	16	68	45	55	53	24	38
8.	53	32	67	68	89	14	92	75
	78	78	68	72	43	97	49	78
9.	49	88	76	39	95	98	49	75
	85	67	98	96	99	79	98	88

Adding Columns

Jack lives in Houston, Texas. His father sells shoes to the merchants in the towns around Houston. During the summer Jack goes with him on trips.

1. On Monday they drove from Houston to Orange. It is 44 miles from Houston to Liberty, 43 miles from Liberty to Beaumont, and 25 miles from Beaumont to Orange. How far did they drive that day?

```
  1
 44
 43
 25
───
112
```

First, we add the ones: 4 and 3 are 7, and 5 are 12. 12 is 1 ten and 2; so we write 2 in one's place and carry 1 (ten).

Now we add the tens: 1 (carried) and 4 are 5, and 4 are 9, and 2 are 11.

They drove 112 miles that day.

2. The next day they went from Orange to Lufkin. From Orange to Beaumont is 25 miles. From Beaumont to Woodville is 58 miles, and from there to Lufkin it is 52 miles. How many miles did they drive on Tuesday?

3. From Lufkin they drove 45 miles to Crockett, 39 miles to Madisonville, and 36 miles to Bryan. How far did they drive in going from Lufkin to Bryan?

Add the ones: 5 and 9 are 14, and 6 are 20.
Write 0 in one's place and carry the 2 (tens).
Add the tens: 2 (carried) and 4 are 6, and 3 are 9, and 3 are 12.
They drove 120 miles on this trip.

$$\begin{array}{r} 2 \\ 45 \\ 39 \\ \underline{36} \\ 120 \end{array}$$

---

4. Here are some other trips that they made together. How many miles did they drive on each trip?

Houston to Conroe........41 miles
Conroe to Huntsville.......30 miles
Huntsville to Livingston....<u>39</u> miles

Houston to Cleveland......46 miles
Cleveland to Livingston....28 miles
Livingston to Lufkin.......<u>47</u> miles

Houston to Hempstead.....50 miles
Hempstead to Navasota....21 miles
Navasota to Huntsville.....<u>43</u> miles

Houston to Huntsville......71 miles
Huntsville to Navasota.....43 miles
Navasota to Houston......<u>71</u> miles

5. Jane looked at the map on page 78 and said, "It is 74 miles from Houston to Livingston."
Was she right?

6. Alice said, "It is exactly 119 miles from Houston to Crockett." Was Alice right?

7. How far is it from Houston to Madisonville?

8. Use the map to find the **distances** between towns. Then make up problems using those distances.

Carrying When We Add

1. Bob counted the people in the parade. There were 30 sailors, 54 soldiers, and 48 Boy Scouts. How many were in the parade?

2. Susan read 38 storybooks at home and 24 books at school during the year. How many books did she read that year?

3. Jack read 95 pages in one book and 78 pages in another book. How many pages did he read in the two books?

4. In a big pasture Jim counted 24 cows, 10 calves, 9 horses, and 6 colts. How many animals did he count?

5. Miss Brown asked Tom to find how many bottles of milk were needed for the first three grades. Tom found that Grade I wanted 29 bottles, Grade II wanted 25 bottles, and Grade III wanted 18 bottles. How many bottles of milk were needed?

6. The fourth-grade class invited the third-grade class to a Halloween party. They found that there would be 38 children from the third grade, 39 children from the fourth grade, and 14 mothers and teachers. How many people in all should they plan for?

Copy and add:

	(a)	(b)	(c)	(d)	(e)	(f)	(g)	(h)	(i)
7.	38	57	68	73	27	36	19	86	98
	64	37	25	20	54	36	87	59	47
	26	65	46	57	63	64	63	34	43
8.	29	36	49	45	42	17	59	66	56
	42	38	23	56	99	29	58	17	54
	89	96	38	78	65	74	56	98	40

Buying at the Grocery Store

1. Alice bought a pound of coffee, a dozen eggs, and a pound of bacon. How much did the things that she bought cost?

$ .80
  .54
  .58
$1.92

2. Susan has on her list: 3 pounds of bananas, 1 dozen rolls, and a head of lettuce. How much money does she need to pay for the things she wants to buy?

3. Jerry asked for a bunch of celery, a pound of butter, and a dozen oranges. How much will these things cost?

4. How much should Helen pay for a bunch of carrots, a box of cookies, and 2 pounds of apples?

5. How much should Tom pay for a loaf of bread, a pound of butter, and a dozen eggs?

6. Bill bought a loaf of bread, a bunch of carrots, a pound of butter, and a bunch of celery. He gave the clerk a dollar bill. Did he give the clerk the right amount of money?

Thinking about Carrying

Edith said, "One morning at camp we had 5 dozen eggs for breakfast."

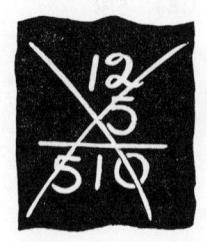

"I know there are 12 eggs in a dozen," said Ted, "and 5 **times** 12 is 510. You girls ate a lot of eggs for breakfast."

Ted thought, "Five twos are ten, and five ones are five."

What is wrong with the way Ted multiplies?

Edith showed Ted where he made his mistake. This is the way Edith multiplied:

```
 12
 ×5
  0

 12
 ×5
 60
```

The sign × means **times**. It tells us to multiply just as the sign + tells us to add and the sign − tells us to subtract.

Edith multiplied: Five twos are ten. She wrote 0 and **carried** the 1 ten. Then she multiplied the tens: Five ones are five. She added the 1 ten that she carried to the 5 tens. She wrote 6 in ten's place.

The girls ate 60 eggs for breakfast.

The answer to a multiplication question is called the **product**.

Tell how these **products** were found:

```
 13    47    24    32    42    66    85    36    57
 ×5    ×2    ×3    ×8    ×6    ×3    ×2    ×3    ×2
 65    94    72   256   252   198   170   108   114
```

1. Copy and multiply:

```
 (a)   (b)   (c)   (d)   (e)   (f)   (g)   (h)   (i)
 84    93    95    42    43    53    42    52    63
 ×3    ×4    ×3    ×9    ×5    ×6    ×7    ×8    ×5
```

More about Carrying

Sometimes when we multiply, we carry 2 tens.
Think: Four sixes are twenty-four.
Write 4 in one's place and carry 2 tens.
Think: Four twos are eight, and two are ten.
10 tens are one hundred. So we write 0 in ten's place and 1 in hundred's place.

```
 26
× 4
───
104
```

Sometimes when we multiply, we carry 3 tens.
Think: Eight fours are thirty-two.
Write 2 in one's place and carry 3 tens.
Think: Eight ones are eight, and three are eleven.

```
 14
× 8
───
112
```

Tell how we carry in each of these examples:

25	34	33	44	34	56	34	55
×4	×5	×7	×9	×8	×4	×3	×6
100	170	231	396	272	224	102	330

Think the product for each of these multiplications. Then add 3. Say, "Two fours are eight, and three are eleven." Say each product again. Then add 2.

4	2	3	8	2	3	4	7	3	2	4
×2	×3	×4	×4	×5	×6	×6	×3	×7	×9	×9

2	5	6	1	3	2	7	6	4	9	3
×2	×1	×2	×3	×3	×4	×2	×3	×4	×4	×5

4	3	8	5	7	5	8	9	6	9	8
×3	×2	×3	×4	×4	×2	×2	×3	×4	×2	×4

1. Multiply:

(a)	(b)	(c)	(d)	(e)	(f)	(g)	(h)	(i)	(j)
47	24	56	32	14	23	63	42	55	74
×2	×3	×4	×8	×9	×7	×5	×6	×5	×4

A Help in Carrying

1. In a camp there are 24 tents with 4 boys in each tent. How many boys are at the camp?

$$\begin{array}{r}\overset{1}{2}4\\ \times 4\\ \hline 96\end{array}$$

First, we multiply the ones: Four 4's are 16. We write 6 in one's place. To remember the 1 (ten) to carry, we write a **little 1** just above the 2 (tens) that are to be multiplied next.

Now we multiply the tens: Four 2's are 8, and the 1 to carry are 9. We write 9 in ten's place. There are 96 boys at the camp.

2. Jack earns money to go to camp. He works 3 days each week for Mr. Brown and gets 25¢ a day for his work. How much does he earn each week?

$$\begin{array}{r}\overset{1}{\$.2}5\\ \times 3\\ \hline \$.75\end{array}$$

We multiply cents the way we multiply tens and ones. We write the cent's answer in cent's place. We write cents in **two places** at the right of the point.

3. The boys went to camp in a bus. Jack said, "The bus is going 45 miles an hour. In 4 hours it will go 180 miles." Is Jack right?

$$\begin{array}{r}\overset{2}{4}5\\ \times 4\\ \hline 180\end{array}$$

Sometimes when we multiply, we carry 2 tens.

Think: Four 5's are 20. Write 0 in one's place and carry 2 tens. Four 4's are 16, and 2 are 18. 18 tens are 1 hundred and 8 tens; so we write 1 in hundred's place and 8 in ten's place.

The bus can go 180 miles in 4 hours.

$$\begin{array}{r}\$\overset{2}{.7}5\\ \times 4\\ \hline \$3.00\end{array}$$

4. Jack takes 4 swimming lessons a week. Each lesson is 75¢. How much do the lessons cost him each week?

84

5. Jack has 45 minutes each day for his lesson, but he uses part of the time to get ready. Actually he swims only 38 minutes. How many minutes does he swim each week?

$$\overset{3}{38} \\ \underline{\times 4} \\ 152$$

Here are some examples partly worked. Finish working each example.

Think: Nine 4's are 36.
Nine 3's are 27, and 3 are 30.

$$\overset{3}{34} \\ \underline{\times 9} \\ 6 \qquad \overset{3}{34} \\ \underline{\times 9} \\ 306$$

	(a)	(b)	(c)	(d)	(e)	(f)	(g)	(h)
6.	¹56 ×3 ―― 8	¹75 ×2 ―― 0	²68 ×3 ―― 4	²43 ×7 ―― 1	³58 ×4 ―― 2	³44 ×8 ―― 2	²23 ×8 ―― 4	¹75 ×3 ―― 5
7.	²29 ×3 ―― 7	²78 ×3 ―― 4	²95 ×4 ―― 0	³59 ×4 ―― 6	³34 ×8 ―― 2	³19 ×4 ―― 6	²24 ×5 ―― 0	³49 ×4 ―― 6

A Test

Now let us see if we can remember to carry without the use of the "little figures." Copy and multiply:

8.	76 ×5	68 ×4	58 ×5	43 ×9	14 ×7	23 ×6	76 ×4	45 ×7
9.	27 ×5	35 ×7	89 ×4	67 ×4	36 ×4	85 ×4	39 ×3	54 ×6
10.	46 ×4	58 ×2	95 ×2	95 ×3	46 ×3	39 ×4	53 ×8	14 ×8
11.	24 ×8	12 ×9	41 ×8	32 ×7	83 ×5	44 ×7	28 ×4	42 ×9

At the Grocery Store

1. Jack helps at the grocery store on Saturdays. He has to multiply and add cents, and he has to be careful when he multiplies and adds so that he will get the right answer.

When he sells some groceries to a customer, he writes the articles and the cost of each on a slip of paper, and then he adds to find how much all the groceries cost. He gives the slip to the customer.

Here are some slips that Jack wrote. See if he added correctly.

Mrs. Brown
Bread......$ .19
Steak......$ .89
Peaches....$ .25
$1.23

Mrs. Camp
Meat.......$ .86
Sugar......$ .45
Milk.......$ .18
$1.49

Mrs. Smith
Oranges....$ .36
Bananas....$ .35
Corn.......$ .30
$1.01

Mrs. Jones
Spinach....$ .15
Cabbage....$ .08
Lettuce....$ .12
$ .35

Mr. Grey
Cake.......$ .46
Beans......$ .24
Flour......$ .17
$ .87

Mrs. Hill
Bread......$ .19
Butter.....$ .52
Eggs.......$ .48
$1.09

Mrs. Bell
Sugar......$ .45
Potatoes...$ .65
Apples.....$ .55
$1.65

Mr. Ben
Soap.......$ .27
Rice.......$ .21
Olives.....$ .19
$ .67

Mr. Hays
Eggs.......$ .72
Ham........$ .80
Bananas....$ .24
$1.80

2. Jack sold 3 cans of peaches to Mrs. White. The price was 25 cents a can. How much should Jack charge Mrs. White for the peaches?

3. Jack sold 3 pounds of butter to Mrs. Hall. The price of the butter was 56 cents a pound. How much did the butter cost?

Bob's Vegetable Stand

1. Bob had such nice celery that his neighbors were glad to buy it from him at 15 cents a bunch. One day he sold 4 bunches. How much did he get for the celery?

2. Bob had 4 small baskets of potatoes to sell. He sold them for 48 cents a basket. How much did he get for the 4 baskets of potatoes?

3. Bob sold 3 big baskets of sweet potatoes for 65¢ a basket. How much did he get for the sweet potatoes?

Copy and multiply:

	(a)	(b)	(c)	(d)	(e)	(f)	(g)
4.	$ .42 7	$ .76 4	$ .38 5	$ .43 9	$ .65 5	$ .21 9	$ .41 8
5.	$ .47 2	$ .34 7	$ .54 6	$ .44 5	$ .14 5	$ .25 8	$ .63 3
6.	$ .33 9	$ .34 8	$ .45 8	$ .67 3	$ .25 4	$ .35 3	$ .12 7
7.	$ .98 4	$ .75 4	$ .35 7	$ .41 2	$ .14 9	$ .12 9	$ .93 2
8.	$ .45 6	$ .80 3	$ .95 4	$ .38 2	$ .98 2	$ .92 5	$ .34 6

Using a Ten When We Subtract

We want to subtract 27 from 43.

Forty-three is 4 tens and 3 ones. Then at the start we have 4 tens and 3 ones. Twenty-seven is 2 tens and 7 ones. So we want to take 2 tens and 7 ones away from 4 tens and 3 ones.

First, we take away the ones. We cannot take 7 ones from 3 ones. We must use 1 of the 4 tens. Now we think, "Seven from thirteen is six."

Next, we take away the tens. We used 1 of the 4 tens; so we take 2 tens from 3 tens. There is 1 ten left.

We have 1 ten and 6 ones left. When we take 27 from 43, we have 16 left.

Carrying Back a Ten

1. Jack is pasting stamps in his stamp book. He has 54 stamps in all. He has pasted 28 of them in his book. How many stamps does he have yet to paste in his book?

To answer the question, we must subtract 28 from 54. At the start we do not have enough ones. So we **carry back** one of the 5 tens and use it with the 4 ones we do have. We now think, "Eight from fourteen is six." We write 6 in one's place.

Since we have used one of our 5 tens, we have only 4 tens. We now think, "Two from four is two." We write 2 in ten's place.

Jack has 26 stamps yet to paste in his book.

$$\begin{array}{r} \overset{4}{\cancel{5}}14 \\ -2\ 8 \\ \hline 2\ 6 \end{array}$$

2. There are 132 children in the fourth grade. The school nurse weighed 85 children today. How many children does the school nurse still have to weigh?

$$\begin{array}{r} \overset{12}{1\cancel{3}}12 \\ 8\ 5 \\ \hline 4\ 7 \end{array}$$

3. Jim has 102 Lincoln-head pennies, and Joe has 55. How many more Lincoln-head pennies has Jim than Joe?

$$\begin{array}{r} \overset{9}{1\cancel{0}}12 \\ 5\ 5 \\ \hline \end{array}$$

4. Susan weighs 66 pounds, and her mother weighs 115 pounds. How much less does Susan weigh than her mother?

$$\begin{array}{r} \overset{10}{1\cancel{1}}15 \\ 6\ 6 \\ \hline \end{array}$$

Copy and subtract:

	(a)	(b)	(c)	(d)	(e)	(f)	(g)	(h)
5.	61 27	55 18	48 9	93 89	92 85	31 12	44 19	84 37
6.	107 79	113 87	115 66	151 94	105 98	173 74	136 59	113 54

Carrying Back a Ten

We sometimes have to subtract ones when we do not have enough ones at the start. We carry back one of the tens and use it with the ones we have.

We use a ten the same way when we have **no ones** at all at the start.

$$\begin{array}{r} 60 \\ -28 \\ \hline 32 \end{array}$$

Suppose we want to subtract 28 from 60. At the start we have 6 tens but no ones, and we want to take away 8 ones. We use 1 of the 6 tens. We think, "8 from 10 is 2."

Now we subtract from the tens. We have used 1 ten. So we take 2 tens from 5 tens.

We now have 3 tens and 2 ones, or 32, left. When we take 28 from 60, we have 32 left.

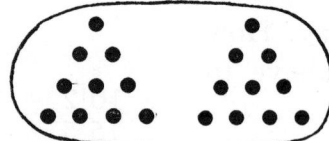

1. Tom had 150 evening papers to deliver. He has already delivered 67 of the papers. How many papers has he yet to deliver?

2. Tell how these subtractions were made:

$$\begin{array}{r} {}^{8}\cancel{9}{}^{1}0 \\ 5\ 7 \\ \hline 3\ 3 \end{array} \qquad \begin{array}{r} {}^{1\ 5}\cancel{16}{}^{1}0 \\ 9\ 8 \\ \hline 6\ 2 \end{array} \qquad \begin{array}{r} {}^{9}\cancel{10}{}^{1}0 \\ 5\ 6 \\ \hline 4\ 4 \end{array} \qquad \begin{array}{r} {}^{1\ 0}\cancel{11}{}^{1}0 \\ 8\ 4 \\ \hline 2\ 6 \end{array} \qquad \begin{array}{r} {}^{1\ 2}\cancel{13}{}^{1}0 \\ 7\ 5 \\ \hline 5\ 5 \end{array}$$

3. Copy and subtract:

(a)	(b)	(c)	(d)	(e)	(f)	(g)	(h)	(i)
80	100	170	170	80	100	90	90	70
32	75	86	91	75	48	38	42	36

Our Own Problems

1. There were 25 words in the spelling test. Each word spelled correctly counted 4 points. The number of words each child spelled correctly is shown below. Find the score of each child in the spelling test.

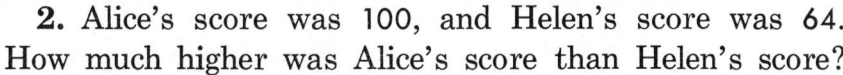

Alice ___ 25	*Jim* ___ 20	*Susan* ___ 19
Jane ___ 24	*Joe* ___ 18	*Helen* ___ 16
Dick ___ 14	*Tom* ___ 17	*Mary* ___ 15

2. Alice's score was 100, and Helen's score was 64. How much higher was Alice's score than Helen's score?

3. Joe's score was 72, and Dick's score was 56. How much less was Dick's score than Joe's score?

4. Mary said, "I made a low score. I made only 60, but I made a better score than Dick. He made 56. So my score was 4 points better than his."
Was Mary right?

5. Alice said, "I made almost **twice** as much as Dick." Was Alice right?

6. "Alice had the best score, and I had the next best," said Jane. "I missed only one word, but Alice did not miss any. So she beat me by ___ points."

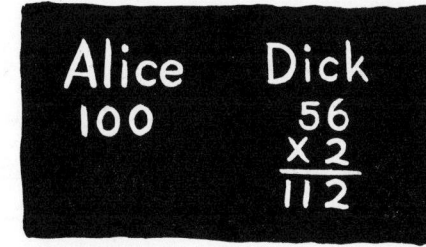

7. Find the difference between these scores:

(a)	(b)	(c)	(d)
Alice 100	*Jane* 96	*Joe* 72	*Jim* 80
Dick 56	*Tom* 68	*Helen* 64	*Mary* 60

Subtracting Cents

Tim, Ed, and Roy are finishing their cars for the soap-box derby.

1. Tim had $1.15 when he went downtown to buy paint for his racer. He bought a pint of paint for 39¢. How much money did he have left?

2. Ed is saving his money to buy a horn for his racer. The horn costs $1.90. Ed has saved 95¢. How much more money must he save before he can buy the horn?

3. Roy had a dollar. He bought a safety reflector for 45¢. How much money did he have left?

Copy and subtract:

	(a)	(b)	(c)	(d)	(e)	(f)
4.	$ .90 .48	$ .75 .36	$ .60 .25	$ .48 .28	$ .86 .56	$ .92 .45
5.	$1.50 .65	$1.65 .78	$1.37 .59	$1.20 .86	$1.65 .98	$1.00 .53
6.	$1.60 .88	$1.83 .65	$1.90 .84	$1.17 .69	$1.14 .76	$1.32 .63
7.	$1.48 .79	$1.50 .91	$1.75 .77	$1.90 .82	$1.37 .58	$1.62 .84

Checking Subtraction

The best check is to do your work carefully. Another check is to add the answer and the number you take away.

Suppose we have to subtract 45 from 93. We subtract and get the answer 48.

To check, we write 45 under 48 and add. Before we add, we cover the 93 at the top. The sum should be the same as the number from which you subtracted. It should be 93.

```
  93 ←
 −45
  48
       Same
  48
 +45
  93 ←
```

Copy, subtract, and check the answers:

	(a)	(b)	(c)	(d)	(e)	(f)	(g)	(h)
1.	95 27	78 39	60 36	70 47	90 38	81 18	91 26	73 44
2.	70 35	96 56	82 54	95 39	112 48	115 79	100 48	104 78
3.	161 86	172 92	153 73	146 86	105 58	150 87	102 78	130 67
4.	$.94 .37	$.98 .49	$.50 .26	$1.12 .57	$1.00 .69			
5.	$1.25 .60	$1.50 .85	$1.48 .70	$1.37 .90	$1.14 .76			

```
$1.10
  .68
$ .42
  .68
$1.10
```

A Test

Read each sentence. Say the word that belongs in the blank.

1. We add tens the way we add <u>ones</u>.
2. We subtract tens the way we subtract ___.
3. In subtracting, when we do not have enough ones at the start, we carry back a ten and use it with the ___ that we already have.
4. When we add ones and have 10 or more as an answer, we ___ the ten to the next column and add it with the other ___.
5. We multiply tens the way we multiply ___.
6. We divide tens the way we divide ___.
7. When we add, or subtract, or multiply, or divide tens, we must write our ___ answer in ___ place.
8. When we have no ones to write, we write ___ in one's place to put our tens in ___ place.
9. When we add tens and ones, first we add the ___, and then we add the ___.
10. When we multiply tens and ones, first we multiply the ___ and then we multiply the tens.
11. When we divide tens and ones, first we divide the ___, and then we divide the ___.

Write and work an example to show that you know the meaning of each sentence above.

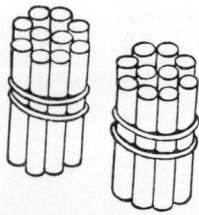

```
  20      40      20         20
 +20     -20      ×2      2)40
 ---     ---     ---         40
  40      20      40
```

[Test]   **Showing That You Know**

1. How do we add tens?

2. Copy and add:

(a)	(b)	(c)	(d)	(e)	(f)	(g)	(h)	
70	90	70	85	98	75	92	87	(46)
80	60	30	85	76	96	98	75	(76)

3. How do we subtract tens?

4. Copy and subtract:

115	104	100	150	186	192	180	178	
87	94	83	87	97	98	92	90	(50)
								(89)

5. How do we multiply tens?

6. Copy and multiply:

34	48	40	45	98	86	54	53	
6	3	6	9	4	5	8	7	(54)
								(82)

7. How do we divide tens?

8. Copy and divide:

(a)	(b)	(c)	(d)	(e)	(f)	(g)	
4)168	5)100	5)205	6)240	7)357	9)189	6)300	(56)
							(57)

9. How do we find part of a number?

10. Find:

(a) ½ of 168   (b) ¼ of 164   (c) ⅓ of 210   (d) ⅙ of 186   (e) ⅕ of 200

(40)

11. The arrow points to what measure on the ruler?

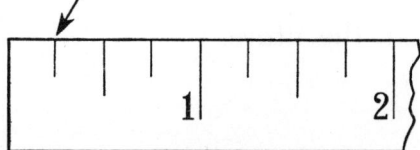 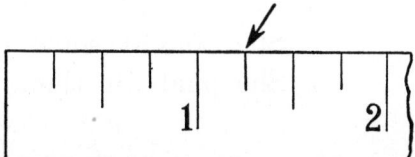

Chapter 6
Reading and Solving Problems

What Happened?

Betty went to the store for her mother. She bought cheese for 57¢, crackers for 14¢, and meat for 89¢. How much did these things cost altogether?

In many problems something happens. In this problem here are the things that happened:

Betty went to the store.
She bought some things at the store.
She paid for them.

Read each problem carefully. Forget about the numbers, but be able to tell in your own words what happens.

1. Jane and June are saving their money to buy a radio. They have already saved $11. The radio they want costs $20. How much more money must they save before they can buy the radio?

2. Mary got a new book for her birthday. There are 192 pages in her book. She has already read 95 pages of it. How many pages has she yet to read?

3. "There goes the Flyer," said Jack. "It goes a mile a minute. That means it goes 60 miles an hour. Our car is going 45 miles an hour."

How much faster is the train going than the car?

4. Last Saturday Helen spent 40 minutes practicing her piano lesson, 30 minutes studying her history lesson, and 25 minutes working some examples in arithmetic. How many minutes in all did Helen spend working on her lessons?

5. Tom saw a book in the store window. The book cost $1.29. Tom wanted to buy the book, but he did not have enough money. He had $.80. How much more money did he need to have enough to buy the book?

6. When Alice went to town, she had $1.60 in her purse. She spent a little here and a little there, but she had bought nothing to take home with her. When she got home, she counted her money. She had 75¢. How much money had she spent?

7. A ticket to the show costs 44¢, and popcorn costs 10¢. Jane has 50¢. Does she have enough to go to the show and buy a box of popcorn?

Kinds of Problems

Something does not always happen in a problem. Often a problem just tells some facts. A **fact** is something that is true.

~~~~~~~~~~~~~~~~~~~~~~~~~~~~~~~~

Jack and his puppy together weigh 90 pounds. Jack alone weighs 72 pounds. How much does the puppy weigh?

~~~~~~~~~~~~~~~~~~~~~~~~~~~~~~~~

Nothing happens in this problem. It just tells us **two facts.** What are the two facts?

Read each problem carefully. In which problems does something happen? Which problems just tell us facts?

1. The class made 4 books about boys and girls of other lands. Each book has 24 pages in it. How many pages are there in the four books?

2. There are 4 pictures on a page, and there are 24 pages in a book. How many pictures are in a book?

3. Joe picked 28 of his best tomatoes. He put them in bags to take to his neighbors. He put 4 tomatoes in each bag. To how many neighbors did he take a bag of tomatoes?

4. Jerry wants to save one fourth of the money he earns. He earned $3.60 this week. How much money should he save?

auditorium

5. In the auditorium at school there are 42 rows of seats. There are 8 seats in each row. How many seats are in the auditorium?

6. Fred had saved 70¢. Then he earned 25¢ on Friday and 85¢ on Saturday. How much **did** Fred have then?

What Does the Problem Tell?

A problem always tells us more than one fact. It may tell us several facts.

~~~~~~

Eight boys went on a picnic on Saturday. The food for the picnic cost $3.28. Each boy paid his share of the money. What was each boy's share?

~~~~~~

Here are the facts that the problem tells:
(*a*) There were eight boys. (*b*) The food cost $3.28. (*c*) Each boy paid the same amount of money.

Read the problem carefully. Find out exactly what the problem tells. *Remember: It may tell several facts.*

1. Mary bought 4 yards of lace for her dress. The lace cost 15¢ a yard. How much should Mary pay for the lace?

2. Ann went to the store for her mother. She bought a loaf of bread for 16¢, a can of peaches for 30¢, and a jar of peanut butter for 20¢. How much did these things cost altogether?

3. Jane earned $1.00. June earned 25¢ less than Jane. How much did June earn?

4. Bill weighs 73 pounds, and his father weighs 161 pounds. Bill's father is how much heavier than Bill?

5. Mrs. Jackson canned 48 jars of peaches, 35 jars of pears, and 37 jars of cherries. How many jars of fruit did she can?

6. Tom put the jars on the shelves in the basement. He put 20 jars on each shelf, and there were 6 shelves. How many jars did he put on the shelves?

Using the Facts

In every problem we use the facts to find out something that we do not know. The problem asks a question to let us know what we are to find out. When we have answered the question, we have **solved** the problem.

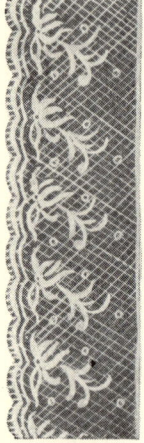

lace

~~~~~~~~~~~~~~~~~~~~~~~~~~~~

The lace for Mary's dress cost 60¢. She gave the clerk 75¢ to pay for the lace. How much change should she get back?

~~~~~~~~~~~~~~~~~~~~~~~~~~~~

The problem tells: *(a)* The lace cost 60¢. *(b)* Mary gave the clerk 75¢ to pay for the lace.

It asks: *How much change should Mary get?*

The question makes us know that we are to find out how much change the clerk should give Mary.

Read each problem. What does it tell? What does it ask?

1. Mary missed 8 of the 20 words in a spelling test. How many words did she spell right?

2. Henry bought a shirt for 95¢, a tie for 50¢, and a handkerchief for 25¢. How much did he pay for them?

3. Tom had $1.20. He paid 65¢ for a tie. How much money did he have left after he paid for the tie?

4. During one week Fred sold 68 papers at 5¢ each. How much did he get for all the papers?

5. James wants to buy a knife that costs $1.48. He has only 75¢. How much more money does he need?

Read each problem again. Now use the facts to find the answer to the question that the problem asks.

The School Picnic

Solve each problem:

1. The children of the third, fourth, and fifth grades of the West School went on a picnic. There were 43 pupils of the third grade who went, 42 pupils of the fourth grade, and 35 pupils of the fifth grade. How many children went on the picnic?

2. Of the 120 pupils who went on the picnic, 61 were boys. How many girls went on the picnic?

3. Some of the 120 pupils went in streetcars and some went in school busses. If 54 pupils went in streetcars, how many went in the school busses?

4. There were 3 bus loads of pupils with 22 pupils in each bus. How many pupils were in the three busses?

5. The children sat down to eat their picnic lunch at 6 long tables. There were 20 pupils at each table. How many pupils were eating at the tables?

Understanding a Problem

Read the problem carefully so that you understand it. Then tell it in your own words.

Jack's father sold all but 18 of his 40 pigs. How many pigs did he sell?

Here is the way Jim told the problem: "Jack's father had 40 pigs. He kept 18 pigs and sold the others. How many pigs did he sell?"

1. Jerry gave away all but 48 of his 100 marbles. How many marbles did he give away?

2. The 34 pupils in the fourth grade and the teacher are going to the zoo. They have hired cars and drivers. Five people can ride in each car with the driver. How many cars will be needed to take them to the zoo?

3. George had tied 8 radishes in each bunch. Mrs. Smith asked him how many radishes she would get in 5 bunches. What should George answer?

4. Four girls made sandwiches. They made 128 sandwiches altogether. Each girl made the same number of sandwiches. How many sandwiches did each girl make?

5. There were 6 boys who brought the oranges. Each boy brought a sack with 24 oranges in it. How many oranges did the boys bring?

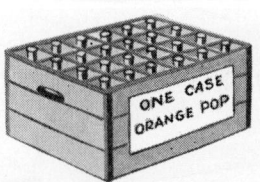

6. The milkman brought 4 cases of chocolate milk. There were 24 bottles in each case. How many bottles of chocolate milk were delivered?

The Important Facts

Some facts that a problem tells are very **important** because we use them to solve the problem. Some facts are not important because we do not use them to solve the problem. As we read a problem, we must learn to choose the important facts.

The girls used 164 yards of paper to make their Indian dresses for the play. They used 4 yards for each dress. How many dresses did they make?

To solve this problem, it is not important to know that: (*a*) The dresses were Indian dresses. (*b*) The girls were going to be in a play.

It is important to know that: (*a*) Each dress took four yards of paper. (*b*) The girls used 164 yards of paper in all. Without these two facts we cannot solve the problem.

Read each problem carefully. Decide which are the important facts. Which facts are not important?

1. Miss Green needed some flowerpots. Jack brought 8, Susan brought 6, Jane brought 4, and Jim brought 7. How many flowerpots did the children bring?

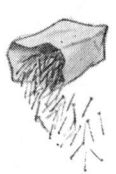

2. Jim had saved his money. He spent part of it for things he needed to build a house for his dog. He spent 90¢ for boards, 55¢ for paint, and 5¢ for nails. How much did he spend in all for these things?

Careful Reading

It is very important to read a problem carefully. If we do not, we may overlook some little word that is very important. We cannot understand the problem until we know the meaning of that word, and we cannot solve the problem unless we understand it.

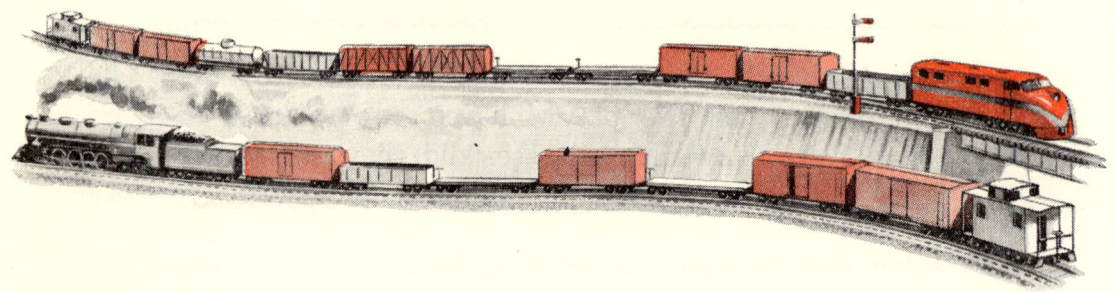

1. Answer these questions about the trains. Watch out for the words **each** and **both**.

    a. How many cars does **each** train have?

    b. How many cars do **both** trains have?

    c. How many flatcars does **each** train have?

    d. How many flatcars do **both** trains have?

2. Jack bought two puzzle games. He paid 65¢ for one and 50¢ for the other. How much did he pay for both games?

3. Jim bought two puzzle games. He paid 65¢ for each game. How much did both games cost?

4. Alice paid 35¢ for a big can of orange juice and 15¢ for a small can of orange juice. How much did she pay for both cans?

5. Alice paid 35¢ **apiece** for two large cans of orange juice. How much did she pay for both cans?

6. Jack earned 90¢ which was 15¢ less than Tom earned. How much did Tom earn?

"Jack earned **less** than Tom. So Tom earned more than Jack. Jack earned 90¢; so Tom earned 15¢ more than that. He earned 15¢ more than 90¢, or $1.05," said Frank.

7. Jim weighs 92 pounds which is 69 pounds less than his father weighs. How much does Jim's father weigh?

8. Joe and Jim together earned $1.60. Joe earned 65¢. How much did Jim earn?

9. A box **full** of apples weighs 100 pounds, and the empty box weighs 16 pounds. How much do the apples weigh?

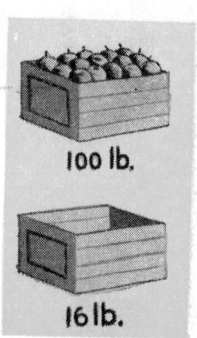

10. The milkman **left** 36 bottles of chocolate milk and 84 bottles of regular milk at school. How many bottles of milk did the milkman leave at school?

11. Joe, Jim, and Jerry worked at the same job. **Together** they earned $2.10. They divided the money equally. How much money did each boy get?

12. Jerry solved 35 examples in arithmetic, and David solved 37 examples. How many examples did both boys solve?

13. David and Alice each solved 37 examples. How many examples did both of them solve?

14. Fred has his chickens in 4 pens. He has 80 chickens in all. There are the same number of chickens in each pen. How many chickens are in each pen?

Important Numbers

Some numbers in a problem are very important. Sometimes numbers in a problem are unimportant because we do not need them to solve the problem. We must think what the problem is about. Then we must use only the numbers we need to find the answer to the question.

~~~~~~~~~~~~~~~~~~~~~~~~~~~~~~~~

Jim and his father fished for **3** hours on the lake. Jim caught **8** fish, and his father caught **24** fish. How many fish did they catch altogether?

~~~~~~~~~~~~~~~~~~~~~~~~~~~~~~~~

To answer the question, it is important to know how many fish Jim caught and how many fish his father caught. So **8** and **24** are the important numbers. We do not have to know how many hours they fished. So the number **3** is not important.

Read each problem carefully. Decide which are the important numbers in each problem. Are there any **unimportant** numbers?

1. Ed saw 3 kinds of horses on his uncle's farm. He saw 4 white horses, 10 red horses, and 7 black horses. How many horses did he see?

2. Betty bought 2 pieces of cloth to make a curtain for the stage. She paid 85¢ for the cloth. She gave the clerk $1.00. How much change should she get?

Facts the Question Tells

Sometimes one of the facts that we need to work a problem is found in the question.

~~~~~~~~~~~~~~~~~~~~~~~~~~~~~~~~~~~~~~~

The children in the fourth grade sold 43 tickets to the school play. How much money did they get for the tickets if they sold them for 8¢ each?

~~~~~~~~~~~~~~~~~~~~~~~~~~~~~~~~~~~~~~~

We cannot solve this problem unless we know the fact that is found in the question: *The tickets sold for* 8 *cents apiece.*

Read each problem carefully. What important fact is found in the question?

1. Helen began to practice her piano lesson at 4:15. At what time will she be through with her lesson if she practices 40 minutes?

2. Helen practices her piano lesson 40 minutes each day. How many minutes does she practice in 6 days?

Sometimes all the facts are found in the question.

3. If Helen's piano lessons cost 75¢ each, how much will 5 lessons cost?

4. Jack takes violin lessons. If he practiced 30 minutes on Friday, 45 minutes on Saturday, and 45 minutes on Sunday, how long did he practice?

Chapter 7
New Multiplications and Divisions

A Quick Way to Count

1. The farmer brings eggs to Jane's mother every Saturday morning. He counts the eggs by threes: **three, six, nine, twelve, fifteen, eighteen,** and so on.

Count by threes to thirty-six.

2. When Jane puts the eggs away, she counts them by twos: **two, four, six, eight, ten,** and so on.

Count by twos to twenty.

3. John said that he could count from two to twenty, but not from four to forty.

"This is the way I learned to count by **fours**," said Jack. "First, I count by twos to twenty and write the numbers. Then I multiply each number by two."

Count by fours to forty.

4. Count by fives to fifty.

```
  2    4    6    8   10
 x2   x2   x2   x2   x2
  4    8   12   16   20

 12   14   16   18   20
 x2   x2   x2   x2   x2
 24   28   32   36   40
```

2	4	6	8	10	12	14	16	18
3	6	9	12	15	18	21	24	27
4	8	12	16	20	24	28	32	36
5	10	15	20	25	30	35	40	45

A Review of Multiplication

"How many multiplications do we know?" asked Betty.

"We know our ones, of course," said Bob.

1	2	3	4	5	6	7	8	9
×1	×1	×1	×1	×1	×1	×1	×1	×1
1	2	3	4	5	6	7	8	9
1	1	1	1	1	1	1	1	1
×1	×2	×3	×4	×5	×6	×7	×8	×9
1	2	3	4	5	6	7	8	9

"And we can count by twos to twenty," said Ruth; "so we know the twos."

"And by threes to thirty," said Joe.

"And by fours to forty," said Ann.

"And by fives to fifty—about the easiest of all," said Tom. "We know the ones, the twos, the threes, the fours, and the fives."

"How many more multiplications do we yet have to learn?" asked Miss Green.

"The sixes, sevens, eights, and nines," said everyone but Nell.

"We already know most of the sixes, sevens, eights, and nines," said Nell. "We learned them with the ones, twos, threes, fours, and fives."

Multiplication Tables

The pupils in Miss Green's room made multiplication tables of the sixes, sevens, eights, and nines. They wrote the answers to the ones they knew.

6 ×1 — 6	6 ×2 — 12	6 ×3 — 18	6 ×4 — 24	6 ×5 — 30	6 ×6 —	6 ×7 —	6 ×8 —	6 ×9 —
7 ×1 — 7	7 ×2 — 14	7 ×3 — 21	7 ×4 — 28	7 ×5 — 35	7 ×6 —	7 ×7 —	7 ×8 —	7 ×9 —
8 ×1 — 8	8 ×2 — 16	8 ×3 — 24	8 ×4 — 32	8 ×5 — 40	8 ×6 —	8 ×7 —	8 ×8 —	8 ×9 —
9 ×1 — 9	9 ×2 — 18	9 ×3 — 27	9 ×4 — 36	9 ×5 — 45	9 ×6 —	9 ×7 —	9 ×8 —	9 ×9 —

"We have 16 more multiplications to learn," said Jane.

"Not as many as 16," said Nell. "Because when we learn 7 sixes are 42, we know that 6 sevens are 42."

```
  6        7
 ×7       ×6
 ——       ——
 42       42
```

Nell was right. Why?

"We have 16 divisions to learn, too, because there is a division that goes with each multiplication," said Bob.

"Don't you remember?" explained Nell. "When we learn one multiplication, we know another multiplication and two divisions."

"What have you to say about the **doubles**?" asked Jack.

What do you think Nell answered?

```
  6          5
 ×5         ×6
 ——         ——
 30         30

    6          5
 5)30       6)30

  5
 ×5         5)25
 ——
 25
```

110

The 6's in Multiplication and Division

Then the children made division tables for the sixes, sevens, eights, and nines.

$$6\overline{)6}^{1} \quad 6\overline{)12}^{2} \quad 6\overline{)18}^{3} \quad 6\overline{)24}^{4} \quad 6\overline{)30}^{5} \quad 6\overline{)36} \quad 6\overline{)42} \quad 6\overline{)48} \quad 6\overline{)54}$$

$$7\overline{)7}^{1} \quad 7\overline{)14}^{2} \quad 7\overline{)21}^{3} \quad 7\overline{)28}^{4} \quad 7\overline{)35}^{5} \quad 7\overline{)42} \quad 7\overline{)49} \quad 7\overline{)56} \quad 7\overline{)63}$$

$$8\overline{)8}^{1} \quad 8\overline{)16}^{2} \quad 8\overline{)24}^{3} \quad 8\overline{)32}^{4} \quad 8\overline{)40}^{5} \quad 8\overline{)48} \quad 8\overline{)56} \quad 8\overline{)64} \quad 8\overline{)72}$$

$$9\overline{)9}^{1} \quad 9\overline{)18}^{2} \quad 9\overline{)27}^{3} \quad 9\overline{)36}^{4} \quad 9\overline{)45}^{5} \quad 9\overline{)54} \quad 9\overline{)63} \quad 9\overline{)72} \quad 9\overline{)81}$$

On a piece of paper that you can keep, write the multiplication and division tables for the sixes, sevens, eights, and nines. Then write the answers to all of the multiplications and divisions that you know.

How many do you still have to learn?

Now let us find the new multiplications and divisions for sixes.

Six sixes are how many? Count the tens. Then see how many ones are left over.

$$\begin{array}{r} 6 \\ \times 6 \\ \hline 36 \end{array} \qquad 6\overline{)36}^{\;6}_{\;36}$$

How many sixes are in 36?

Seven sixes are how many?

How many sixes are in 42?

Write the new multiplications and new divisions for sixes in your table.

Thinking about Multiplications

> 2 sixes are 12
> 4 sixes are 24
> 6 sixes are 36

"Let us do some thinking about the new multiplications. Let's begin with the sixes. Six sixes are how many? We already know that 2 sixes are 12, and 4 sixes are 24. So we know that 6 sixes are 36," said Miss Green.

Nell got the idea right away.

Do you get the idea?

Nell said, "I understand, and I know another way to find how many 6 sixes are. I know that 5 sixes are 30, and 6 sixes would be one more six. So 6 sixes are 36."

"I know another way," said Ned. "3 sixes are 18, and 6 sixes are 2 times 18, or 36."

"Let us write our different ways on the board," said Nell. "Then maybe someone can think of another way."

What is another way to find how many 6 sixes are?

Miss Green			Nell		Ned	
6 ×2 — 12	6 ×4 — 24	12 24 — 36	6 ×5 — 30	30 +6 — 36	6 ×3 — 18	18 ×2 — 36
	6 ×6 — 36			6 ×6 — 36		6 ×6 — 36

"I can find how many 9 sixes are," said Betty. "Nine sixes are the same as 5 sixes and 4 sixes."

Billy said, "Nine sixes are the same as 3 times three sixes."

Tell how Betty and Billy found that 9 sixes are 54.

```
           Betty                          Billy
   6     6    30     6           6     18       6
  x5    x4   +24    x9          x3    x3      x9
  ——    ——   ———    ——          ——    ——      ——
  30    24    54    54          18    54      54
```

Seven sixes are how many?
Seven sixes are the same as 4 sixes and 3 sixes.
Seven sixes are the same as 5 sixes and 2 sixes.

```
  6     6    24     6           6     6    30     6
 x4    x3   +18    x7          x5    x2   +12    x7
 ——    ——   ———    ——          ——    ——   ———    ——
 24    18    42    42          30    12    42    42
```

Eight sixes are how many?
8 sixes are the same as 4 sixes and 4 sixes.
8 sixes are the same as 2 times 4 sixes.

```
  6     6    24     6           6    24     6
 x4    x4   +24    x8          x4   x2     x8
 ——    ——   ———    ——          ——   ——     ——
 24    24    48    48          24   48     48
```

Say the answers:

```
  6    6    6    6    6    6    6    6    6
 x2   x4   x1   x7   x5   x8   x9   x3   x6
 ——   ——   ——   ——   ——   ——   ——   ——   ——

  7    8    6    4    9    5    2    1    3
 x6   x6   x6   x6   x6   x6   x6   x6   x6
 ——   ——   ——   ——   ——   ——   ——   ——   ——
```

Multiplication and Division Families

Most multiplications and divisions go in families.

If you know $\begin{array}{r}6\\ \times 1\\ \hline 6\end{array}$, you also know $\begin{array}{r}1\\ \times 6\\ \hline 6\end{array}$ $6\overline{)6}^{\,1}$ $1\overline{)6}^{\,6}$

Look at the multiplication in each box. Then say the answers to the questions in that box.

$\begin{array}{r}6\\ \times 2\\ \hline 12\end{array}$ $6\overline{)12}$ $\begin{array}{r}2\\ \times 6\\ \hline 12\end{array}$ $2\overline{)12}$	$\begin{array}{r}6\\ \times 4\\ \hline 24\end{array}$ $6\overline{)24}$ $\begin{array}{r}4\\ \times 6\\ \hline 24\end{array}$ $4\overline{)24}$
$\begin{array}{r}6\\ \times 5\\ \hline 30\end{array}$ $6\overline{)30}$ $\begin{array}{r}5\\ \times 6\\ \hline 30\end{array}$ $5\overline{)30}$	$\begin{array}{r}6\\ \times 3\\ \hline 18\end{array}$ $6\overline{)18}$ $\begin{array}{r}3\\ \times 6\\ \hline 18\end{array}$ $3\overline{)18}$
$\begin{array}{r}6\\ \times 7\\ \hline 42\end{array}$ $6\overline{)42}$ $\begin{array}{r}7\\ \times 6\\ \hline 42\end{array}$ $7\overline{)42}$	$\begin{array}{r}6\\ \times 6\\ \hline 36\end{array}$ $6\overline{)36}$ $\begin{array}{r}6\\ \times 6\\ \hline 36\end{array}$ $6\overline{)36}$
$\begin{array}{r}6\\ \times 8\\ \hline 48\end{array}$ $6\overline{)48}$ $\begin{array}{r}8\\ \times 6\\ \hline 48\end{array}$ $8\overline{)48}$	$\begin{array}{r}6\\ \times 9\\ \hline 54\end{array}$ $6\overline{)54}$ $\begin{array}{r}9\\ \times 6\\ \hline 54\end{array}$ $9\overline{)54}$

Use the table to help you learn and remember the multiplications and divisions for sixes.

Table of Sixes

$\begin{array}{r}6\\ \times 1\\ \hline 6\end{array}$	$\begin{array}{r}6\\ \times 2\\ \hline 12\end{array}$	$\begin{array}{r}6\\ \times 3\\ \hline 18\end{array}$	$\begin{array}{r}6\\ \times 4\\ \hline 24\end{array}$	$\begin{array}{r}6\\ \times 5\\ \hline 30\end{array}$	$\begin{array}{r}6\\ \times 6\\ \hline 36\end{array}$	$\begin{array}{r}6\\ \times 7\\ \hline 42\end{array}$	$\begin{array}{r}6\\ \times 8\\ \hline 48\end{array}$	$\begin{array}{r}6\\ \times 9\\ \hline 54\end{array}$
$6\overline{)6}^{\,1}$	$6\overline{)12}^{\,2}$	$6\overline{)18}^{\,3}$	$6\overline{)24}^{\,4}$	$6\overline{)30}^{\,5}$	$6\overline{)36}^{\,6}$	$6\overline{)42}^{\,7}$	$6\overline{)48}^{\,8}$	$6\overline{)54}^{\,9}$

Problems

1. Bob has an order for 9 bunches of green onions. He ties 6 onions in each bunch. How many onions does he need for this order? Nine 6's are how many?

2. He sells radishes at 6¢ a bunch. How much should he get for 7 bunches? for 8 bunches?

3. Bob has 48 fancy plums left. He wants to put them into little boxes. How many boxes will he need if he puts 6 plums in a box? How many 6's are in 48?

4. Bob sold 6 oranges at 5¢ each. How much was he paid for the oranges?

5. Jack asked Bob to sell 6 of his pumpkins at the stand. Jack sold the pumpkins at 9¢ each.

"Thanksgiving is over, and your pumpkins were hard to sell, but I sold them for 9¢ apiece. Here is a half dollar and four pennies," said Bob.

Did Bob give Jack the right amount of money?

6. At 6¢ each, how many apples can Jane buy for 30¢?

7. Tom stopped to help Bob at the stand. Bob counted 42 carrots. Then he tied them in bunches with 6 carrots in a bunch. How many bunches did he make?

Problems

1. Pears cost 6¢ each. How much will 4 pears cost? How much will 7 pears cost? How much will 9 pears cost?

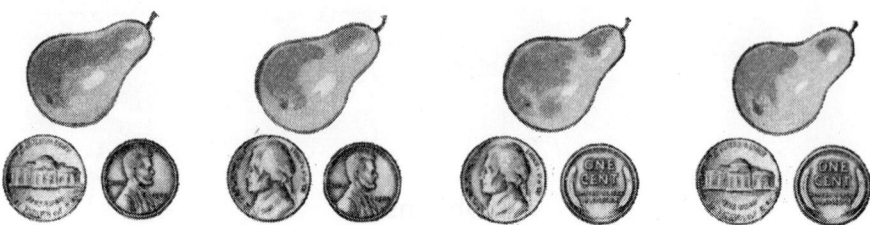

2. Jim thinks he can catch more fish if he has a hook that looks like a bug. The one he wants costs 54¢. If he can save 6¢ a week from his allowance, in how many weeks can he buy the fishhook?

3. Jack bought a card of fishhooks for 48¢. There were 6 hooks on the card. How much did each hook cost?

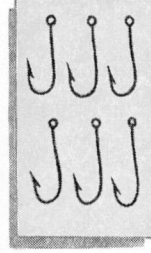

4. The girls want to make 6 paper leaves to paste on each window in their room at school. There are 8 windows. How many paper leaves do they need to make?

5. The girls need 6 sheets of colored paper to make the leaves. At 8¢ a sheet, how much should the paper cost them?

6. Dick is visiting in Florida. He wants to take two oranges home to each of six friends. How many oranges should he get?

7. Jane got a box of cards for 48¢. There were 8 cards in the box. How much did she pay for each card?

8. Bill wants to change his 30 pennies for nickels. How many nickels should he get for his pennies?

Practice

1. Say the answers for these questions:

6 ×3	3 ×6	6)18	3)18	5 ×3	3 ×5	5)15	3)15
4 ×3	3 ×4	4)12	3)12	5 ×6	6 ×5	5)30	6)30
6 ×4	4 ×6	6)24	4)24	6 ×2	2 ×6	6)12	2)12
6 ×6	5 ×5	6)36	5)25	5 ×4	4 ×5	5)20	4)20
7 ×5	5 ×7	7)35	5)35	8 ×5	5 ×8	8)40	5)40
3 ×8	8 ×3	3)24	8)24	4 ×8	8 ×4	4)32	8)32

Copy the examples, and find the answers:

	(a)	(b)	(c)	(d)	(e)	(f)
2.	6)126	5)150	6)360	5)255	6)240	6)300
3.	6)366	6)246	5)55	3)183	2)164	8)168

This sign (÷) also tells us to divide. 28 ÷ 4 means "divide 28 by 4." We read it: 28 divided by 4, or how many 4's are in 28?

Copy and find the answers:

	(a)	(b)	(c)	(d)	(e)
4.	350 ÷ 7	120 ÷ 6	426 ÷ 6	420 ÷ 7	168 ÷ 4
5.	126 ÷ 3	189 ÷ 3	186 ÷ 6	155 ÷ 5	300 ÷ 5

The 7's in Multiplication and Division

Think the answers to these multiplication questions:

7
×6 Six sevens are how many?
     6 sevens are the same as 3 sevens and 3 sevens.

| 7
×3
――
21 | 7
×3
――
21 | 21
+21
――
42 | 7
×6
――
42 | 7
×4
――
28 | 7
×3
――
21 | 28
+21
――
49 | 7
×7
――
49 |

7
×7 Seven sevens are how many?
     7 sevens are the same as 4 sevens and 3 sevens.
     Can you think of another way
     to find how many 7 sevens are?

7
×8 Eight sevens are how many?
     8 sevens are 2 times 4 sevens.
     8 sevens are 5 sevens and 3 sevens.

| 7
×5
――
35 | 7
×2
――
14 | 35
+14
――
49 |

| 7
×4
――
28 | 28
×2
――
56 | 7
×8
――
56 | 7
×3
――
21 | 21
×3
――
63 | 7
×9
――
63 |

7
×9 Nine sevens are how many?
     9 sevens are the same as 3 times 3 sevens.
     9 sevens are the same as 5 sevens and 4 sevens.

Table of Sevens

| 7
×1
――
7 | 7
×2
――
14 | 7
×3
――
21 | 7
×4
――
28 | 7
×5
――
35 | 7
×6
――
42 | 7
×7
――
49 | 7
×8
――
56 | 7
×9
――
63 |

| 1
7)7 | 2
7)14 | 3
7)21 | 4
7)28 | 5
7)35 | 6
7)42 | 7
7)49 | 8
7)56 | 9
7)63 |

Multiplication and Division Families

If you know $\begin{array}{r}6\\ \times 7\\ \hline 42\end{array}$, you also know $6\overline{)42}^{\,7}$ $\begin{array}{r}7\\ \times 6\\ \hline 42\end{array}$ $7\overline{)42}^{\,6}$

Look at the multiplication in each box. Then say the answers to the questions in that box.

$\begin{array}{r}7\\ \times 1\\ \hline 7\end{array}$ $7\overline{)7}$ $\begin{array}{r}1\\ \times 7\\ \hline \end{array}$ $1\overline{)7}$		$\begin{array}{r}7\\ \times 4\\ \hline 28\end{array}$ $7\overline{)28}$ $\begin{array}{r}4\\ \times 7\\ \hline \end{array}$ $4\overline{)28}$	
$\begin{array}{r}7\\ \times 5\\ \hline 35\end{array}$ $7\overline{)35}$ $\begin{array}{r}5\\ \times 7\\ \hline \end{array}$ $5\overline{)35}$		$\begin{array}{r}7\\ \times 3\\ \hline 21\end{array}$ $7\overline{)21}$ $\begin{array}{r}3\\ \times 7\\ \hline \end{array}$ $3\overline{)21}$	
$\begin{array}{r}7\\ \times 2\\ \hline 14\end{array}$ $7\overline{)14}$ $\begin{array}{r}2\\ \times 7\\ \hline \end{array}$ $2\overline{)14}$		$\begin{array}{r}7\\ \times 8\\ \hline 56\end{array}$ $7\overline{)56}$ $\begin{array}{r}8\\ \times 7\\ \hline \end{array}$ $8\overline{)56}$	
$\begin{array}{r}7\\ \times 9\\ \hline 63\end{array}$ $7\overline{)63}$ $\begin{array}{r}9\\ \times 7\\ \hline \end{array}$ $9\overline{)63}$		$\begin{array}{r}7\\ \times 7\\ \hline 49\end{array}$ $7\overline{)49}$ $\begin{array}{r}7\\ \times 7\\ \hline \end{array}$ $7\overline{)49}$	

Work the examples below:

	(a)	(b)	(c)	(d)	(e)	(f)	(g)	
1.	16 ×6	27 ×6	38 ×6	49 ×6	54 ×6	62 ×6	43 ×6	Carry 6 39 ×7 ——— 273
2.	64 ×7	75 ×7	86 ×7	59 ×7	48 ×7	37 ×7	44 ×7	

	(a)	(b)	(c)	(d)	(e)	(f)	(g)
3.	$7\overline{)490}$	$7\overline{)210}$	$7\overline{)420}$	$7\overline{)140}$	$7\overline{)630}$	$7\overline{)280}$	$7\overline{)350}$
4.	$7\overline{)560}$	$7\overline{)497}$	$7\overline{)287}$	$7\overline{)637}$	$7\overline{)357}$	$7\overline{)427}$	$7\overline{)217}$

Finding Laundry Costs

Alice helped get the laundry ready to send to the Chief Wash Company. She made a list of the things she sent.

1. How much does it cost to have 1 shirt washed? How much does it cost to have 4 shirts washed?
2. How much does it cost to have 8 sheets washed?
3. Find the cost to wash:
    - a. 4 aprons
    - b. 16 face towels
    - c. 13 bath towels
    - d. 24 handkerchiefs
    - e. 16 napkins
    - f. 4 pillowcases
4. If you know the cost of one thing, how do you find the cost of 2 or more of the same kind of thing?

Problems

1. There are 7 days in a week.
How many days are there in 6 weeks?
How many days are there in 8 weeks?
How many days are there in 9 weeks?

2. How many weeks are in 49 days?
How many weeks are there in 35 days?
How many weeks are there in 28 days?
How many weeks are there in 63 days?

3. There are 5 school days in a week. How many weeks are there in 35 school days?

4. Jim has 42 marbles. He wants to put them in bags with 7 marbles in each bag. How many bags will he use?

5. Ann has 56 cents. She wants to buy some chairs for her doll house. If the chairs cost 7¢ apiece, has she enough money to buy 8 chairs?

6. Betty wants to buy 6 of the 7-cent chairs, too. She has 35¢. Has she enough money to buy them?

7. How much should Mrs. Small pay for 7 oranges if they cost 6¢ apiece?

8. Jane has 63 stamps to paste in her book. If she puts 9 stamps on each page, how many pages of her book will she use for the stamps?

9. Jane bought 8 buttons for her new dress. The buttons cost 7¢ each. How much did her buttons cost?

10. Mrs. East buys 7 quarts of milk each day. How many quarts does she buy in a week?

11. Sally bought 8 six-cent stamps for air-mail letters. How much did she have to pay for them?

Problems

1. Mary bought a box of Christmas cards for 49 cents. There were 7 cards in the box. How much did each card cost?

2. Sue bought 8 Christmas cards that cost 7¢ each. How much did she pay for them?

3. Ann has 63¢. Has she enough money to buy 9 of the 7-cent Christmas cards?

4. Betty has a half dollar. Can she buy 7 cards?

5. Alice has a half dollar. She wants to buy 8 of the cards. Has she enough money for that many cards?

Sometimes a problem tells us the price of 1 thing. Then it asks us to find the cost of 2 or more things.

When we know the cost of 1 thing, we multiply to find the cost of 2 or more of the same thing.

Sometimes a problem tells us how much money we have and the price of one thing. Then it asks us to find how many of these things we can buy.

When we know how much money we have and the cost of one thing, we divide to find how many of these things we can buy.

6. Joe has 54¢. How many 6-cent apples can he buy?

7. It costs 5¢ to ride on the merry-go-round. Jack has 35¢. How many times can he ride?

8. At 7¢ a pint, how many pints of milk can Jack buy for 28 cents?

9. How many 6-cent candy bars can Jim get for 42¢?

When we know how many there are in all and how many groups there are, we divide to find how many there are in each group.

10. Helen is pasting pictures in her scrapbook. She has filled all the pages but 7. She has 42 pictures. If she puts the same number of pictures on each page, how many pictures will she put on each page?

11. "There are 28 cookies for 4 of us," said Alice. "Each of us will get ___ cookies."

12. Mary has 45 pieces of candy. She wants to put them in paper bags. She has 5 paper bags. How many pieces should she put in each bag?

Chapter 8
Measures

Using a Timetable

Look at the timetable and tell:

1. When each train leaves Chicago.
2. The time each train gets to Milwaukee.
3. When each train stops in Evanston.
4. When you can catch a train at Kenosha for Milwaukee.

Stations	Train 837 A.M.	Train 239 A.M.	Train 161 P.M.	Train 875 P.M.
Leaves Chicago	9:00	10:30	7:30	10:00
Arrives Evanston	9:17	10:44	7:47	10:23
" Waukegan	9:41	11:06	8:20	11:10
" Kenosha	9:58	11:20	8:40	——
" Racine	10:10	11:32	8:55	——
" Milwaukee	10:35	11:55	9:30	——

```
 9:17 A.M.
 9:00 A.M.
 17 min.
```

5. How long does it take train 837 to run from Chicago to Evanston?

```
11:20 A.M.
    15
11:35 A.M.
```

6. Train 239 is due to arrive in Kenosha at 11:20, but it is 15 minutes late. What time will it arrive in Kenosha?

Reading and Writing Time

Column 1 tells the time. Column 2 shows how we write the time. Column 3 tells how we read the time.

Column 1	Column 2	Column 3
7 minutes past 5	5:07	Five seven
Half past 6	6:30	Six thirty
A quarter after 1	1:15	One fifteen
A quarter to 4	3:45	Three forty-five
8 o'clock	8:00	Eight o'clock
10 minutes of 6	5:50	Five fifty
23 minutes after 2	2:23	Two twenty-three

1. Write the following times in figures:

Four ten   Ten four   One thirty   Five fifteen
Eleven twenty-one   Two eight   Seven fifty   Six o'clock

This clock might show 12 o'clock **noon** or 12 o'clock **midnight**. How can we tell what it shows?

We write A.M. after the time if it is before noon —from midnight until noon. School starts at 8:30 A.M.

We write P.M. after the time if it is after noon— from noon until midnight. School ends at 4.00 P.M.

2. Which of the following mean morning? Which mean afternoon?

9:00 A.M.   3:15 A.M.   6:30 P.M.   2:25 A.M.
10:40 P.M.   1:10 P.M.   12:08 A.M.   11:45 A.M.

3. The time from midnight to noon and on to midnight is one **day**. How many hours are there in a day?

A

B

Telling Time

1. What time does Clock A show?

When the minute hand points to 3, it has moved one quarter of the distance around the clock. So in addition to saying it is three fifteen, or it is 15 minutes after 3, we may also say it is a **quarter past** 3, or a **quarter after** 3.

2. What time does Clock B show?

Sometimes we say it is a **quarter of** 4. Can you tell why?

3. What time does each clock show?

4. Walter has a new watch. How is it different from most watches? What time does his watch show? Can he tell the exact time by his watch?

Walter looked at the clock in the station and said, "Five, ten, fifteen, twenty, twenty-five, thirty, thirty-one, thirty-two, thirty-three. It is **three thirty-three**."

To tell the **exact** time, we count by 5's to the last number the minute hand has passed. Then we count on by ones to the minute hand.

What time does each watch show?

Roman Numerals

Long ago the Romans lived in what is now Italy. They used the letters I, V, and X to write numbers. These letters are called **Roman numerals**.

Do we still use Roman numerals?

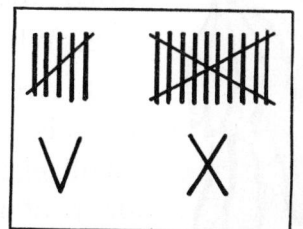

I means 1.　　　　　VI means 6.
II means 2.　　　　 VII means 7.
III means 3.　　　　VIII means 8.
IIII or IV means 4.　IX means 9.
V means 5.　　　　 X means 10.

When I is used after V, it means that 1 is added to 5. So VI means 6. What does VII mean? What does VIII mean? When I is used after X, it means that 1 is added to 10. So XI means 11. What does XIII mean? What does XV mean?

When I is used before V, it means 1 is subtracted from 5. So IV means 4, and XIV means 14. When I is used before X, it means 1 is subtracted from 10. So IX means 9, and XIX means 19.

What do these Roman numerals mean?
XII　XIII　XIV　XV　XVI　XVII　XVIII　XIX

XX means 20.
XXI means 21.
XXIV means 24.
XXV means 25.
XXIX means 29.
XXX means 30.
XXXIX means 39.

What time does each clock show?

Use Roman numerals to write these numbers:
3　13　23　33　9　19　29　39　20　24　7　15　36　4

127

Number of Things

1. How many things make a **dozen**?

We usually buy eggs by the dozen. Can you name other things that we buy by the dozen?

2. What does **doz.** mean?

3. Are all eggs the same size? Suppose the price of eggs is 48¢ a dozen. Would you rather have a dozen small eggs or a dozen large eggs? Why? Sometimes the price of a dozen small eggs is less than the price of a dozen large eggs. Can you tell why? In many places if eggs are sold at a certain price per dozen, they must weigh a certain amount. Do you know why?

4. We used to buy oranges, bananas, and other fruit by the dozen. Now we usually buy such things by the pound. Can you tell why this change was made?

5. If the price of eggs is 48¢ a dozen, what should 4 dozen eggs cost? 5 dozen eggs? 6 dozen eggs?

6. How many cupcakes should you get if you bought $\frac{1}{4}$ of a dozen? $\frac{1}{3}$ of a dozen? $\frac{1}{2}$ of a dozen?

7. When roasting ears cost 50¢ a dozen, how much will 5 dozen cost? 6 dozen? 8 dozen?

8. Mrs. West cut 8 dozen roses. How many roses did she cut?

JANUARY							FEBRUARY							MARCH							APRIL						
S	M	T	W	T	F	S	S	M	T	W	T	F	S	S	M	T	W	T	F	S	S	M	T	W	T	F	S
		1	2	3	4	5						1	2							1			1	2	3	4	5
6	7	8	9	10	11	12	3	4	5	6	7	8	9	2	3	4	5	6	7	8	6	7	8	9	10	11	12
13	14	15	16	17	18	19	10	11	12	13	14	15	16	9	10	11	12	13	14	15	13	14	15	16	17	18	19
20	21	22	23	24	25	26	17	18	19	20	21	22	23	16	17	18	19	20	21	22	20	21	22	23	24	25	26
27	28	29	30	31			24	25	26	27	28	29		23	24	25	26	27	28	29	27	28	29	30			
														30	31												

MAY							JUNE							JULY							AUGUST						
S	M	T	W	T	F	S	S	M	T	W	T	F	S	S	M	T	W	T	F	S	S	M	T	W	T	F	S
				1	2	3	1	2	3	4	5	6	7			1	2	3	4	5						1	2
4	5	6	7	8	9	10	8	9	10	11	12	13	14	6	7	8	9	10	11	12	3	4	5	6	7	8	9
11	12	13	14	15	16	17	15	16	17	18	19	20	21	13	14	15	16	17	18	19	10	11	12	13	14	15	16
18	19	20	21	22	23	24	22	23	24	25	26	27	28	20	21	22	23	24	25	26	17	18	19	20	21	22	23
25	26	27	28	29	30	31	29	30						27	28	29	30	31			24	25	26	27	28	29	30
																					31						

SEPTEMBER							OCTOBER							NOVEMBER							DECEMBER						
S	M	T	W	T	F	S	S	M	T	W	T	F	S	S	M	T	W	T	F	S	S	M	T	W	T	F	S
	1	2	3	4	5	6				1	2	3	4							1		1	2	3	4	5	6
7	8	9	10	11	12	13	5	6	7	8	9	10	11	2	3	4	5	6	7	8	7	8	9	10	11	12	13
14	15	16	17	18	19	20	12	13	14	15	16	17	18	9	10	11	12	13	14	15	14	15	16	17	18	19	20
21	22	23	24	25	26	27	19	20	21	22	23	24	25	16	17	18	19	20	21	22	21	22	23	24	25	26	27
28	29	30					26	27	28	29	30	31		23	24	25	26	27	28	29	28	29	30	31			
														30													

The Calendar

1. Say the names of the months. How many months are in a year? How many months are in 4 years?

2. Look at the calendar. Which of the months have 30 days? Which of the months have 31 days?

3. Which month has neither 30 days nor 31 days? How many days has it?

Once every 4 years, February has 1 more day, or 29 days. A year in which February has 29 days is called **leap year**.

4. Say the names of the days. These seven days are called a **week**.

5. Christmas always comes on December 25. What day is it this year? What day is the Fourth of July?

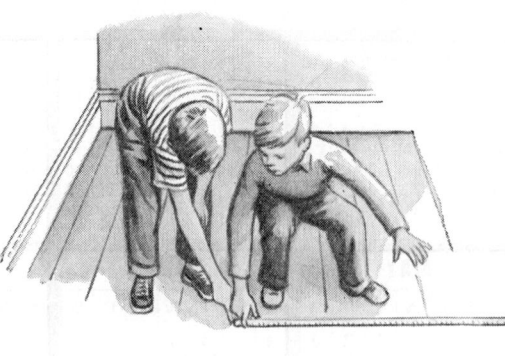

Measuring Length

We measure length with a foot ruler or a yardstick.

How many inches are marked off on a ruler? Is the 12 on your ruler? Can you tell why not? How many inches are marked off on your yardstick? How many inches are in a yard?

12 inches (in.) = 1 foot (ft.) 3 feet = 1 yard (yd.)
36 inches = 1 yard

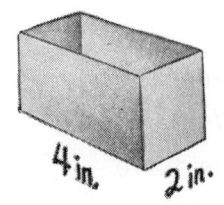

How many feet are in a yard?

What part of a yard is a foot?

We say that the **length** of the box is 4 inches and the **width** is 2 inches. Why do we call the length of one side length and the length of the other side width?

On the ruler below each inch is divided into 4 equal parts, or fourths. Each part is one fourth of an inch.

1. Show $1\frac{1}{4}$ inches on your ruler. Show $3\frac{1}{2}$ inches.
2. How long is the line?

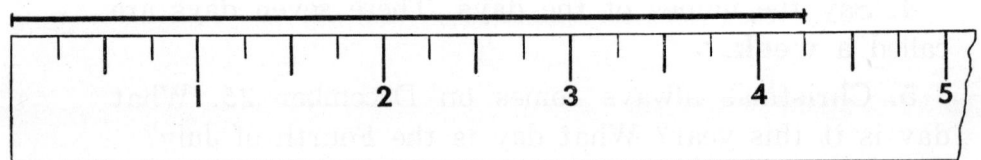

Measuring Liquids

Such things as milk, water, syrup, and gasoline are called **liquids**. We have certain measures for liquids just as we have for time and for length.

**2 cups = 1 pint (pt.)   2 pints = 1 quart (qt.)
4 quarts = 1 gallon (gal.)**

Measure water with real measures to see if:
a. Two cups of water will just fill a pint bottle.
b. Two half pints of water will just fill a pint bottle.
c. Two pints of water will just fill a quart bottle.
d. Four quarts of water will just fill a gallon jug.

1. Name several things we measure in cups or half pints; in pints; in quarts; in gallons.

2. What should you pay for 5 quarts of milk at 18¢ a quart?

3. A gallon of gasoline costs 24¢. How much will 6 gallons cost? How much will 8 gallons cost?

4. Mr. Brown bought 6 quarts of oil for his car. How much was his bill if he paid 35¢ a quart for the oil?

5. Alice filled 3 cans with milk. One can held 6 quarts, one held 8 quarts, and one held 2 quarts. How many quarts did she put into the 3 cans?

How many gallons did she put into the 3 cans?

131

Weight

1. What measure do we use when we tell how much we weigh? What measure do we use when we buy meat?

2. Name some things we buy by the **pound**.

> We have a measure for things that weigh less than a pound. It is called an **ounce**.
> There are 16 ounces (oz.) in a pound (lb.).

3. Look on the wrapper of a loaf of bread. How much does the bread weigh? Do all loaves weigh the same?

4. Look for weights of things on boxes and cans on the kitchen shelves or at the grocery store. Write the names of several things with their weights.

5. How many ounces are there in a half pound of butter? How many ounces are there in a quarter of a pound of butter? $\frac{1}{4}$ of 16 oz. = ?

6. Mrs. Allen put 8 ounces of mustard seed and 6 ounces of celery seed in her pickles. Did she use a pound of the seeds?

7. Onions cost 4¢ a pound. How much should 8 pounds cost?

8. Watermelon costs 5¢ a pound. How much should a watermelon cost that weighs 26 pounds?

9. Postage on letters is 3¢ an ounce. What should it cost to mail a 2-oz. letter? a 3-oz. letter?

Dry Measure

Farmers and merchants sometimes measure and sell fresh berries and small fruit by the quart. Sometimes they measure and sell potatoes, grain, and fruit by the peck or bushel. Such measures are called **dry measures**. Do you know why?

2 pints = 1 quart
8 quarts = 1 peck (pk.)
4 pecks = 1 bushel (bu.)

1. Jack went with his father to a fruit stand.

"Look," said Jack. "Apples are selling for two prices. They are selling for 50¢ a peck and $1.80 a bushel."

How much will 4 pecks of apples cost at 50¢ a peck?

Which is cheaper to buy, 4 pecks at 50¢ a peck or 1 bushel at $1.80?

2. Cherries are selling for 16¢ a quart. Jack's mother bought 8 quarts. How much did the cherries cost her?

3. Strawberries are selling for 24¢ a quart. How much will 6 quarts cost?

4. A peck of potatoes weighs 15 pounds. How much will a bushel of potatoes weigh?

5. Can you carry 10 pounds of sugar and a peck of potatoes? How many pounds will you have to carry?

Facts Hidden in Certain Words

Sometimes we cannot solve a problem until we know the facts that are hidden in certain words. A **dozen** means "12 things." So the word dozen has the fact "12 things" hidden in it. Always watch for words with hidden facts.

Each afternoon Tom delivers papers. He gets 40¢ a day for his work. How much does he make in a week?

We cannot solve this problem unless we know that a week means "seven days." Seven days is the fact that is hidden in the word **week**.

Read each problem carefully. What word in each problem has a hidden fact in it? What is the hidden fact?

1. During the month of July the milkman delivered 88 pints of milk to Mrs. Brown. How many quarts was that?

2. Jack helped his father dig 65 bushels of potatoes. They put the potatoes into small sacks to sell at the market. Each sack held a peck. How many pecks of potatoes did they have?

3. Helen bought 6 yards of ribbon. How many feet of ribbon did she buy?

4. Jane cut 8 inches from a yard of ribbon. How many inches of ribbon did she have left?

5. Bill may play outside for an hour. When he has played 45 minutes, how much longer does he still have to play?

Estimating Answers

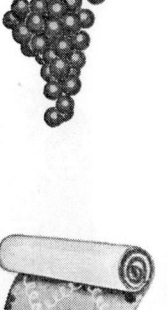

About how much will 5 pounds of grapes cost at 29¢ a pound?

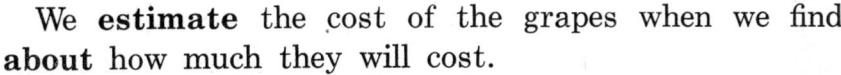

We **estimate** the cost of the grapes when we find **about** how much they will cost.

The grapes will cost about $1.50. 29¢ is about 30¢, and at 30¢ a pound, the grapes would cost $1.50.

1. "This paper is 19¢ a yard. Six yards will cost about $1.20," said Alice.

Is her **estimate** about right? What is the cost?

2. Mr. Brown's car used 7 gallons of gasoline on a trip. About how much did the gasoline cost at 28¢ a gallon? Did it cost about $1.50, $2.00, or $2.50?

3. Dick worked 6 hours at the store on Saturday. At 39¢ an hour, did he earn more or less than $2.50?

4. Jim had $1.00. He spent 49¢. Did he have about 50¢, 60¢, or 75¢ left?

5. A model airplane costs 98¢. Will 2 airplanes cost about $2.00, $1.50, or $1.00?

6. There are 168 children in the fourth grade. The school nurse has weighed 80 of them. Has she weighed about half of them? What is $\frac{1}{2}$ of 168?

7. Jack swam the length of the swimming pool 4 times. The pool is 90 feet long. How far did Jack swim?

8. Jane can swim the length of the pool. She wants to enter the swimming races. Should she enter the 25-yard race, the 50-yard race, or the 75-yard race?

Sensible Answers

1. Charles gives one fourth of the money he makes to his mother. Last week he made $2.48 selling papers and running errands. How much did he give her?

Simon said, "Charles gave his mother one fourth of $2.48. He gave her $62."

Did Simon make a mistake in dividing or in thinking about dollars and cents? Does $62 seem about right? Is it a sensible answer?

Tom said, "Sixty-two dollars is too much. Charles made only $2.48. We think of $2.48 as 248 cents, and one fourth of 248 cents is 62 cents."

Solve these problems. Then decide whether or not the answers make sense.

2. A crane weighs 10 pounds when he stands on one leg. How much will he weigh when he stands on two legs?

"Twenty pounds!" answered Simon.

3. At 98¢ each, how much will 4 books cost? Will they cost about $4? Is $3.92 a sensible answer?

4. Mr. Brown gave Jerry $1.50 for a new fountain pen. Jerry bought one at the drug store for 59¢. How much did he save? Did he save about 50¢, 70¢, 80¢, or 90¢?

5. Dick saw two caps in the store. One was marked $1.35, and the other was marked 87¢. What is the **difference** in the price of the caps—58¢, 48¢, or 38¢?

6. Tom said, "I had 75¢ and spent 32¢ for a ticket to the show. How much money do I have now?"

Simon said, "You have about a dollar."

Did Simon's answer make sense? Why not?

The Thermometer

When we want to know how hot or how cold it is, we look at a thermometer. We measure **temperature** in **degrees**.

The little marks on the thermometer show the degrees. Find the mark for zero degrees. There are 5 marks between 0 degrees and 10 degrees. Each mark means 2 degrees.

What temperature does the thermometer show?

68 degrees is written 68°. The sign ° means degrees.

The liquid in many thermometers is **mercury**. The mercury is inside a glass tube. When it gets warmer, the column of mercury rises. When it gets colder, the column of mercury goes down. When the top of the mercury stands at 90°, it is hot. When the mercury goes down to 32°, water freezes. When it goes down to zero (0°), or below 0°, it is very cold.

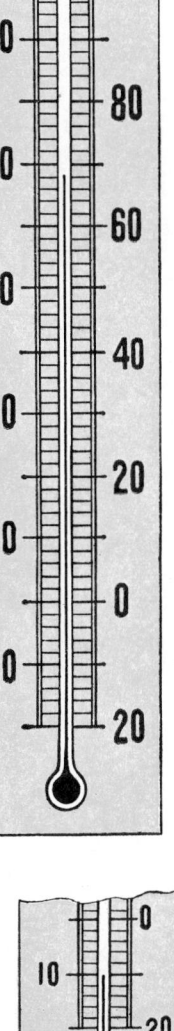

1. Is 100° hot or cold?

2. Water boils at 212°, and it freezes at ____°.

3. One morning at 9 o'clock the temperature was 10° above zero. At noon it was 30° above zero. How much warmer was it?

4. Parts of 5 thermometers are shown below. What temperature does each thermometer show?

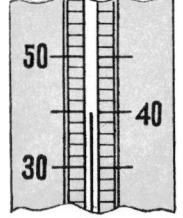 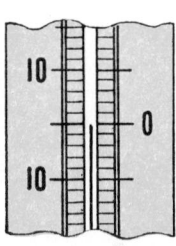 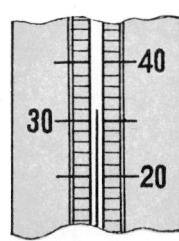 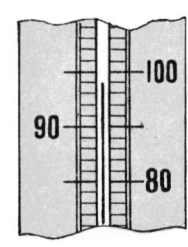

Chapter 9
The Eights and Nines

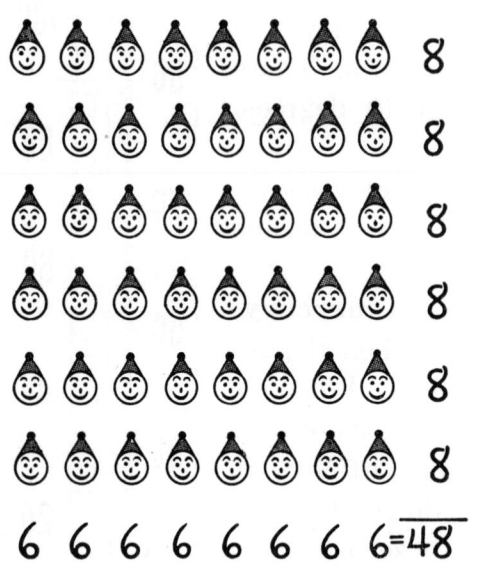

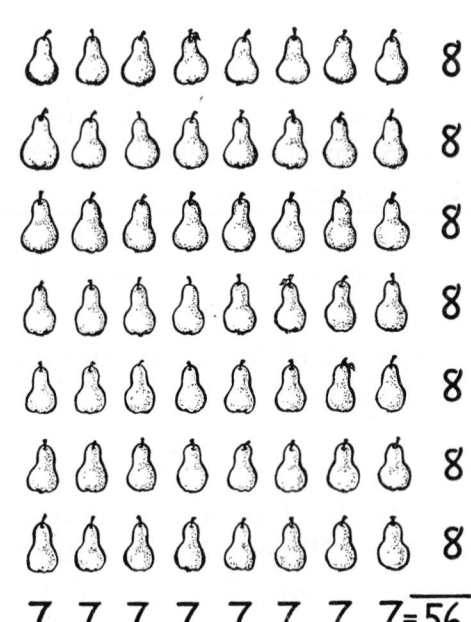

The 8's in Multiplication and Division

Six 8's are how many? Seven 8's are how many?
Eight 6's are how many? Eight 7's are how many?
How many 8's in 48? How many 8's in 56?
How many 6's in 48? How many 7's in 56?

Say the answers:

8 ×5	8)24	6 ×8	8)40	4 ×8	8)32	4)32	8 ×4	5 ×8
8 ×6	6)48	8 ×7	8)48	7 ×8	8)56	7)56	8 ×3	3 ×8

Thinking about Multiplications

Albert said, "I do not need to use a picture or dots to find the answer to a multiplication question. I can think the answer."

Tell how Albert thinks the answers to these questions:

8 eights are how many?

8 eights are the same as 2 times 4 eights.

8 eights are also the same as 5 eights and 3 eights.

| 8
×8
— | 8
×4
32 | 32
×2
64 | 8
×5
40 | 8
×3
24 | 40
+24
64 | 8
×8
— |

How many 8's are in 64? Eight 8's are 64; so there are eight 8's in 64.

9 eights are how many?

9 eights are the same as 5 eights and 4 eights.

9 eights are the same as 3 times 3 eights.

| 8
×9
— | 8
×5
40 | 8
×4
32 | 40
+32
72 | 8
×3
24 | 24
×3
72 | 8
×9
— |

How many 8's are in 72? 8)̅7̅2̅

Nine 8's are 72; so there are nine 8's in 72.

Now we know:

8   8   9   9   8
×8   8)64   ×9   ×8   8)72   9)72
64   72   72

Say the answers:

8   8   8   8   8
×6   ×5   ×8   ×7   ×9   8)48   8)72   8)56   8)64

139

The Eights

Use the table to help you learn and remember the multiplications and divisions for eights.

```
                        Table of Eights
    8      8      8      8      8      8      8      8      8
   ×1     ×2     ×3     ×4     ×5     ×6     ×7     ×8     ×9
   ──     ──     ──     ──     ──     ──     ──     ──     ──
    8     16     24     32     40     48     56     64     72

     1      2      3      4      5      6      7      8      9
   ───    ────   ────   ────   ────   ────   ────   ────   ────
   8)8    8)16   8)24   8)32   8)40   8)48   8)56   8)64   8)72
```

1. Try to say the answers without looking at the table:

8 ×1	4 ×8	8)40	3)24	8 ×6	5 ×8	4)32		8)64
8 ×3	8 ×8	8)24	8)56	2 ×8	6 ×8	8)8	2)16
8 ×2	3 ×8	8)32	8)16	8 ×4	8 ×7	9)72	5)40
8 ×9	8 ×5	8)48	6)48	7 ×8	8 ×9	7)56	8)72

2. Copy the examples below and find the answers:

```
Carry 7
  39
  ×8
 ───
 312
```

	(a)	(b)	(c)	(d)	(e)	(f)	(g)
	19	28	37	46	55	64	99
	×8	×8	×8	×8	×8	×8	×8

	(a)	(b)	(c)	(d)	(e)	(f)	(g)
3.	8)160	8)640	8)400	8)80	8)320	8)240	8)720
4.	8)560	8)728	8)648	8)480	8)168	8)248	8)568

Camp Fire Girls

1. Jane has won 64 honor beads. She is putting them on leather strings. She wants 8 beads on each string. How many strings of beads will she have?

2. Betty has 9 strings of beads. On each string she has 8 beads. How many honor beads has Betty won?

3. Eight of the girls are planning their notebooks of the nature hikes. They will need 8 sheets of paper for each notebook. How many sheets of paper should they buy for all the notebooks?

4. The girls have invited some friends to go with them on their Saturday hike. Sue thinks if each girl brings 6 sandwiches, there will be enough for everyone. There are 8 girls. How many sandwiches will that be?

5. Ann thinks that 56 apples will be enough. Only 7 of the girls can bring apples. How many apples should each girl bring?

6. Helen is a new member of the group. She wants to earn beads as fast as she can. She thinks she can earn 8 beads each week. How many weeks will it take her to earn 72 beads?

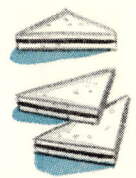

The 9's in Multiplication and Division

We know all of the multiplications and divisions for **nines** but ×9 and 9)81̄.

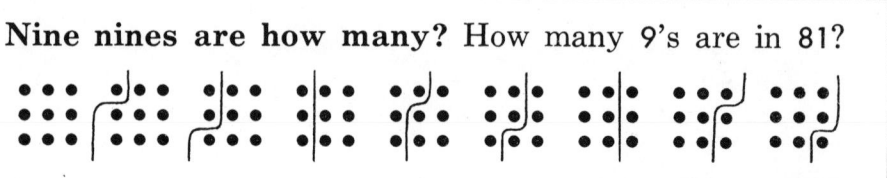

Nine nines are how many? How many 9's are in 81?

"I do not use dots," said John. "I think the answer. 10 nines are 90. 9 nines are 1 nine less than 10 nines. So 9 nines are 9 less than 90, or 9 nines are 81."

Then he wrote 9 nines in a column. He said, "9 nines are 81. I count the nines and know there are 9 nines in 81."

Tell how we think these answers:

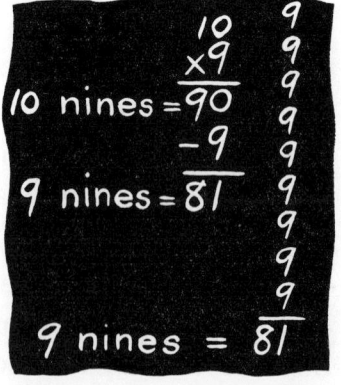

9 ×6 —	9 ×3 27	27 ×2 54	9 ×6 54	9 ×7 —	9 ×3 27	9 ×4 36	27 +36 63	9 ×7 63
9 ×8 —	9 ×4 36	36 ×2 72	9 ×8 72	9 ×5 —	9 ×3 27	9 ×2 18	27 +18 45	9 ×5 45
9 ×4 —	9 ×3 27	27 +9 36	9 ×4 36	9 ×3 —	10 ×3 30	30 −3 27	9 ×3 27	

Use the table to help you learn and remember the multiplications and divisions for nines.

Table of Nines

9 ×1 — 9	9 ×2 — 18	9 ×3 — 27	9 ×4 — 36	9 ×5 — 45	9 ×6 — 54	9 ×7 — 63	9 ×8 — 72	9 ×9 — 81
1 9)9	2 9)18	3 9)27	4 9)36	5 9)45	6 9)54	7 9)63	8 9)72	9 9)81

Try to give the answers without looking at the table:

9 ×3	9)27	3 ×9	3)27	9 ×7	9)63	7 ×9	7)63
9 ×5	9)45	5 ×9	5)45	9 ×9	9)81	9 ×9	9)81
9 ×4	9)36	4 ×9	4)36	9 ×6	9)54	6 ×9	6)54
9 ×2	9)18	2 ×9	2)18	9 ×8	9)72	8 ×9	8)72

Copy the examples below and find the answers:

	(a)	(b)	(c)	(d)	(e)	(f)	(g)	(h)	(i)
1.	50 ×9	60 ×9	40 ×9	30 ×9	70 ×9	90 ×9	80 ×9	10 ×9	20 ×9
2.	54 ×9	94 ×9	15 ×9	82 ×9	33 ×9	71 ×9	65 ×9	90 ×9	23 ×9

	(a)	(b)	(c)	(d)	(e)	(f)	(g)
3.	9)90	9)180	9)630	9)540	9)810	9)450	9)720
4.	9)549	9)639	9)729	9)189	9)270	9)819	9)99

Learning about Eighths

The girls in the fourth grade made a movie for the children in the first grade. They put 4 pictures on a page. So they divided a sheet of paper into **fourths**.

When several children had finished reading the story of Pinocchio, they decided to make a movie of it. They need 8 pictures to tell the story. They want to mark and cut a large sheet of paper into eight equal parts.

What part of the whole sheet of paper will they use for each picture? What is one of 8 equal parts called?

1. First, they cut the sheet of paper into two equal parts. Each piece was one half ($\frac{1}{2}$) of the whole sheet.

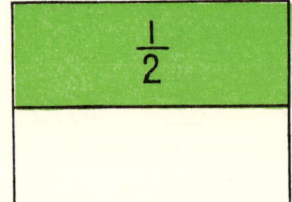 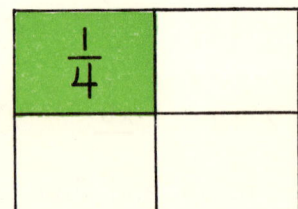 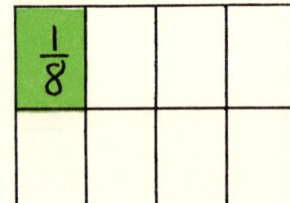

2. Next they cut each **half** into two equal pieces. Then each piece was one fourth ($\frac{1}{4}$) of the whole sheet. They had 4 pieces of paper the same size.

3. Then they cut each **fourth** into two equal pieces. They had 8 pieces the same size. They had divided the sheet of paper into 8 equal parts. When anything is cut into 8 equal parts, each part is called **one eighth**. How do we write one eighth?

4. Mrs. Brown has 64 doughnuts. She has 8 boxes. If she puts the same number of doughnuts in each box, how many will there be in each box?

5. Jane told Ann that she had spent $\frac{1}{7}$ of her money for a pencil. Jane had 35¢ before she bought the pencil. How much did she pay for the pencil?

What is **one seventh** of 35? $\frac{1}{7}$ of 35¢ = ?

6. Mary has 48 books. Her new bookcase has 6 shelves. She is going to put the same number of books on each shelf. What part of the books will she put on each shelf? How many books will she put on each shelf? $\frac{1}{6}$ of 48 = ?

> We divide by 6 to find $\frac{1}{6}$ of a number.
> We divide by 8 to find $\frac{1}{8}$ of a number.

7. Quickly say the answers to these parts of numbers:

$\frac{1}{6}$ of 30 = ?	$\frac{1}{7}$ of 63 = ?	$\frac{1}{8}$ of 40 = ?	$\frac{1}{6}$ of 54 = ?
$\frac{1}{9}$ of 54 = ?	$\frac{1}{5}$ of 30 = ?	$\frac{1}{7}$ of 35 = ?	$\frac{1}{6}$ of 36 = ?
$\frac{1}{9}$ of 81 = ?	$\frac{1}{5}$ of 35 = ?	$\frac{1}{9}$ of 45 = ?	$\frac{1}{7}$ of 42 = ?
$\frac{1}{6}$ of 48 = ?	$\frac{1}{8}$ of 48 = ?	$\frac{1}{7}$ of 49 = ?	$\frac{1}{8}$ of 72 = ?
$\frac{1}{6}$ of 42 = ?	$\frac{1}{5}$ of 45 = ?	$\frac{1}{5}$ of 40 = ?	$\frac{1}{8}$ of 64 = ?
$\frac{1}{7}$ of 56 = ?	$\frac{1}{8}$ of 56 = ?	$\frac{1}{9}$ of 72 = ?	$\frac{1}{9}$ of 63 = ?

Problems

1. Pupils in the first and second grades at Oak Grove School need 8 rows of seats in the auditorium. There are 9 seats in a row. How many pupils are in the first and second grades?

2. There are 81 pupils in the third and fourth grades. When they sit 9 in a row, how many rows of seats do they need?

3. One cold day there were only 63 of the first and second graders at school. How many rows did they need in the auditorium that day?

Remember: There are 9 seats in a row.

4. Last year the pupils gave 6 plays. Nine pupils took part in each play. In all how many pupils took part in the plays?

5. On Washington's Birthday the 72 first- and second-grade pupils gave a flag drill. They stood in rows with 8 pupils in each row. How many rows were there?

Multiplication Baseball

Make a chart like the one below.

Choose sides so that there will be two teams. A player on one team is the pitcher. Each player on the other team has his turn at bat.

The pitcher points to a block, such as A. Then the player at bat must give the answers:

Four fives are twenty.   *Five fours are twenty.*
Fours in twenty, five.   *Fives in twenty, four.*

If the player gives all four answers right, he makes a run for his team. If the player at bat makes a mistake, he is out. When there are three outs, the teams change sides.

Give the answers for Blocks B; C; D; E; F; G; H.

At the Carnival

1. Nine boys went together to the carnival. They each had to pay 5¢ at the gate. How much did they pay at the gate altogether?

2. Mrs. White took 7 girls to the carnival. At the gate she had to pay 5¢ for each girl and 5¢ for herself. How much did she pay for the girls and herself?

3. It cost 7 cents to ride the Ferris wheel. Mr. Ben bought tickets for 6 boys. How much did he pay for their rides?

4. The 7 girls came along just as the boys started their ride. Mr. Ben gave Helen 50¢ to buy tickets for all the girls. At 7¢ each, did Helen have enough money to pay for the girls' rides?

5. A ride on the merry-go-round costs 6¢. How much should Bill pay for 6 rides?

6. Tom said that he would buy tickets for as many girls as he could with his money. He had 48¢. At 6¢ a ticket, for how many girls could he buy tickets?

7. Ann decided to spend 30¢ for rides on the merry-go-round. How many times can she ride if each ride costs 6 cents?

8. The grab bag was a lot of fun. The children never knew what they might get. Each grab cost 8 cents. Jack's father paid for a grab for himself and 7 of the boys. How much did he pay for the grabs?

9. Four of the girls tried the grab bag. How much did the girls pay altogether for the grabs?

How much did one grab cost? Problem **9** does not tell you, but problem **8** does.

10. Noisemakers are part of the fun at a carnival. Six of the boys bought big whistles that were 9¢ each. How much did all the whistles cost?

11. Five of the girls paid 6¢ each for squawkers. How much did they spend in all for squawkers?

12. A box of snappers cost 45¢. The 9 boys shared the cost of a box equally. How much was each boy's share?

"Oh! didn't we have a lot of fun?" said Helen.

"Yes," said Ann. "But didn't we waste a lot of money?"

A Game of Products

For this game you need to know the products that are the answers to multiplication questions. Here are some useful products:

In the twenties: 20, 21, 24, 25, 27, 28.
In the thirties: 30, 32, 35, 36.
In the forties: 40, 42, 45, 48, 49.
In the fifties: 54, 56.
In the sixties: 63, 64.
In the seventies: 72.
In the eighties: 81.

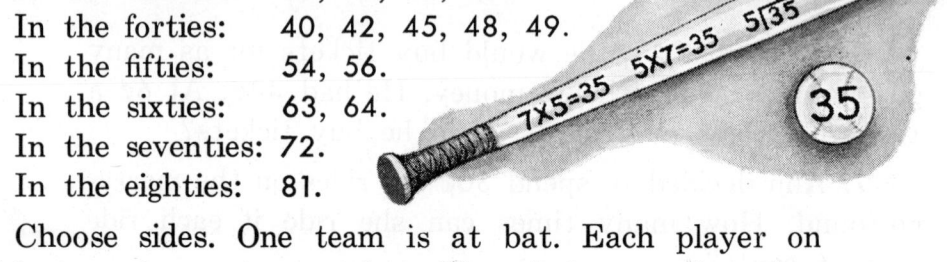

Choose sides. One team is at bat. Each player on this team has a turn at bat. The pitcher on the other team tosses a product. It must be the answer to a multiplication question. Let us say that the pitcher tosses thirty-five, either by saying or by writing it. The player at bat must answer:

Five sevens are thirty-five.
Seven fives are thirty-five.
Fives in thirty-five, seven.
Sevens in thirty-five, five.

$$\begin{array}{cccc} 7 & 5 & 5 & 7 \\ \times 5 & \times 7 & 7\overline{)35} & 5\overline{)35} \\ \hline 35 & 35 & 35 & 35 \end{array}$$

The answers may be in any order, but all four of them must be right to count a run. For any mistake the player is out. The teams change places after three are out.

Say the answers:

$$\begin{array}{cccccccc} 3 & 8 & 9 & 6 & 7 & 7 & 9 & 8 \\ \times 9 & \times 7 & \times 6 & \times 8 & \times 9 & \times 6 & \times 9 & \times 9 \\ \hline \end{array}$$

$7\overline{)49}$ $9\overline{)72}$ $8\overline{)56}$ $7\overline{)63}$ $6\overline{)54}$ $6\overline{)42}$ $9\overline{)81}$ $8\overline{)64}$

$8\overline{)48}$ $6\overline{)36}$ $9\overline{)63}$ $8\overline{)72}$ $7\overline{)56}$ $9\overline{)54}$ $6\overline{)48}$ $7\overline{)42}$

Do You Know? [Self-test]

Write the answers on folded paper:

2	6	4	1	3	2	3	8	3
×2	×4	×6	×7	×2	×3	×3	×3	×8
7	4	2	4	4	8	5	2	4
×4	×7	×4	×2	×8	×4	×2	×5	×4
3	5	4	1	2	9	2	7	8
×5	×3	×9	×6	×9	×2	×7	×2	×1
1	9	1	9	3	6	2	3	6
×5	×1	×9	×3	×9	×2	×6	×6	×3
3	7	2	8	3	4	4	5	6
×7	×3	×8	×2	×4	×3	×5	×4	×1
9	5	5	6	8	6	5	9	1
×5	×9	×5	×8	×6	×5	×6	×4	×8
8	5	6	9	7	5	9	8	7
×5	×8	×9	×6	×5	×7	×8	×9	×7
8	9	7	6	6	7	8	7	9
×8	×7	×9	×6	×7	×6	×7	×8	×9

Tom did not know the answer to $\begin{array}{r}9\\ \times 4\\ \hline\end{array}$. He used dots to find the answer.

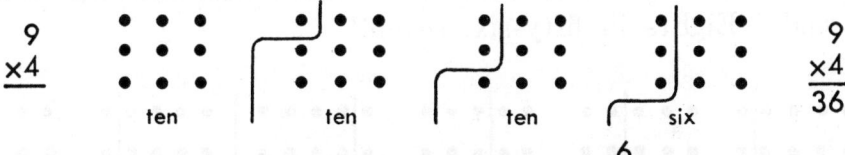

Alice did not know the answer to $\begin{array}{r}6\\ \times 7\\ \hline\end{array}$. She thought the answer: "Seven sixes are the same as 4 sixes and 3 sixes. Four sixes are 24, and 3 sixes are 18. 24 and 18 are 42. So seven sixes are 42."

Find the answers that you did not know. Study them.

Do You Know? [Self-test]

Write the answers on folded paper. If you do not know an answer, do not guess. Go on to the next question.

(a)	(b)	(c)	(d)	(e)	(f)	(g)	(h)	(i)
4)16	2)2	4)12	8)16	4)32	6)18	9)27	3)3	6)12
1)3	4)8	5)10	3)12	4)20	9)18	5)15	1)8	3)21
2)8	6)6	7)14	1)2	5)20	6)24	7)21	2)4	1)1
3)9	8)8	3)24	1)5	8)24	9)36	8)32	2)6	1)9
3)6	9)9	2)14	7)7	4)28	4)24	3)18	1)6	4)4
5)5	1)4	2)16	1)7	3)15	2)18	2)12	4)36	2)10
3)27	7)49	5)25	5)30	6)42	8)48	6)30	7)28	6)48
7)35	8)40	6)36	8)56	8)64	9)45	7)42	5)40	6)54
9)63	5)45	7)63	8)72	7)56	9)72	9)81	9)54	5)35

Jim did not know the answer to 8)56. He used dots to find the answer. Then he studied that division. He said, "Eights in fifty-six, seven."

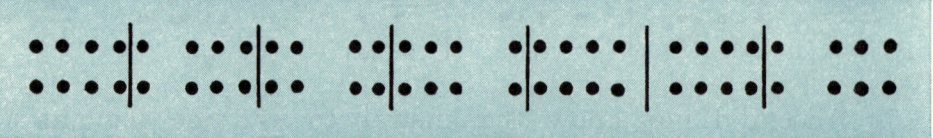

How many eights are in 56? Seven 8's are 56. There are seven 8's in 56.

Find the answers that you did not know. Study them.

A Test

1. Write the answers to these multiplication questions: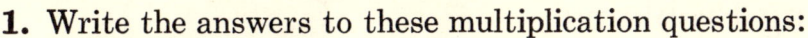

6	5	9	8	5	5	7	6	8	6
×5	×7	×7	×8	×5	×8	×8	×6	×4	×8

7	6	5	7	8	8	9	7	8	5
×5	×9	×6	×7	×9	×5	×8	×6	×6	×9

6	9	4	9	7	8	9	4	9	4
×7	×9	×7	×5	×9	×7	×6	×9	×4	×8

(114)
(118)
(140)
(143)

2. Write the answers to these division questions:

5)25 6)36 7)63 8)32 5)30 7)35 8)48 9)63 6)30

7)21 7)56 8)56 5)35 9)45 8)72 5)40 7)42 8)40

9)81 6)54 8)64 5)45 6)48 7)49 9)72 6)42 9)54

Copy and finish:

	(a)	(b)	(c)	(d)	(e)	(f)	(g)
3.	61 8)488 48	6 6)366 36	70 8)560 56	8 7)567 56	7 7)497	8 9)720	8)728
4.	46 ×8 68	56 ×6 36	72 ×8 6	75 ×4 00	80 ×8 0	51 ×8	92 ×8

(56)
(57)

Copy and find the answers:

	(a)	(b)	(c)	(d)	(e)	(f)
5.	38 × 8	480 ÷ 8	88 × 8	92 × 8	568 ÷ 8	55 × 4
6.	28 × 9	486 ÷ 6	58 × 8	57 × 7	400 ÷ 8	90 × 9
7.	80 × 7	360 ÷ 6	19 × 7	40 × 8	405 ÷ 5	50 × 8

(82)
(85)

Chapter 10
Solving Problems

Each problem tells two or more facts. Each problem also asks a question. We must know exactly what the problem tells so that we will know what to do to answer the question.

Mrs. White is buying 3 quarts of milk at 16¢ a quart. How much should she pay for the milk?

Read the problem carefully.
What does the problem ask us to find?
How much Mrs. White should pay for the milk.

What do we do to answer the question?
We multiply the price of 1 quart by the number of quarts that Mrs. White bought.

What two facts must we get from the problem?
 1. *The price of 1 quart of milk.*
 2. *The number of quarts Mrs. White bought.*

Does the problem tell us the facts we need?
Now solve the problem. Use what the problem tells to find the answer to the question that it asks.

Multiplying Dollars and Cents

When we have to multiply two numbers, we usually find it easier to multiply the larger number by the smaller number. So when we have dollars or cents as one of the numbers, we do our multiplying the easier way.

1. Charles worked 26 days in August. He was paid $2 for each day's work. How much was Charles paid that month?

```
  $.03          75
    75        $.03
   ———       ——————
    15       $2.25
  2 1
 ——————
 $2.25
```

2. Susan bought 75 postage stamps at 3¢ each. How much did she pay for them?

3. There are 34 members in the fourth-grade Good Citizens' Club. Each member pays 5¢ a month dues. How much do they all pay a month for dues?

4. During a shoe sale 46 pairs of shoes were sold at $5 a pair. How much money did the shoes bring?

5. Season tickets to the football games cost $3 each. At the Miller School 89 tickets were bought by the pupils. How much was paid by the pupils for season tickets?

6. Last Sunday Jack sold 42 papers at 8¢ each. How much did he get for the papers?

7. During the week Tom sold 98 papers at 4¢ each. How much did he get for these papers?

8. There are 37 girls in the Bird Club. Each girl pays 7¢ dues each week. How much dues do all the girls pay each week?

Chinese branch money

Ancient stone money

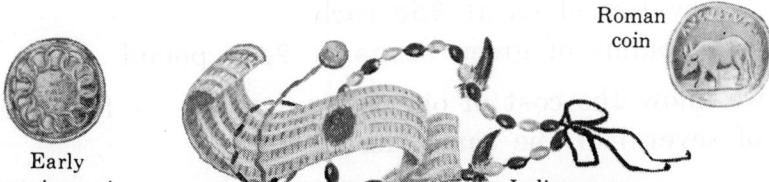

Early American coin

Roman coin

Indian money

Primitive Aztec money

For Sale: Fruits and Vegetables

The Bells have a fruit and vegetable stand by the side of the road. The Bell children help their parents during the summer months. They have to find the cost of the fruits and vegetables they sell to people.

Find the cost of:
1. 3 dozen ears of corn at 50¢ a dozen
2. 6 pounds of cabbage at 6¢ a pound
3. 6 pecks of potatoes at 75¢ a peck
4. 5 quarts of lima beans at 16¢ a quart
5. 3 pecks of apples at 45¢ a peck
6. 8 bunches of beets at 6¢ a bunch
7. 12 pounds of tomatoes at 9¢ a pound
8. 6 bunches of onions at 5¢ a bunch
9. 5 heads of lettuce at 13¢ a head
10. 6 cantaloupes at 15¢ each
11. 4 watermelons at 85¢ each
12. 15 pounds of green beans at 9¢ a pound

If we know the cost of one thing, how do we find the cost of several of the same thing?

Dividing Dollars

1. Ralph makes $6 a week helping at the store after school and on Saturday. How many weeks will he have to work to make $120?

Think: Ralph makes $6 a week. He will work until he makes $120. We want to know how many weeks he will work. We must find how many sixes are in 120. There are 20 sixes in 120; so Ralph must work 20 weeks to make $120.

$$\begin{array}{r} 20 \\ \$6 \overline{) \$120} \\ \underline{12} \\ 0 \end{array}$$

2. Mr. Brown traded in his old car for a new one. He now owes $287 on the new car. He is saving $7 each week to pay what he still owes. In how many weeks will he save enough to pay all he owes on the new car?

3. Fred earns money by mowing lawns. He decided to buy a gasoline lawn mower that costs $100. He is saving $5 a month to pay for it. In how many months will he save enough to buy the lawn mower?

lawn mower

4. Jack said, "I bought a bicycle for $27. I am paying $3 a week on it. In ____ weeks the bicycle will be mine."

5. Alice is saving her money to buy a pony and saddle. She needs $120 before she can buy the pony and saddle. If she saves $4 a week, how many weeks will it take her to save enough money to buy them?

6. June is saving money to buy a flute. The price of the flute is $72. If she saves $8 a week, in how many weeks will she have enough money to buy the flute?

saddle

7. Mrs. Smith bought a sewing machine. She still owes $90 on it. How long will it take her to pay for the machine if she pays $9 a week?

Dividing Dollars and Cents

1. A grocer paid $2.70 for a box of oranges. In the box were 9 dozen oranges. How much did each dozen cost?

```
      $.30
  9)$2.70
     2 7
        0
```

$2.70 is the same as 270 cents. So when we divide 270 cents by 9, we get 30 cents. We write 30 cents like this: $.30.

2. Jim, Joe, and Tom gather up and sell old papers and magazines to buy Savings Stamps. Last week they sold $2.73 worth of paper and divided the money equally. How much did each boy get as his share?

3. Fred had $1.60. He bought Saving Stamps with half of his money. How much did the Savings Stamps cost?

4. Tom had $2.40. He gave one third of his money to the Red Cross. How much did he give to the Red Cross?

5. Lois got $2.70 for her birthday. She wants to put $\frac{1}{3}$ of it in her bank. How much should she put in her bank?

6. Alice, Sue, and Jerry bought a present for their dad. It cost $2.40. What was each child's share of the cost?

7. Four boys mowed Mrs. Smith's lawn and raked the leaves. She gave them $1.60. The boys divided the money equally. How much did each boy get?

Dividing by Cents

1. Jimmy Dale makes 2¢ on each paper he sells. How many papers must he sell to make $1.68?

```
    84                                                    84
2)168      We think of $1.68 as 168 cents,        $.02)$1.68
 16        and of $.02 as 2 cents. We divide        16
 ──        $1.68 by $.02 the way we divide         ──
  8        168 by 2.                                 8
  8                                                  8
```

2. One evening Henry made 68¢ selling papers. He kept 2¢ for each paper that he sold. How many papers did he sell that evening?

```
    34     Check: When Henry sold 30 papers, he       34
2)68       made 60¢. To make 8 more cents, he    $.02)$.68
 6         would have to sell 4 more papers. Henry   6
 ──        made 68 cents; so he sold 34 papers.     ──
  8                                                  8
  8                                                  8
```

3. Frank planned to save 5¢ a day so that he could buy a knife that cost $1.50. How long will it take him to save enough money to buy the knife?

4. The pupils in the Oak Grove School gave a play to get money to buy records for their record player. They sold tickets at 5¢ each. Alice counted her money and said, "I have two dollars and five cents. How many tickets did I sell?"

5. Jane may keep 8¢ for each magazine she sells. She wants to buy a dress that costs $4.80. How many of the magazines must Jane sell to pay for the dress?

6. Alice wanted to plant some rosebushes. She could get some small ones at the dime store for 8¢ apiece. She had $3.20. How many rosebushes could she buy?

records

How Do We Find the Answer?

1. George had 86 Savings Stamps before he bought 14 more. How many Savings Stamps had he then?

2. Jack weighs 58 pounds. The nurse told him that he was 14 pounds underweight. How many pounds should he weigh?

3. Jack's father asked, "How much money did your mother give you this morning?"

Jack said, "I don't know, but I can find out. I spent 42¢ to go to the show, and I have 48¢ left. So Mother gave me 90¢."

Was Jack right?

4. Tom has 68 stamps in his collection. Tom has 45 fewer stamps than Joe has. How many stamps does Joe have?

5. Jim sold 86 papers today, and Joe sold 74. How many papers did both boys sell?

6. Alice made 24 white paper flowers and 36 red paper flowers. How many flowers did she make?

7. Mr. West paid 85¢ for his lunch and 55¢ for Jim's lunch. How much did he pay for the two lunches?

8. Mrs. West spent 90¢ for ribbon and 24¢ for buttons. How much did she spend for both?

9. Henry watched the birds at the birdbath. Today he counted 15 robins, 10 blue jays, 3 red birds, and 26 sparrows. How many birds did he count altogether?

How Do We Find the Answer?

1. Jack had saved $1.65. He bought a ball for 68¢. How much money did he have left?

2. Walter wants to buy a pair of rubber boots that cost $1.67. He has 90¢. How much more money does he need?

3. Joe had 90 marbles. He sold 36 marbles to Bob. Then how many marbles did Joe have?

4. Jane made 72 valentines, and June made 96 valentines. How many more valentines did June make than Jane?

5. Joe bought a book for $.86. He gave the clerk $1.00. How much change should the clerk give Joe?

6. When Joe bought his book, he gave the clerk $1.00. The clerk gave him 14¢ change. How much did the book cost?

7. There are 52 white keys and 36 black keys on a piano. How many keys are there in all? How many more white keys are there than black keys?

8. Mr. West paid $1.25 for his ticket to the baseball game. Bobby paid $.85 for his ticket. What was the difference in price between these tickets?

9. Harry is 10 years old, and his father is 45 years old. How much younger is Harry than his father?

10. The school nurse weighed 125 children. Of this number 38 were underweight. How many children were not underweight?

11. This morning our thermometer read 65°, and this afternoon it read 72°. How much warmer did it get?

How Do We Find the Answer?

1. Bill has 3 baskets of apples in his wagon. He has 48 apples in each basket. How many apples does he have?

2. Each page of Jane's stamp book holds 64 stamps. She has 8 pages full of stamps. How many stamps has she in her stamp book?

3. Mr. Brown bought 4 tickets to the circus. Each ticket cost 87¢. How much did he pay for them?

4. Our car can go 18 miles on one gallon of gasoline. At that rate, how far can it go on 8 gallons?

5. If you know the price of a dozen eggs, how can you find the cost of several dozen eggs?

6. Bobby and Betty bought 6 plates for their mother and gave them to her on her birthday. Each plate cost 77¢. How much did they spend for plates?

7. "How much do the dolls cost?" asked Alice.

"The little doll costs 68¢, and the big doll costs just **twice** as much," answered the clerk.

How much does the big doll cost?

8. The 8 boys in our class made a sand table. Each boy carried 12 buckets of sand. How many buckets of sand did they carry in all?

9. The girls are making animals out of bars of soap. They used 50 bars of soap. At 5¢ a bar, how much did the soap cost?

What Do We Do?

We add, subtract, multiply, or divide to find the answer to the question that the problem asks. We decide what to do by thinking about what the problem tells and what the question asks.

Read each problem. Do we add, subtract, multiply, or divide to solve the problem?

1. Alice weighed 81 pounds last year. Now she weighs 87 pounds. How many pounds has she gained?

2. Helen has 60 Savings Stamps. Joe said, "You have 12 more stamps than I have."
How many Savings Stamps does Joe have?

3. Ellen went to the store. She paid 38¢ for butter, 56¢ for bacon, 33¢ for eggs, and 18¢ for brown sugar. How much did Ellen pay for these things?

4. Lee has $8. He plans to earn enough to buy a bicycle that costs $56. How much money must he earn before he has enough to buy the bicycle?

5. Jane had $1.50. She spent 85¢ and put the rest in the bank. How much did she put in the bank?

6. Mr. Dan has some canned peaches for sale. He is selling 3 cans for 96¢. What will one can cost?

7. Jack is buying a kite that costs 45¢. He has $1.00. If he gives the clerk $1.00, how much change should he get?

8. There is room for 4 kodak pictures on each page of Mary's scrapbook. During her vacation this summer, she took 84 pictures. How many pages of her scrapbook will these pictures fill?

Making Pictures

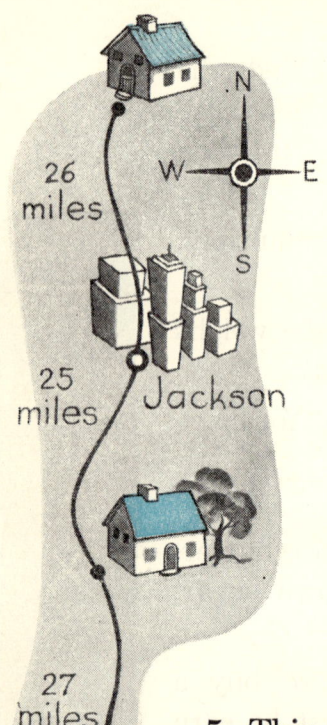

Sometimes we can draw a picture to help us understand a problem.

1. Mary lives 26 miles north of the town of Jackson, and Susan lives 25 miles south of Jackson. How far apart do the girls live?

2. Susan lives 25 miles south of Jackson, and Betty lives 52 miles south of Jackson. How far apart do the girls live?

3. Mary lives 26 miles north of Jackson, and Betty lives 52 miles south of Jackson. How far apart do these girls live?

4. It is 51 miles from Mary's house to Susan's house. It is 27 miles from Betty's house to Susan's house. How much closer to Susan does Betty live than Mary?

5. This lot is 65 feet wide, but the other lot is 25 feet wider. How wide is the other lot?

6. May and Martha live on Elm Street. May lives 3 blocks north of the stop-and-go light. Martha lives 6 blocks south of the light. How far apart do they live?

7. At noon the temperature was 40°, but the next morning it was 4° above zero. How many degrees had the temperature dropped?

8. At 8 o'clock one morning the temperature was 32°. At 4 o'clock that afternoon it was 60°. How much warmer had it gotten?

9. Joe lives 4 blocks east and 5 blocks south of the school. How far does he live from the school?

What Is the Question?

These number stories are not problems because there are no questions. Ask a question to change each number story into a problem. Then solve the problem.

~~~~~~~~~~~~~~~~~~~~~~~~~~~~~~~~~~~

Martha weighs 57 pounds. Ben is 17 pounds heavier than Martha.

~~~~~~~~~~~~~~~~~~~~~~~~~~~~~~~~~~~

We might ask: *How much does Ben weigh?*

1. Two years ago Jim weighed 69 pounds. He now weighs 84 pounds.

2. Mr. Brown is 32 years old, and Jane is 9 years old.

3. Bob is 56 inches tall, and Susan is 48 inches tall.

4. George weighed 83 pounds with his overcoat on. When he took off his overcoat, he weighed only 79 pounds.

5. Dan's father bought 4 cows for $60 apiece.

6. A set of bird pictures cost $.85, and a set of animal pictures cost $.75.

7. Jean colored 64 pictures, and Marie colored 88.

8. Mr. West has 143 chickens. He has 95 white chickens, and the rest of them are black.

9. Jane's mother plans to make 120 sandwiches for the school picnic. She has already made 60 sandwiches.

10. Jane made a score of 94 on a test. Tom made a score of 56 on the same test.

11. One morning 3 groups of airplanes flew over our house. There were 26 airplanes in each group.

What Is Missing?

A problem always tells 2 or more important facts.

Mary's mother needs some ice cream for the party. At 45¢ a quart, how much will she pay for it?

This number story is not a problem. It tells only one of the facts we need to answer the question. We know that the ice cream costs 45¢ a quart, but we do not know how many quarts are needed.

Read each number story. Tell what else we need to know before there is a problem to solve. Then supply the missing fact and solve the problem.

1. Jane paid 38¢ for a pound of coffee. How much money did she have left after she paid for the coffee?

2. Jim swam the length of the swimming pool 5 times. How far did he swim?

3. Jack had 45¢. He went to the store to buy some seeds for his vegetable garden. How many packages of seeds can he buy?

4. The boys and girls collected pictures of Mexico. The boys collected 28 pictures, and the girls collected the rest. How many pictures did they collect altogether?

5. Mr. James needs 6 long pieces of wire. How many feet of wire does he need in all?

6. Jim saw two dart games in the store window. One of them cost $1.15. The other one did not cost that much. How much more did the one dart game cost than the other?

Making Problems

1. Had $1.00. Bought a knife for $.65. Make a problem in **subtracting**.

~~~~~~~~~~~~~~~~~~~~~~~~~~~~~

Jack had $1.00 that his father gave him for a birthday present. Jack spent $.65 for a pocket-knife. How much money did he have left?

~~~~~~~~~~~~~~~~~~~~~~~~~~~~~

2. A pound of butter for 43¢; a dozen eggs for 35¢; and some bacon for 38¢. Make a problem in **adding**.

3. Paid $3.60 for 4 shirts; cost of each was the same. Make a problem in **dividing**.

4. Bought 3 neckties; cost of each was 65¢. Make a problem in **multiplying**.

5. Had $1.62 in purse; went shopping and spent 75¢. Make a problem in **subtracting**.

6. In first spelling list, 90 words; in second spelling list, 62 words. Make a problem in **subtracting**.

7. In first spelling list, 90 words; in second spelling list, 62 words. Make a problem in **adding**.

8. In auditorium, 50 rows of seats; in each row, 8 seats. Make a problem in **multiplying**.

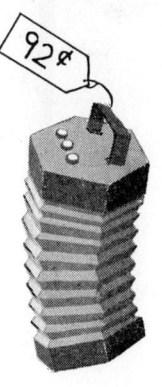

9. Set out 180 tomato plants; 9 plants in a row. Make a problem in **dividing**.

10. Cost of baseball and bat, $2.70; 9 boys on the team. Make a problem in **dividing**.

11. Gasoline costs 24¢ a gallon; bought 5 gallons. Make a problem in **multiplying**.

Chapter 11
The Uneven Divisions

How Many Are Left Over?

1. There were 9 cookies on the plate when the four girls came in from play. Each girl took 2 cookies, and 1 cookie was left on the plate.

2. Jack said, "If I had 11 cookies to give to 4 boys, I could give each boy 2 cookies, and there would be 3 cookies left over."

3. How many will each get? How many are left over?
 a. Divide 7 flowers among 4 girls.
 b. Divide 8 books among 3 girls.
 c. Divide 13 balloons among 5 children.
 d. Divide 15 marbles among 6 boys.

Uneven Divisions

1. How many children are in the band? How many groups of 2 are there? The boy in front is the leader. He has no partner.

We could ask a question like this:

How many twos are in nine? 2)9

Think: How many 2's are in 9? We know that four 2's are 8 and that five 2's are 10 or more than 9. There are four 2's in 8; so there are four 2's in 9 with something left over. We write 4 above the 9.

$$\begin{array}{r} 4 \\ 2\overline{)9} \end{array}$$

We multiply: Four 2's are 8. We write 8 under the 9 and draw a line.

$$\begin{array}{r} 4 \\ 2\overline{)9} \\ \underline{8} \end{array}$$

We subtract to find how many are left. 8 from 9 is 1. We write 1 under 8.

There are four 2's in 9, and 1 **left over**.

$$\begin{array}{r} 4 \\ 2\overline{)9} \\ \underline{8} \\ 1 \end{array}$$

2. How many 4's are in 9? •••• •••• •

We find that there are two 4's in 9, and 1 left over, or **1 remainder**.

$$\begin{array}{r} 2 \\ 4\overline{)9} \\ \underline{8} \\ 1 \end{array}$$

3. How many 3's are in 11? ••• ••• ••• ••

The answer is 3, and 2 remainder.

$$\begin{array}{r} 3 \\ 3\overline{)11} \\ \underline{9} \\ 2 \end{array}$$

Dividing by Two and Three

1. Say the answer to each division question:

$2\overline{)2}$ $2\overline{)4}$ $2\overline{)6}$ $2\overline{)8}$ $2\overline{)10}$ $2\overline{)12}$ $2\overline{)14}$ $2\overline{)16}$ $2\overline{)18}$

There is nothing left over; so we say that the numbers divide evenly by 2.

2. Count by 2's from 2 to 18. All the numbers you said divide evenly by 2. They are called **even** numbers. What is an even number?

3. Say the answer to each division question. How many are left over?

Think: How many twos are in 11? The next number smaller than 11 that can be divided evenly by 2 is 10. There are five 2's in 11 with some left over.

$$\begin{array}{r} 5 \\ 2\overline{)11} \\ \underline{10} \\ 1 \end{array}$$

Say: Twos in eleven, five and **1** remainder.

$2\overline{)3}$ $2\overline{)5}$ $2\overline{)7}$ $2\overline{)9}$ $2\overline{)11}$ $2\overline{)13}$ $2\overline{)15}$ $2\overline{)17}$ $2\overline{)19}$

There is one left over in each division above. The numbers do not divide evenly by 2. We say they are the uneven divisions.

4. Count by 2's from 3 to 19. These numbers have one left over when we divide by 2. They are **odd** numbers.

5. Say the answer to each division question:

$3\overline{)3}$ $3\overline{)6}$ $3\overline{)9}$ $3\overline{)12}$ $3\overline{)15}$ $3\overline{)18}$ $3\overline{)21}$ $3\overline{)24}$ $3\overline{)27}$

6. Say the answers to these division questions. How many are left over?

$3\overline{)4}$ $3\overline{)5}$ $3\overline{)7}$ $3\overline{)8}$ $3\overline{)10}$ $3\overline{)11}$ $3\overline{)13}$ $3\overline{)14}$ $3\overline{)16}$
$3\overline{)17}$ $3\overline{)19}$ $3\overline{)20}$ $3\overline{)22}$ $3\overline{)23}$ $3\overline{)25}$ $3\overline{)26}$ $3\overline{)28}$ $3\overline{)29}$

Dividing by Four

If you know the answers to all parts of the first three questions, you are ready to divide by 4.

1. Say the products for these multiplication questions:

$$\begin{array}{ccccccccc} 4 & 4 & 4 & 4 & 4 & 4 & 4 & 4 & 4 \\ \times 1 & \times 5 & \times 3 & \times 9 & \times 6 & \times 8 & \times 2 & \times 7 & \times 4 \end{array}$$

2. Say the answers to these division questions:

4)4   4)8   4)12   4)16   4)20   4)24   4)28   4)32   4)36

3. Count by 4's from 4 to 36. These numbers divide evenly by 4.

4. Say the number **smaller** than each of these numbers, and **nearest** to it, that will divide evenly by 4.

a. 6   9   5   11   17   18   23   19   25   30   35
b. 10 7   14 15   39   13   27   21   33   22   31

5. Jack picked 18 apples to put into boxes to sell at the fruit stand. If he puts 4 apples in a box, how many boxes will he have to sell? How many **extra** apples will he have?

```
    4
4)18
   16
    2
```

6. Say the answers to these division questions.
Remember: The remainder is part of the answer.

4)9   4)10   4)11   4)5   4)17   4)15   4)13   4)7   4)6

Write your work for these division examples:

	(a)	(b)	(c)	(d)	(e)	(f)	(g)	(h)	(i)
7.	4)21	4)29	4)35	4)19	4)33	4)39	4)23	4)38	4)18
8.	4)14	4)37	4)25	4)30	4)27	4)22	4)26	4)34	4)31

Dividing by Five

1. Say the products for these multiplication questions:

5	5	5	5	5	5	5	5	5
×1	×2	×3	×4	×5	×6	×7	×8	×9

2. Say the answers to these division questions:

5)5   5)10   5)15   5)20   5)25   5)30   5)35   5)40   5)45

3. Count by 5's from 5 to 50.

4. Say the number smaller than each of these numbers, and nearest to it, that will divide evenly by 5.

Remember: Any number ending with 0 or 5 divides evenly by 5.

a.	7	21	33	36	26	11	14	44	17	31
b.	9	32	27	12	16	28	23	13	22	18
c.	8	24	38	41	19	29	43	34	39	42

5. Jerry had 17 radishes from his garden. He tied them in bunches of 5 radishes each. How many bunches did he have?

$$\begin{array}{r} 3 \\ 5\overline{)17} \\ \underline{15} \\ 2 \end{array}$$

6. How were these examples worked?

$$\begin{array}{r} 1 \\ 5\overline{)7} \\ \underline{5} \\ 2 \end{array} \quad \begin{array}{r} 2 \\ 5\overline{)12} \\ \underline{10} \\ 2 \end{array} \quad \begin{array}{r} 5 \\ 5\overline{)26} \\ \underline{25} \\ 1 \end{array} \quad \begin{array}{r} 6 \\ 5\overline{)33} \\ \underline{30} \\ 3 \end{array} \quad \begin{array}{r} 7 \\ 5\overline{)39} \\ \underline{35} \\ 4 \end{array} \quad \begin{array}{r} 8 \\ 5\overline{)44} \\ \underline{40} \\ 4 \end{array} \quad \begin{array}{r} 9 \\ 5\overline{)48} \\ \underline{45} \\ 3 \end{array}$$

Find the answers:

	(a)	(b)	(c)	(d)	(e)	(f)	(g)	(h)	(i)
7.	5)6	5)13	5)18	5)21	5)24	5)31	5)41	5)29	5)19
8.	5)23	5)28	5)32	5)22	5)43	5)38	5)16	5)34	5)47
9.	5)49	5)11	5)36	5)46	5)37	5)27	5)42	5)14	5)9

Problems

1. Jane and 3 of her friends bought a box of cookies. There were 18 cookies in the box. How many cookies were there for each of the four girls? Were there any extra cookies? If so, how many were there?

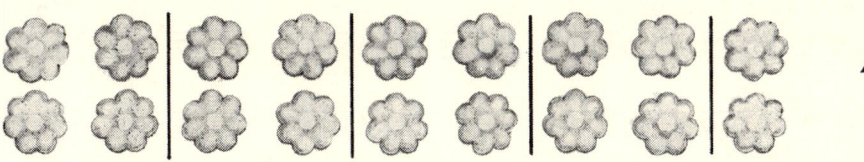

How many 4's in 18? How many are left over?

2. The 4 girls bought a bottle of olives. There were 35 olives in the bottle. How many olives was each girl's share? Were there any extra olives? If so, how many?

3. Jim plans to save one third of the money he earns. One Saturday he earned 25¢. How many cents should he save? Does 25 divide evenly by 3? How much is left over?

4. Sue baked 15 cupcakes. She wants to take one half of them to her Aunt Helen. How many cupcakes should she take? Does 15 divide evenly by 2? Do you suppose Sue will take the extra cupcake to her aunt, or will she eat it herself?

5. Betty and Alice are making doll dresses for their Christmas dolls. They are going to put 3 buttons on each dress. They have 22 buttons. For how many dresses do they have buttons? Will any buttons be left over?

6. The boys are making toy wagons for the Christmas boxes. They will put 4 wheels on each wagon. They have made 33 wheels. For how many wagons do they have wheels? How many wheels do they have left over?

Even Divisions	Uneven Divisions					Even Divisions
$\overset{1}{6\overline{)6}}$	$6\overline{)7}$	$6\overline{)8}$	$6\overline{)9}$	$6\overline{)10}$	$6\overline{)11}$	$\overset{2}{6\overline{)12}}$
$\overset{2}{6\overline{)12}}$	$6\overline{)13}$	$6\overline{)14}$	$6\overline{)15}$	$6\overline{)16}$	$6\overline{)17}$	$\overset{3}{6\overline{)18}}$
$\overset{3}{6\overline{)18}}$	$6\overline{)19}$	$6\overline{)20}$	$6\overline{)21}$	$6\overline{)22}$	$6\overline{)23}$	$\overset{4}{6\overline{)24}}$
$\overset{4}{6\overline{)24}}$	$6\overline{)25}$	$6\overline{)26}$	$6\overline{)27}$	$6\overline{)28}$	$6\overline{)29}$	$\overset{5}{6\overline{)30}}$
$\overset{5}{6\overline{)30}}$	$6\overline{)31}$	$6\overline{)32}$	$6\overline{)33}$	$6\overline{)34}$	$6\overline{)35}$	$\overset{6}{6\overline{)36}}$
$\overset{6}{6\overline{)36}}$	$6\overline{)37}$	$6\overline{)38}$	$6\overline{)39}$	$6\overline{)40}$	$6\overline{)41}$	$\overset{7}{6\overline{)42}}$
$\overset{7}{6\overline{)42}}$	$6\overline{)43}$	$6\overline{)44}$	$6\overline{)45}$	$6\overline{)46}$	$6\overline{)47}$	$\overset{8}{6\overline{)48}}$
$\overset{8}{6\overline{)48}}$	$6\overline{)49}$	$6\overline{)50}$	$6\overline{)51}$	$6\overline{)52}$	$6\overline{)53}$	$\overset{9}{6\overline{)54}}$

Dividing by Six

Look in the table under "Even Divisions." See $\overset{1}{6\overline{)6}}$. Then look under "Uneven Divisions." When we see $6\overline{)7}$, $6\overline{)8}$, $6\overline{)9}$, $6\overline{)10}$, and $6\overline{)11}$, we think back to $6\overline{)6}$.

What even division should you think back to when you see each of these questions? Now say the answers.

$6\overline{)9}$ $6\overline{)44}$ $6\overline{)13}$ $6\overline{)25}$ $6\overline{)31}$ $6\overline{)41}$ $6\overline{)22}$ $6\overline{)51}$ $6\overline{)49}$

$6\overline{)7}$ $6\overline{)19}$ $6\overline{)23}$ $6\overline{)47}$ $6\overline{)35}$ $6\overline{)11}$ $6\overline{)38}$ $6\overline{)29}$ $6\overline{)15}$

$6\overline{)43}$ $6\overline{)34}$ $6\overline{)50}$ $6\overline{)32}$ $6\overline{)56}$ $6\overline{)39}$ $6\overline{)26}$ $6\overline{)52}$ $6\overline{)40}$

Dividing by Seven

Do you know the multiplications and divisions for 7's?

```
  7      3       3       7       7       5        5       7
 ×3     ×7    7)21    3)21     ×5      ×7     7)35     5)35
 --     --                     --      --
 21     21                     35      35

  7      6       6       7       7       2        2       7
 ×6     ×7    7)42    6)42     ×2      ×7     7)14     2)14
 --     --                     --      --
 42     42                     14      14

  7      4       4       7       7       7        7       1
 ×4     ×7    7)28    4)28     ×7    7)49       ×1     7)7
 --     --                     --               --
 28     28                     49                7

  7      8       8       7       7       9        7       9
 ×8     ×7    7)56    8)56     ×9      ×7     9)63     7)63
 --     --                     --      --
 56     56                     63      63
```

"I spent my vacation at my uncle's farm. I was there 32 days," said Harry. "That was 4 weeks and 4 days."

```
    4
 7)32
   28
   --
    4
```

Tell how these numbers were divided. Then copy each example without the work and answer. Find the answer.

```
   2       3       8       5       9       4       6       7
7)15    7)24    7)60    7)38    7)65    7)34    7)47    7)51
  14      21      56      35      63      28      42      49
  --      --      --      --      --      --      --      --
   1       3       4       3       2       6       5       2
```

Copy and find the answers:

	(a)	(b)	(c)	(d)	(e)	(f)	(g)
1.	7)39	7)62	7)54	7)66	7)40	7)50	7)23
2.	7)53	7)36	7)11	7)18	7)58	7)26	7)43
3.	7)44	7)61	7)17	7)22	7)31	7)57	7)55
4.	7)48	7)32	7)25	7)19	7)27	7)68	7)37

Dividing by Eight

Use these multiplications and divisions to find the quotients and remainders for the examples below.

```
  8       3         8       5         8       2         8       7
 ×3    8)24        ×5    8)40        ×2    8)16        ×7    8)56
 ―――              ―――              ―――              ―――
  24               40                16                56

  8       4         8       6         8       8         8       9
 ×4    8)32        ×6    8)48        ×8    8)64        ×9    8)72
 ―――              ―――              ―――              ―――
  32               48                64                72
```

	(a)	(b)	(c)	(d)	(e)	(f)	(g)
1.	8)26	8)17	8)42	8)28	8)66	8)37	8)12
2.	8)78	8)19	8)34	8)9	8)51	8)30	8)70
3.	8)15	8)52	8)77	8)63	8)27	8)46	8)39
4.	8)20	8)31	8)45	8)57	8)23	8)10	8)68
5.	8)54	8)14	8)25	8)74	8)44	8)18	8)22
6.	8)29	8)33	8)59	8)41	8)65	8)73	8)21
7.	8)71	8)43	8)13	8)35	8)47	8)60	8)53
8.	8)38	8)69	8)50	8)49	8)55	8)79	8)62
9.	8)36	8)11	8)58	8)67	8)75	8)61	8)76

10. Which of these numbers can be divided by 8 without a remainder—18, 24, 36, 40, 50, 54, 68, 74?

11. The 32 children in our room were going to clean up the playground. They were divided into 8 squads. How many children were there in each squad?

Dividing by Nine

Use these multiplications and divisions to find the quotients and remainders for the examples below.

$$\begin{array}{c} 9 \\ \times 5 \\ \hline 45 \end{array} \qquad 9\overline{)45}^{\,5} \qquad \begin{array}{c} 9 \\ \times 2 \\ \hline 18 \end{array} \qquad 9\overline{)18}^{\,2} \qquad \begin{array}{c} 9 \\ \times 6 \\ \hline 54 \end{array} \qquad 9\overline{)54}^{\,6} \qquad \begin{array}{c} 9 \\ \times 9 \\ \hline 81 \end{array} \qquad 9\overline{)81}^{\,9}$$

$$\begin{array}{c} 9 \\ \times 3 \\ \hline 27 \end{array} \qquad 9\overline{)27}^{\,3} \qquad \begin{array}{c} 9 \\ \times 7 \\ \hline 63 \end{array} \qquad 9\overline{)63}^{\,7} \qquad \begin{array}{c} 9 \\ \times 8 \\ \hline 72 \end{array} \qquad 8\overline{)72}^{\,9} \qquad \begin{array}{c} 9 \\ \times 4 \\ \hline 36 \end{array} \qquad 9\overline{)36}^{\,4}$$

	(a)	(b)	(c)	(d)	(e)	(f)	(g)	(h)
1.	9)41	9)34	9)21	9)60	9)85	9)51	9)66	9)24
2.	9)14	9)43	9)76	9)25	9)87	9)56	9)35	9)28
3.	9)12	9)42	9)30	9)61	9)80	9)49	9)23	9)16
4.	9)65	9)52	9)44	9)26	9)15	9)32	9)75	9)88
5.	9)77	9)40	9)67	9)53	9)11	9)20	9)46	9)86
6.	9)73	9)22	9)10	9)38	9)50	9)68	9)83	9)71
7.	9)59	9)17	9)33	9)39	9)13	9)19	9)29	9)31
8.	9)37	9)62	9)64	9)74	9)47	9)55	9)78	9)82
9.	9)84	9)48	9)57	9)79	9)58	9)70	9)69	9)89

10. Which of these numbers can be divided by 9 without a remainder—17, 28, 36, 48, 54, 64, 72, 82?

11. Chris has 84 tomato plants. He wants to set 9 plants in each row. How many full rows will he have? How many extra plants will he have?

Chapter 12
Carrying in Division

Are We Ready?

1. Uncle George gave his three nephews, Tom, Charles, and Fred, 75 cents to be divided equally among them. How much did each boy get?

How many quarters make 75 cents? $\frac{1}{3}$ of 75¢ is 25¢.

2. Tom had 60¢ in all. He spent $\frac{1}{5}$ of his money for a newspaper and a magazine. How much did he spend?

$\frac{1}{5}$ of 50¢ = 10¢
$\frac{1}{5}$ of 10¢ = 2¢
$\frac{1}{5}$ of 60¢ = 12¢

How much did Tom spend? $\frac{1}{5}$ of 60¢ is how many cents?

3. Charles had 90¢ in all. He spent $\frac{1}{2}$ of it for a tie. How much did he pay for the tie?

Ninety cents is 9 dimes, or 18 nickels.
$\frac{1}{2}$ of 18 nickels is 9 nickels, or 45 cents.
So $\frac{1}{2}$ of 90¢ is 45¢.

There is an easier way to solve the problems:

$$3\overline{)75¢} \qquad 5\overline{)60¢} \qquad 2\overline{)90¢}$$

But before we can solve them, we must learn how to **carry tens** when we divide.

Carrying When We Divide

Joe was selling tickets for the school play when he met Jim on the street. "How many tickets do you have to sell?" asked Jim. "I can't buy a ticket, but I can help you sell them. Let me have half of them."

"I have 7 bundles with 10 tickets in each bundle and 4 extra tickets; so I have 74 tickets in all," answered Joe.

Joe gave Jim half of the tickets, and he kept half of the tickets. How many tickets did each boy have to sell?

Gave Jim   Had left   Joe kept

This is the way Joe divided the tickets:

First, he divided the bundles. There were 7 bundles; so he gave Jim 3 bundles, kept 3 bundles, and had 1 bundle left over.

Joe still had 1 bundle and 4 extra tickets to divide. He opened the 1 bundle of 10 tickets and put them with the 4 loose tickets. Then he had 14 loose tickets; so he took 7 tickets and gave Jim 7 tickets.

Jim has   Joe has

Each boy has 3 bundles (tens) and 7 loose tickets. Each boy has $\frac{1}{2}$ of the 74 tickets. $\frac{1}{2}$ of 74 is how many? How many tickets did each boy have to sell?

Dividing Tens and Ones

Now let us show a division with figures.

Dividing Tens

Dividing Tens

Step 1
```
   2
3)75
```

Step 2
```
   2
3)75
   6
```

Step 3
```
   2
3)75
   6
   1
```

Step 4
```
   2
3)75
   6
  15
```

1. We will divide the tens first. We think, "Threes in seven, two." We know there are more than 2 threes, but not as many as 3 threes in 7. We write 2 in ten's place in the answer.

2. Next we multiply: Two threes are six. We write 6 under 7 and draw a line under 6. We notice to make sure that the number we write (6) is **not more** than the number just above it (7).

3. Now we subtract: Six from seven is one. We write 1 directly under the 6. This means that after dividing 6 of the 7 tens, we have 1 ten left to be divided. We notice that the 1 is **less** than the 3.

4. We also have the 5 ones to be divided. We bring down the 5 (ones) and write 5 beside the 1 (ten). We really **carry back** the 1 **ten** and use it with the 5 ones to make 15 ones.

Dividing Ones

Dividing Ones

Step 1
```
  25
3)75
   6
  15
```

Step 2
```
  25
3)75
   6
  15
  15
```

1. Now we divide the ones. We have 15 ones. We think, "Threes in fifteen, five." We write 5 in one's place.

2. We multiply: Five threes are 15. We write 15 under 15 and draw a line.

We have finished dividing 75 by 3.
Our answer is 25.

Steps in Carrying

Dividing Tens

1. First, we **divide** the **tens**. There are 9. We think, "Twos in nine, four." We write 4 in ten's place in the answer.

2. We **multiply**: Four twos are eight. We write 8 under 9 and draw a line. We notice that 8 is **not more** than the 9 just above it.

3. We **subtract**: Eight from nine is one. We write 1 below the line under 8. This means that we still have 1 ten left to divide. We notice that this 1 is **less** than 2.

4. We **bring down** the 0 and write it beside the 1 (ten). We have 10 (ones) to divide.

Dividing Ones

1. Now we **divide** the 10 **ones**. We think, "Twos in ten, five." We write 5 in one's place in the answer.

2. We **multiply**: Five twos are ten. We write 10 under 10 and draw a line.

We have finished dividing 90 by 2.
Our answer is 45.

Step 1

$$\begin{array}{r}4\\2\overline{)90}\end{array}$$

Step 2

$$\begin{array}{r}4\\2\overline{)90}\\8\end{array}$$

Step 3

$$\begin{array}{r}4\\2\overline{)90}\\\underline{8}\\1\end{array}$$

Step 4

$$\begin{array}{r}4\\2\overline{)90}\\\underline{8}\\10\end{array}$$

Step 1

$$\begin{array}{r}45\\2\overline{)90}\\\underline{8}\\10\end{array}$$

Step 2

$$\begin{array}{r}45\\2\overline{)90}\\\underline{8}\\10\\10\end{array}$$

Copy and divide:

	(a)	(b)	(c)	(d)	(e)	(f)	(g)	(h)
1.	2)50	2)70	2)90	5)80	5)90	6)90	4)60	5)60
2.	3)48	4)56	5)85	6)84	7)91	8)96	7)84	6)96
3.	2)98	3)54	5)65	6)72	7)98	4)68	4)92	5)75

More about Carrying

1. Fred helped his father set out 275 tomato plants in their garden. They set them out in 5 rows, and they put the same number of plants in each row. How many plants did they put in each row?

Dividing Tens

275 is 27 tens and 5 ones.

First, we **divide** the 27 tens: Fives in twenty-seven, five. We write 5 in ten's place in the answer.

We **multiply**: Five fives are twenty-five. We write 25 under 27. We notice that 25 is not more than 27.

We **subtract**: Twenty-five from twenty-seven is two. We write 2 under the 5. We notice that 2 is less than 5.

Dividing Ones

We divide the ones. We **bring down** the 5 (ones). We write the 5 beside the 2 (tens). We have 25 ones to divide: Fives in twenty-five, five. We write 5 in one's place in the answer.

We multiply: Five fives are twenty-five.

They set out 55 tomato plants in each row.

```
      5
  5)275

      5
  5)275
     25

      5
  5)275
     25
      2

      5
  5)275
     25
     25

     55
  5)275
     25
     25

     55
  5)275
     25
     25
     25
```

2. Tell how these numbers were divided:

```
      38          87          64          85          84
  5)190       4)348       6)384       7)595       8)672
     15          32          36          56          64
     40          28          24          35          32
     40          28          24          35          32
```

3. Copy and divide:

(a) 8)336   (b) 9)243   (c) 8)232   (d) 9)405   (e) 8)504   (f) 9)567

Checking in Division

Sometimes we make mistakes when we divide. But if we do our work carefully, we can find and correct our mistakes as we go along.

The best check is to do your work carefully.

At first Simon thought there were six 4's in 23. He wrote 6 in ten's place in the answer. Then he thought, "Six 4's are 24." He wrote 24 under 23. Then he **compared** 24 with 23 above it. He saw that 24 was more than 23; so he knew he had made a mistake.

```
Wrong
     6
4)232
    24
```

He divided again. This time he thought, "There are five 4's in 23." He wrote 20 under 23, and noticed that 20 was **less** than 23. He subtracted 20 from 23. He checked to see that the 3 was less than the 4.

```
Right
     5
4)232
    20
     3
```

Copy the example and finish working it.

Another check is to multiply the answer by the divisor.

See how Jim divided and checked his example. He worked carefully. He found that the answer was 57, but he checked another way to be sure that the answer was right. To check the answer, he multiplied 57 by 3. Why was he sure that his answer was right?

```
              57  quotient
divisor 3)171
          15
           21
           21

           57  quotient
           ×3  divisor
          171
```

Divide and check each answer:

	(a)	(b)	(c)	(d)	(e)	(f)	(g)
1.	9)252	4)328	5)455	9)504	6)228	6)384	8)432
2.	6)474	3)234	4)388	5)460	8)704	6)276	6)192

Dividing Dollars and Cents

1. Jim bought a box of neckties for $1.95. There were 3 ties in the box. How much did each tie cost?

```
    $.65         65¢
3)$1.95      3)195¢
  18           18
  ──           ──
   15           15
   15           15

Check:   $.65
         ×3
        ─────
        $1.95
```

We think of $1.95 as 195¢. If 195¢ is divided by 3, the answer is 65¢. We may write 65¢ as $.65.

Notice where we put the point in our answer. There must be two places for cents after the point.

2. Study these examples. See where the points are placed in the answers.

```
    $.69         $.55         $.63         $.96         $.75         $.95
4)$2.76      4)$2.20      5)$3.15      5)$4.80      4)$3.00      6)$5.70
  24           20           30           45           28           54
  ──           ──           ──           ──           ──           ──
   36           20           15           30           20           30
   36           20           15           30           20           30
```

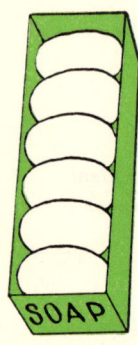

3. Ann bought a box of soap for $1.50. There were 6 bars of soap in the box. How much did each bar of soap cost?

4. Betty and Sue paid $1.30 for a pair of gloves for their father. They shared the cost equally. How much was each girl's share?

5. Father gave the four children $3.00 to spend at the fair. They divided the money equally. How much did each child have to spend?

6. Mrs. Smith bought 3 dozen eggs for $1.05. How much did she pay for each dozen?

Each Paid His Share

1. The members of the school baseball team bought some balls, bats, and gloves for $5.85. Each of the 9 boys on the team paid his share of the expense, which was $\frac{1}{9}$ of $5.85. How much was each boy's share?

2. While the boys were playing ball, they accidentally broke a window in Mr. Bell's garage. It cost $3.15 to replace the window. The 9 boys divided the cost equally. How much did each boy pay?

Copy and divide.

	(a)	(b)	(c)	(d)	(e)	(f)
3.	2)$.90	3)$.75	4)$1.36	5)$1.25	8)$3.84	6)$2.28
4.	7)$1.75	8)$2.80	9)$2.25	2)$1.50	8)$6.64	3)$1.95
5.	4)$3.00	5)$3.75	6)$3.90	7)$5.25	9)$7.65	5)$6.80
6.	9)$3.87	4)$3.56	4)$2.72	5)$3.65	9)$8.37	5)$2.45
7.	6)$5.64	6)$4.56	7)$3.36	7)$6.23	9)$4.23	8)$3.04

Practice in Dividing

Be sure that you know these divisions before you try to work the examples below.

							
6)12 ⎯2	6)18 ⎯3	6)24 ⎯4	6)30 ⎯5	6)36 ⎯6	6)42 ⎯7	6)48 ⎯8	6)54 ⎯9
7)14 ⎯2	7)21 ⎯3	7)28 ⎯4	7)35 ⎯5	7)42 ⎯6	7)49 ⎯7	7)56 ⎯8	7)63 ⎯9
8)16 ⎯2	8)24 ⎯3	8)32 ⎯4	8)40 ⎯5	8)48 ⎯6	8)56 ⎯7	8)64 ⎯8	8)72 ⎯9
9)18 ⎯2	9)27 ⎯3	9)36 ⎯4	9)45 ⎯5	9)54 ⎯6	9)63 ⎯7	9)72 ⎯8	9)81 ⎯9

In these examples we do not carry. Copy and divide:

	(a)	(b)	(c)	(d)	(e)	(f)
1.	5)105	6)186	7)147	8)248	9)189	2)106
2.	4)208	5)255	6)306	7)350	8)408	9)450
3.	4)240	5)350	6)420	7)497	8)480	9)540
4.	4)288	5)400	6)546	7)560	7)567	8)640
5.	9)630	9)720	9)819	7)217	6)240	6)300
6.	8)240	8)320	4)328	9)279	4)360	5)455

$$\begin{array}{r}83\\3\overline{)249}\\24\\\hline 9\\9\end{array}$$

In these examples we carry. Copy and divide:

	(a)	(b)	(c)	(d)	(e)	(f)
7.	8)176	5)215	6)258	9)387	7)224	5)170
8.	7)238	8)272	9)198	6)144	8)336	7)161
9.	9)891	6)192	8)344	7)294	9)387	5)275
10.	6)198	9)108	8)496	9)486	6)204	7)203

$$\begin{array}{r}38\\8\overline{)304}\\24\\\hline 64\\64\end{array}$$

Christmas Shopping

1. Susan bought a box of handkerchiefs for $1.25. There were 5 handkerchiefs in the box. How much did each handkerchief cost?

2. Jack bought 7 ties that cost $.65 each. How much did he pay for the ties?

3. Helen bought 6 books to give to her friends. The price of each book was 85¢. How much did the books cost?

4. Harry bought a set of storybooks. The set of books cost $4.75, and there were 5 books in the set. What was the cost of each book?

5. Alice bought 5 boxes of games to give to the children in the hospital. She paid $2.25 for the games. How much did each box cost if the price of each was the same?

6. Sally spent 18¢ for a handkerchief, 65¢ for a book, and 35¢ for a game. How much did Sally spend?

7. Copy and divide:

(a) 8)472　(b) 8)544　(c) 9)702　(d) 8)608　(e) 9)801　(f) 9)522　(g) 9)675

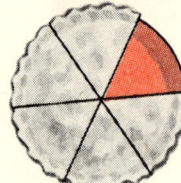

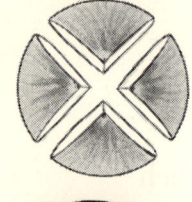

Equal Parts

Read each statement. Say the words that belong in the blanks:

1. The apple has been divided into ____ equal parts. Each part is ____ ____ of the apple.

2. Someone has eaten ____ ____ of the pie. When anything is divided into 6 equal parts, each part is called ____ ____.

3. Someone has eaten ____ ____ of the ice cream. When anything is divided into 5 equal parts, each part is called ____ ____.

4. There is ____ ____ of a melon in each piece.

5. The circle has been divided into ____ equal parts. ____ ____ of the circle is black.

6. To find $\frac{1}{3}$ of a number, we divide by ____.

7. There are 12 cupcakes in the picture. One ____ of all the cupcakes are on the plate.

Find:

	(a)	(b)	(c)	(d)
8.	$\frac{1}{2}$ of $.76	$\frac{1}{6}$ of $5.04	$\frac{1}{3}$ of $1.74	$\frac{1}{4}$ of $2.76
9.	$\frac{1}{5}$ of $3.85	$\frac{1}{7}$ of $5.25	$\frac{1}{8}$ of $5.04	$\frac{1}{8}$ of $3.76

10. Charles bought 56 pages of drawing paper and used $\frac{1}{4}$ of it to make a science booklet. How many pages did he use?

A Fruit Basket

The 8 girls in our class bought a pretty basket and filled it with fresh fruit. They sent the basket of fruit to Mary Brown, who was at home with the measles.

1. Find the cost of the fruit:
 $\frac{1}{2}$ dozen oranges at 36¢ a dozen
 3 pounds of grapes at 15¢ a pound
 1 pound of apples at 3 pounds for 42¢
 4 pounds of bananas at 17¢ a pound

2. The basket cost 55¢. What was the cost of the fruit and the basket together?

3. The girls shared the expense equally. What was each girl's share?

4. Copy and add:

(a)	(b)	(c)	(d)	(e)	(f)	(g)	(h)	(i)
25	13	60	$.90	$.78	$.86	$.77	40	39
32	95	70	.18	.65	.95	.80	71	82
64	82	96	.47	.36	.84	.96	22	91

5. Copy and subtract:

156	170	165	$1.00	$1.05	$.80	$.85	98	110
88	93	78	.86	.98	.24	.28	39	88

A Test in Carrying Tens

Do you know how to **carry** tens in adding and multiplying? Copy these examples on paper and work them.

Add in row **1**; multiply in rows **2** and **3**.

	(a)	(b)	(c)	(d)	(e)	(f)	(g)
1.	32 46 75	24 65 73	46 33 95	78 25 49	$ .64 .50 .48	$ .65 .75 .98	$ .88 .65 .67
2.	38 ×2	22 ×9	96 ×5	47 ×6	76 ×4	84 ×8	68 ×7
3.	$ .25 ×3	$ .75 ×4	$ .35 ×6	$ .94 ×8	$ .85 ×7	$ .96 ×4	$ .87 ×8

Do you know how to **carry back** tens and use them with ones when you subtract and divide?

Subtract in rows **4** and **5**; divide in rows **6** and **7**.

4.	83 67	172 94	162 96	151 87	162 98	181 99	153 78
5.	$1.60 .85	$1.50 .98	$1.75 .96	$1.10 .86	$1.70 .75	$1.90 .92	$1.23 .65

	(a)	(b)	(c)	(d)	(e)	(f)
6.	4)9	5)17	7)91	3)108	9)207	8)360
7.	7)$1.54	5)$1.15	8)$4.40	9)$6.57	6)$4.92	8)$4.48

Find:

	(a)	(b)	(c)	(d)	(e)
8.	½ of 92	⅑ of 396	⅐ of 168	⅓ of 228	¼ of 380
9.	⅙ of $1.38	⅛ of $1.36	⅕ of $4.60	⅛ of $.96	⅑ of $.72

Earning Money

Billy and Bobby cleaned up the attic for a playroom. They sold some of the "junk" that was stored in the attic and used the money to buy things for their playroom.

1. The boys sold 5 folding chairs to Mrs. Rose for $2.25. How much did they get for each chair?

2. They sold 24 old books for 5¢ each. How much did they get for the books?

3. They also sold a basket of dishes for 75¢. How much did they get for all of the things they sold?

Copy and multiply:

	(a)	(b)	(c)	(d)	(e)	(f)	(g)	(h)
4.	50 × 3	70 × 6	60 × 8	40 × 9	82 × 4	58 × 6	$.75 × 6	$.53 × 7
5.	28 × 5	37 × 7	45 × 2	63 × 4	19 × 6	73 × 7	$.98 × 4	$.24 × 8

Copy and divide:

	(a)	(b)	(c)	(d)	(e)	(f)
6.	4)248	3)276	2)128	5)75	6)156	8)$6.80
7.	9)810	7)630	9)828	7)644	8)672	9)$2.25
8.	9)162	8)144	7)119	6)108	5)140	3)$1.41

Chapter 13
Working with Hundreds

A Thousand

Miss White sent Bobby and Betty to the school supply room to get some paper and pencils for the class to use. There they saw stacks and stacks of paper, hundreds of pencils, boxes of chalk, and books.

"How many sheets of paper are there in one of these packages?" asked Bobby.

"There are 100 sheets in each package," answered Betty. "There are 10 packages; so there are 10 hundreds."

We have a special name—**thousand**—for 10 hundreds. One thousand means 10 hundreds, and it also means 100 tens. We write one thousand like this: 1000. The 000 put the 1 in thousand's place.

Reading and Writing Numbers

The figure 1 tells us **one**.
What does the figure 1 in these places tell us?

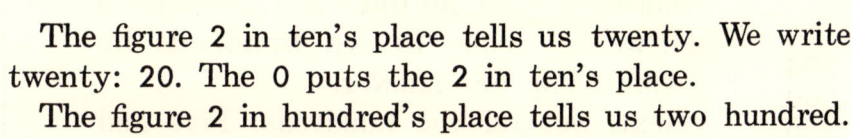

10	1 *ten*	In what place is 1 written?
100	_____	In what place is 1 written?
1000	_____	In what place is 1 written?

The figure 2 in ten's place tells us twenty. We write twenty: 20. The 0 puts the 2 in ten's place.

The figure 2 in hundred's place tells us two hundred. We write: 200. The 00 put the 2 in hundred's place.

The figure 2 in thousand's place tells us two thousand. We write: 2000. The 000 put the 2 in thousand's place.

We say:	We mean:	We write:
Forty	4 tens	40
Four hundred	4 hundreds	400
	40 tens	
One thousand	1 thousand	1000
	10 hundreds	
	100 tens	
Four thousand	4 thousands	4000
	40 hundreds	
	400 tens	
One thousand five hundred . .	1 thousand and 50 tens	1500
	15 hundreds	
	150 tens	
Four thousand four hundred .	4 thousands and 40 tens	4400
	44 hundreds	
	440 tens	

Read each number and tell what it means:
30   800   2000   5000   1600   2800   3090   7002

Adding Hundreds

1. Bobby took 5 packages of paper, and Betty took 3 packages of paper. Bobby had 500 sheets, and Betty had 300 sheets. How many sheets of paper did they have in all?

> 500
> 300
> ───
> 800
>
> Since there are **no ones** and **no tens** to add, we get ready to add **hundreds** by writing 00 in our answer.
>
> Next, we add the hundreds: Five and three are eight. We write 8 in hundred's place.
>
> Bobby and Betty had 800 sheets of paper.

2. Bobby and Betty put the 800 sheets of paper on the table. Then Bobby went back to the supply room and got 700 more sheets of paper. He put them in a pile beside the 800 sheets. How many sheets of paper were on the table?

There are no ones and no tens to add. Why do we write zeros in the one's and ten's places in the sum?

 800
 700
────
1500

Add the hundreds: 8 and 7 are 15. 15 hundreds are 1 thousand and 5 hundreds. So we write 1 in thousand's place and 5 in hundred's place.

There were 1500 sheets of paper on the table.

3. Mr. Jackson, the supply clerk, said that there were 550 sheets of red paper and 800 sheets of green paper on one of the shelves. How many sheets of colored paper were on this shelf?

Adding Hundreds

1. Tell how these numbers were added:

800	504	503	632	680	740	665	900
300	305	700	465	908	737	704	856
1100	809	1203	1097	1588	1477	1369	1756

> We add hundreds the way we add ones and tens.

Find the sums:

	(a)	(b)	(c)	(d)	(e)	(f)	(g)	(h)
2.	100	150	703	600	140	272	442	613
	300	220	104	237	400	726	423	363
3.	534	783	729	972	401	625	813	960
	551	312	420	104	645	500	271	212
4.	810	952	715	900	806	508	600	758
	411	511	500	300	560	660	600	640
5.	800	956	844	364	930	950	412	643
	760	843	645	735	450	638	787	735
6.	143	276	654	268	804	505	770	396
	954	822	840	931	854	990	807	802

7. Ray and his father drove 363 miles on Monday and 420 miles on Tuesday. How many miles did they drive in the two days?

8. Mrs. Jones sold 480 eggs one week and 600 eggs the next week. How many eggs did she sell in all?

9. One afternoon at the carnival 622 children's tickets and 432 grown people's tickets were sold. How many carnival tickets were sold that afternoon?

Subtracting Hundreds

Many of the pupils who go to Lincoln School must go on the bus. If they buy their tickets at school, they get a special price. The tickets come in rolls with one hundred tickets in a roll.

1. The bus man brought 1500 tickets the first month. Nine rolls of tickets, or 900 tickets, were left. How many of the tickets were sold?

```
 1500
 -900
  600
```

There are no ones to subtract, and there are no tens to subtract. So we write 0 in one's place and 0 in ten's place. We need them to keep the hundred's figure in its place.

Now subtract the hundreds.

Six hundred tickets were sold.

2. One month they started with 1569 tickets. On the second Friday of the month there were 815 tickets left. How many tickets had been sold in those two weeks?

```
 1569
 -815
  754
```

First, subtract the ones. Next subtract the tens. Then subtract the hundreds. Be sure to write the figures in their proper places.

> We subtract hundreds the way we subtract ones and tens.

Subtracting Hundreds

1. Mr. East had 375 tomato plants. He sold 144 of them. How many tomato plants did he have then?

Subtract the ones.
Write 1 in one's place.
Subtract the tens.
Write 3 in ten's place.
Subtract the hundreds.
Write 2 in hundred's place.

```
 375
-144
 231
```

We subtract hundreds just as we subtract ones.

2. Tell how we subtract these numbers:

```
569    900    860    380    758    564    218    439
342    500    430    200    351    513    216    126
227    400    430    180    407     51      2    313
```

Copy and subtract:

	(a)	(b)	(c)	(d)	(e)	(f)	(g)	(h)
3.	845 311	986 714	678 427	697 140	559 408	800 400	750 320	586 181
4.	645 633	596 535	847 205	768 565	438 436	307 201	986 916	490 190
5.	178 168	395 145	497 286	789 539	695 445	750 650	378 175	680 330
6.	463 200	785 283	408 100	568 323	873 830	962 162	709 505	398 360
7.	760 140	900 300	878 645	976 533	688 253	669 222	888 642	259 134

Subtracting Hundreds

```
 1800
  900
 ————
  900

 1109
  704
 ————
  405
```

1. Tell how these numbers were subtracted:

← Why do we write 00 in our answer?

Why do we write 0 in one's place? →

← Why do we write 0 in ten's place?

Why do we write 00 in our answer? →

```
 1290
  850
 ————
  440

 1440
  740
 ————
  700
```

Copy and subtract. Then check each answer:

	(a)	(b)	(c)	(d)	(e)	(f)	(g)	(h)
2.	978 106	840 510	952 630	1085 744	657 314	1265 522	1297 654	1208 706
3.	433 202	878 322	461 310	1095 440	1086 100	1376 534	1409 505	1867 954
4.	1169 755	1074 660	1397 605	1273 771	1452 951	1091 521	1677 965	1808 908
5.	1120 520	1395 473	1100 300	1708 905	1270 350	1108 602	1897 955	1318 513
6.	1300 900	1575 800	1478 654	1109 203	1200 400	1560 660		
7.	1375 805	1008 808	1597 992	1650 850	1366 766	1180 850		
8.	1500 700	1680 780	1400 800	1289 953	1788 847	1260 840		
9.	1386 780	1408 805	1528 724	1344 940	1509 901	1141 801		
10.	1728 820	1888 901	1534 804	1659 719	1433 730	1121 400		

```
Subtract
  1008
   903
  ————
   105

Check
   903
   105
  ————
  1008
```

Multiplying Hundreds

1. On the table there are 5 packages of paper. In each package there are 500 sheets of paper. How many sheets of paper are there in all?

There are no ones and no tens to multiply. Why do we write 0 in one's place and 0 in ten's place in the answer?

When we multiply the hundreds by 5, we get 25 hundreds. This means 2 thousand 5 hundred. So we write 2 in thousand's place and 5 in hundred's place.

```
 500
  ×5
2500
```

There are 2500 sheets of paper in the five packages.

2. In the big carnival tent there were 3 spaces for seats. In each space there were 432 seats. How many seats were in the big tent?

Multiply the ones. Next multiply the tens. Then multiply the hundreds. Write each number in its proper place. There are 4 figures in the product. The figure in the fourth place is 1. What does it mean? In what place do we write it?

```
 432
  ×3
1296
```

There are 1296 seats in the big tent.

> We multiply hundreds the way we multiply tens and ones.

3. Multiply:

(a)	(b)	(c)	(d)	(e)	(f)	(g)	(h)	(i)
400	422	700	800	332	612	711	834	523
7	4	8	8	3	4	7	2	3

Multiplying Hundreds

1. Mrs. Adams can put 144 eggs in each case. How many eggs will she need to fill 2 cases?

> To find how many eggs she will need, we multiply 144 by 2.
> First, we multiply the ones by 2.
> Next, we multiply the tens by 2.
> Last, we multiply the hundreds by 2.
> Mrs. Adams will need 288 eggs.
>
> 144 eggs
> ×2
> 288 eggs

2. Jane has 4 new books. Each book has 121 pages. How many pages are in the four books?

120
3
360

3. We go 120 miles each time we make a trip to Jonesville. Last week we went 3 times. How many miles would that be?

4. Jim's father drove 234 miles to a lake. How far was it both ways?

5. Joe ran 110 yards. There are 3 feet in 1 yard. How many feet did Joe run?

6. Tell how these numbers are multiplied:

234	114	100	120	$1.10	$3.20	$3.10
×2	×2	×5	×4	×5	×4	×5
468	228	500	480	$5.50	$12.80	$15.50

7. Multiply:

(a)	(b)	(c)	(d)	(e)	(f)	(g)
$2.41	$4.20	$5.30	821	702	632	720
2	3	3	4	4	3	4

Zeros in Multiplication

We multiply hundreds the way we multiply tens and ones. We must write each part of our answer in its proper place. We use zeros when we need them.

1. Jim and his father are flying to Washington, D.C. It is 404 miles to Washington by air. How far is it to Washington and back?

Multiply the ones: Two 4's are 8. Write 8. Next multiply the tens. There are no tens to multiply; so we write 0 in ten's place in the answer. Why? Last, multiply the hundreds.

```
 404
   2
 808
```

2. "How far is it around the race track?" asked Joe. "It is 440 yards," answered Mr. Woods, the principal.

Joe rode his bicycle around the track twice. How far did he ride?

Multiply the ones. There are no ones; so we write 0 in one's place in the answer. Why?

```
 440
   2
 880
```

```
 501                                        520
   5     How do we multiply 501 by 5?         4
2505     How do we multiply 520 by 4?      2080
```

Copy and multiply:

	(a)	(b)	(c)	(d)	(e)	(f)	(g)	(h)
3.	802	504	540	720	703	510	602	501
	3	2	2	4	3	6	4	9
4.	601	810	920	801	620	801	503	710
	9	8	4	5	3	8	3	7

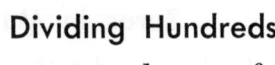

Dividing Hundreds

1. There are 8 packages of paper on the table. Mary has put them into 2 piles with the same number of packages in each pile. How many packages are in each pile?

2. There are 100 sheets of paper in each package. So there are 8 hundreds, or 800 sheets of paper. Mary put them into 2 equal piles. How many sheets of paper are there in each pile?

```
  4 hundreds
2)8 hundreds
```

First, we divide the hundreds the way we divide tens and ones. We write the answer in hundred's place.

```
   400
2)800
   8
   ‾‾
    00
```

Next, since there are no tens and no ones to divide, we write 00 in the answer to put 4 in hundred's place.

3. On the counter in the supply room there are 24 packages of paper. Betty put them into 3 equal piles. How many packages are in each pile?

4. There are 100 sheets of paper in each package; so there are 24 hundreds, or 2400 sheets of paper. Betty put them into 3 equal piles. How many sheets of paper are in each pile?

```
    8 hundreds
3)24 hundreds
```

We think of 2400 as 24 hundreds. How many 3's in 24? We write the 8 in hundred's place. Since there are no tens and no ones to divide, we write 00 in the answer to put the 8 in hundred's place.

```
    800
3)2400
   24
   ‾‾
    00
```

How do we divide hundreds?

Problems and Practice

1. Each night Mr. West put his pennies into a bank at home. At Christmas he opened the bank to divide the pennies among his three children. There were 693 pennies to be divided. How many pennies should each of them get?

2. There is room for 1296 seats in the big tent at the carnival, and there are 3 places where these seats can be put. If the places are all the same size, how many seats is there room for in each place?

```
    231                                                    432
3)693      We divide hundreds the way we divide       3)1296
  6        tens and ones. But we must write each        12
  ‾        part of the answer in its proper place.      ‾
  9        Where do we write the hundred's figure?       9
  9                                                      9
  ‾                                                      ‾
  3                                                      6
  3                                                      6
```

3. Mr. Brown paid $28.88 for 4 tickets to Chicago. How much did each ticket cost?

We divide dollars and cents the way we divide other numbers. We must write the dollars and cents in their proper places.

```
   $ 7.22
4)$28.88
  28
  ‾
   8
   8
   ‾
    8
    8
```

4. Alice, Jane, and Martha belong to the Sewing Club. They paid $15.69 for cloth to make aprons. They divided the cost equally. How much was each girl's share?

Copy and divide:

	(a)	(b)	(c)	(d)	(e)	(f)
5.	3)900	9)1800	5)2500	4)3600	9)7200	7)5600
6.	6)3666	4)3684	3)2769	8)7288	9)4599	8)5688

Zeros in Dividing

> We use zeros when we need them to put each part of our answer in its proper place.

1. "This is a big book. There are 804 pages in it, and I am just **halfway** through it," said Jane.

How many pages of the book has she read?

```
  402
2)804
  8
  04
   4
```

First, we divide the hundreds: Twos in 8, 4. We write 4 in hundred's place in the answer.

Next, we divide the tens. There are no tens to divide; so we write 0 in our answer.

Last, we divide the ones: Twos in 4, 2. We write 2 in one's place in the answer.

The 0 in 402 holds the "empty" ten's place, and it puts the 4 in hundred's place and the 2 in one's place.

2. Our school is giving a play about Daniel Boone. Jane, Martha, Sue, and Alice are making the tickets. There are 840 seats in the auditorium, and there must be a ticket for each seat. How many tickets should Jane make if she makes her share of the tickets?

```
  210
4)840
  8
  4
  4
  0
```

First, divide the hundreds: Fours in 8, 2. Write 2 in hundred's place in the answer.

Next, divide the tens: Fours in 4, 1. Write 1 in ten's place in the answer.

Last, divide the ones. There are no ones to divide. We write 0 in one's place in the answer.

Is each part of our answer in its place?

Problems and Practice

1. Tell how these examples are divided:

```
    720          301           510
4)2880       6)1806        8)4080
  28           18             40
   8            06             8
   8             6             8
   0                           0
```

2. Four boys plan to buy a new football. The one they want costs $4.08. Tomorrow each boy will bring his share of the money. How much should each boy bring?

3. Only $\frac{1}{6}$ of the 1866 people at the basketball game were women and girls. How many women and girls were at the game?

4. There are 455 children in our school. Of this number $\frac{1}{5}$ are in the first grade. How many children are in the first grade?

5. Jim read 1260 words in 6 minutes. At that rate, how many words did he read in one minute?

Copy and divide:

	(a)	(b)	(c)	(d)	(e)	(f)
6.	4)2488	4)3608	4)2880	5)3050	6)4206	6)5460
7.	6)2466	7)4970	8)4008	7)6370	9)5409	7)3507

	(a)	(b)	(c)	(d)	(e)
8.	$\frac{1}{3}$ of 1209	$\frac{1}{4}$ of 2080	$\frac{1}{5}$ of 4050	$\frac{1}{6}$ of 3660	$\frac{1}{4}$ of 888
9.	$\frac{1}{7}$ of 5670	$\frac{1}{8}$ of 880	$\frac{1}{9}$ of 909	$\frac{1}{7}$ of 1477	$\frac{1}{8}$ of 4808
10.	4)$36.04	3)$9.60	2)$2.40	2)$8.04	6)$18.06
11.	8)$24.00	2)$12.80	5)$15.50	7)$21.07	9)$36.90

Easy Problems

1. Jim bought 4 fifteen-cent tablets. How much did he pay for them? How much change did he get from a dollar bill? Count Jim's change.

2. Jack bought 3 bird books that cost 25¢ each. How much did he pay for the books? How much change did he get from a dollar?

3. Mr. West can travel in his car 16 miles on a gallon of gasoline. He has about 3 gallons of gasoline in the tank. Can he go on a 30-mile trip without buying gasoline?

4. After school Bill earns 45¢ an hour doing errands for Mr. Owen. Bill works 2 hours each day. How much does he earn a day?

5. Jane made 60 cookies. She put them in 5 boxes, the same number of cookies in each box. How many did she put in each box?

6. Glen bought a knife for 75¢ and a ruler for 15¢. How much did both cost?

7. Tom and Carl gathered 3 bushels of walnuts. They sold them for $1.00 a bushel and divided the money equally. How much did they get for the walnuts? How much was each boy's share?

8. Ann made 3 dozen cookies. How many is that?

9. Ben had 38 marbles. He gave one half of them to Joe. How many marbles did Ben keep?

10. Meg wants a scarf that costs 98¢. She has 75¢. How much more money does she need?

11. Bob bought a bird, a snowman, a bell, and a Santa Claus to hang on the Christmas tree. How much did these things cost?

A Problem Test

1. Sue made 41 blotters. She gave one to each of the 27 pupils in her class. How many blotters did she have left?

2. Mary and Ann decided to make penwipers for the 28 pupils in the class. They have 15 of them made. How many more should they make?

3. Jack is 11 years old, and his older brother is 19 years old. What is the difference in their ages?

4. The Wells family drove 192 miles in 6 hours. How far did they drive in one hour?

5. Jack bought a book for $.85 and 2 tablets for $.15. How much did he pay for them?

6. Bill bought a book for 85¢ and 2 tablets for 15¢ each. How much did he pay for them?

7. Joe and Bob bought a tennis net for $6.84. They shared the cost equally. What did each boy pay?

8. How much will 4 books cost at $1.12 each?

9. Members of the Bell family are planning a trip of 176 miles. How fast will they travel per hour if they make the trip in 4 hours?

10. Jane has a dollar. She wants to buy a box of handkerchiefs that costs 60¢. If she buys the handkerchiefs, how much money will she have left? Will she have enough to go to the show? A ticket will cost 35¢.

Chapter 14
More about Carrying

Carrying to Ten's Column

1. There are 325 pupils who go to our school and 568 who go to the East School. How many children go to both schools?

$$\begin{array}{r} \overset{1}{3}25 \\ 568 \\ \hline 893 \end{array}$$

Ben worked the problem and explained: We think: "Five and eight are thirteen." We write the 3 in one's place in the answer and carry the 1 (ten).

We add the tens: One and two are three, and six are nine.

Last, we add the hundreds: Three and five are eight.

There are 893 pupils in both schools.

"What is that *little 1* you have in ten's column?" asked Miss Green. "Do you need to write it?"

"That is the 1 ten I carried," answered Ben. "No, I can add without using the little 1. I can remember to carry it."

2. The children at Lake School bought 246 bottles of milk on Tuesday and 244 bottles on Wednesday. How many bottles of milk did they buy on those two days?

3. The milkman delivered 246 bottles of milk to Lake School on Tuesday, and he had 28 bottles left in his car. How many bottles of milk did he have when he came to the school?

4. On Wednesday the milkman left 244 bottles of milk at Lake School, and he had 16 bottles left in his car. How many bottles of milk did he have when he came to Lake School?

Copy and add:

	(a)	(b)	(c)	(d)	(e)	(f)	(g)
5.	335	324	746	237	225	375	929
	548	266	236	548	549	415	56
6.	325	704	207	436	739	238	329
	659	29	708	208	255	37	57
7.	842	253	537	822	316	555	738
	439	538	757	368	45	116	259
8.	428	419	849	235	528	347	567
	453	373	141	527	162	613	319
9.	517	644	435	824	746	537	625
	579	437	748	266	835	656	646

Carrying Tens When We Add

1. There are three schools in Fulton. In East School there are 435 children. In Center School there are 207 children, and in West School there are 228 children. How many children are there in the three schools?

```
  2
435
207
228
───
870
```

Add the ones: 5 and 7 are 12, and 8 are 20. Write 0 in one's place and carry 2 (tens).

Add the tens: 2 (carried) and 3 are 5, and 2 are 7. Write 7 in ten's place.

Add the hundreds: 4 and 2 are 6, and 2 are 8. Write 8 in hundred's place.

There are 870 children in the three schools.

```
$2.54
$2.08
$1.26
```

2. The ice cream for Jane's party cost $2.54. The cakes cost $2.08, and the favors cost $1.26. How much did Jane spend for her party?

3. Ray's father sends milk in big cans to the cheese factory. He weighs each can before he sends it. Today the three cans weighed 102 pounds, 106 pounds, and 108 pounds. How much did the three cans of milk weigh?

4. Jim and his father drove 406 miles the first day, 256 miles the second day, and 325 miles the third day. How far did they drive in the three days?

Copy and add:

	(a)	(b)	(c)	(d)	(e)	(f)	(g)	(h)
5.	425	736	538	947	617	348	308	120
	334	449	232	426	645	405	208	348
	729	514	223	123	237	507	207	425
6.	409	388	304	533	335	666	545	237
	348	405	458	209	536	500	49	229
	338	506	508	208	404	304	205	514

Carrying to Hundred's Column

1. Helen read *If I Were Going* and *Through the Green Gate*. There are 337 pages in *If I Were Going* and 191 pages in *Through the Green Gate*. How many pages did Helen read?

First, add the ones: 7 and 1 are 8.
Then add the tens: 3 and 9 are 12. 12 tens are 1 hundred and 2 tens. Write 2 in ten's place and carry 1 (hundred).
Now add the hundreds: 1 (carried) and 3 are 4, and 1 are 5.
Helen read 528 pages in her books.

```
  1
337
191
---
528
```

2. Susan read *The Five-and-a-Half Club* and *Through the Green Gate*. There are 254 pages in *The Five-and-a-Half Club* and 191 in *Through the Green Gate*. How many pages did Susan read in these two books?

3. Jim read *Singing Wheels*. It has 373 pages in it. He also read *In Reindeer Land*, which has 336 pages in it. How many pages did he read?

4. Tom read *Runaway Home*, a book of 373 pages. Then he read *Young Prince Hubert*, a book of 230 pages. How many pages did Tom read?

5. Alice read *After the Sun Sets* and *Young Prince Hubert*. There are 299 pages in the first book and 230 pages in the other book. How many pages did she read?

6. Joe read *Robin Rides Away* and *Singing Wheels*. How many pages did he read? *Robin Rides Away* has 256 pages in it, and *Singing Wheels* has 373 pages.

Money

We write:	We read:
$4.25	Four dollars and twenty-five cents
$10.00	Ten dollars
$50.60	Fifty dollars and sixty cents
$2.05	Two dollars and five cents
$.65	Sixty-five cents
$18.07	Eighteen dollars and seven cents

Write the following amounts of money in figures, using the dollar sign and the point:

Five dollars and five cents
Sixteen dollars and eighteen cents
Twenty dollars and forty cents
Eight hundred sixty-five dollars
Four hundred six dollars and fifteen cents
Seven hundred fifty dollars
One hundred dollars and ten cents
Eighty-eight dollars and eighty cents

Read these amounts of money, saying **and** for the point:

| $5.80 | $105.75 | $67.08 | $110.01 | $92.60 |
| $10.10 | $150.06 | $95.38 | $225.70 | $800.02 |

Tell the price of each article:

Adding Money

1. Jack bought some meat for 86 cents and tomato juice for 64 cents. How much should he pay for them?

```
  86¢      $ .86     Jack should pay 150¢.
  64¢      $ .64
 ────     ──────
 150¢      $1.50     Jack should pay $1.50.
```

Tell how we add these amounts of money:

$ .63	$ .55	$2.15	$.90	$4.37	$.06	$1.89
$ .98	$ .48	$1.75	$.06	$1.72	$.02	$3.50
$1.61	$1.03	$3.90	$.96	$6.09	$.08	$5.39

2. Mary had $2.05. Her mother gave her $1.00. How much money did Mary have then?

3. Jim bought a sweater for $4.95 and a cap for $1.50. How much should he pay for them?

4. Ann's dress cost $3.98 and her shoes $2.80. How much did the dress and shoes cost together?

5. Betty bought a pair of sun glasses for $1.25 and a zipper bag for $1.80. How much did she pay for both of them?

Add these amounts of money. Check each answer.

	(a)	(b)	(c)	(d)	(e)	(f)	(g)
6.	$ .57	$ .48	$2.39	$5.27	$ .56	$ .42	$ .75
	$ .63	$ .28	$1.24	$3.63	$1.09	$ .85	$ .39
7.	$ .23	$ .07	$ .97	$4.14	$3.59	$6.05	$1.52
	$ .86	$ .49	$ .41	$3.39	$1.50	$2.39	$1.67

Carrying Twice

1. Tom is going on a camping trip. He saw these prices in a store. How much must he pay for a blanket and a cap?

$$\begin{array}{r} \overset{1\ 1}{\$4.68} \\ 1.79 \\ \hline \$6.47 \end{array}$$

2. Tom's father bought him a raincoat and a belt. How much did these things cost?

3. Jim also went to camp. His mother bought him a shirt and a sweater. How much should she pay for them?

4. Jim's father bought him a belt and a lantern. How much did he pay for them?

5. How much will a raincoat and a sweater cost?

6. How much will a shirt, a cap, and a belt cost?

7. How much will a sweater, a shirt, and a cap cost?

8. Copy and add:

(a)	(b)	(c)	(d)	(e)	(f)	(g)	(h)
468	394	557	449	766	678	338	273
465	286	356	258	245	327	562	328

Carrying When We Multiply

1. It is 236 miles from Pittsburgh to Baltimore. Dave drove with his father from Pittsburgh to Baltimore and back to Pittsburgh. How far did they drive?

To answer the question, we multiply 236 by 2.

Think: Two 6's are 12. Write the 2 in one's place, and carry the 1 in your mind.

Think: Two 3's are 6, and 1 are 7. Write 7 in ten's place.

Think: Two 2's are 4. Write 4 in hundred's place in the answer.

Dave and his father drove 472 miles.

$$\begin{array}{r} \overset{1}{2}36 \\ \times 2 \\ \hline 472 \end{array}$$

---

2. Copy and multiply:

(a)	(b)	(c)	(d)	(e)	(f)	(g)	(h)
225	306	213	325	112	215	514	709
3	7	5	2	8	6	4	9

3. Tom went to visit his grandmother in Columbus, Ohio. When Tom got on the bus, he asked the driver how far it was from Chicago to Columbus. The driver said, "It is 315 miles from Chicago to Columbus and 315 miles from Columbus to Chicago. You will travel ____ miles before you get back home."

4. "We are going to Niagara Falls," said Jane. "It is 526 miles from here to Niagara Falls. We will drive over 1000 miles there and back."

Was Jane right? How far will they drive?

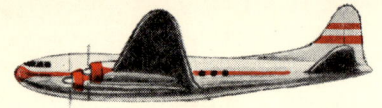

Carrying to Tens

1. A small airplane flew 112 miles in one hour. At this rate how far would it fly in 4 hours?

```
 112
× 4
───
 448
```

First, multiply the ones and next, the tens. We multiply the hundreds the way we multiply ones and tens.

2. A bigger and faster airplane flew 224 miles in one hour. At this rate how far would it fly in 3 hours?

```
 224
× 3
───
 672
```

First, multiply the ones: Three 4's are 12. Remember to carry 1 (ten) and add it to the tens after you multiply them. Then multiply the hundreds.

3. Another small airplane flew 116 miles in one hour. At this rate how far would it fly in 4 hours?

```
 116
× 4
───
   4
```

Finish working the problem. How many tens do you get when you multiply the ones? What will you do with the 2 tens?

4. Another large plane was very fast. It flew 408 miles in one hour. How far would it fly in 5 hours?

Multiply the ones: Five 8's are 40.

```
 408
× 5
────
2040
```

There are no tens to multiply; so write the 4 (carried) in ten's place.

Then multiply the hundreds: Five 4's are 20. 20 hundreds are 2 thousands. Write 0 in hundred's place to put the 2 in thousand's place.

We carry 2, 3, 4, 5, 6, 7, or 8 the way we carry 1.

Making Sandwiches

The girls of the fourth grade met at school at 8:30 Saturday morning to make the sandwiches for the picnic. How many sandwiches do you suppose they made?

Ann asked, "How many pupils are going?"

Jane asked, "How many sandwiches shall we make for each pupil?"

Miss White said, "We must plan for one hundred sixty pupils, and we should make three sandwiches for each pupil. How many sandwiches should we make in all?"

Jane answered, "160 pupils and 3 sandwiches for each pupil. That would be ____ sandwiches."

"Remember the teachers," said Miss Green. "We like sandwiches too. Perhaps we should make 20 extra sandwiches."

How many sandwiches did the girls make?

"Five hundred sandwiches!" said Helen. "It will take a lot of bread for that many sandwiches."

Can you guess how many slices of bread Helen said they would need for 500 sandwiches? Exactly how many slices of bread do they need?

$$\begin{array}{r} 160 \\ \times 3 \\ \hline 480 \end{array}$$

$$\begin{array}{r} 480 \\ +20 \\ \hline 500 \end{array}$$

217

Carrying to Hundreds

Jack helped Mr. West carry packages of drawing paper, books, and paper towels to the fourth-grade room.

1. There are 8 packages of drawing paper, and there are 24 sheets in each package. How many sheets of drawing paper are there?

2. There are 14 packages of readers, and there are 5 readers in each package. How many readers are there?

3. There are 6 packages of paper towels with 150 towels in each package. How many paper towels are there?

```
 150
   6
 ―――
 900
```

There are no ones to multiply by 6; so we write 0 in one's place in the answer. Why?

Next, we multiply the tens: Six 5's are 30. We write 0 and carry 3.

Then we multiply the hundreds: Six 1's are 6, and 3 (carried) are 9.

There are 900 towels in the 6 packages.

Copy and multiply:

	(a)	(b)	(c)	(d)	(e)	(f)	(g)	(h)
4.	22 9	34 6	35 7	46 8	36 9	38 8	49 8	39 9
5.	253 3	352 4	541 8	490 7	670 6	381 7	480 9	290 9

We carry to hundreds the way we carry to tens.

```
  2         2          3          3          4          4
 25        250         26        261         35        350
  5          5          6          6          8          8
―――       ―――――       ―――        ―――――       ―――        ―――――
125       1250        156        1566        280        2800
```

Mistakes in Thinking

Each example on the board is **wrong**. The children made mistakes in thinking about carrying. Find each mistake and correct it.

Jack thought: Two 8's are 16. Write 16. Two 5's are 10. Write 10. The answer is 1016.

Jack's thinking was bad. Where did he make his mistake?

```
 58
  2
----
1016
```

Jane thought: Four 6's are 24. Write 2 and carry 4. Four 5's are 20, and 4 are 24. The answer is 242.

Jane's thinking was bad, too. Where did she make her mistake?

```
  4
 56
  4
----
 242
```

Jim thought: Two 4's are 8. Write 8. There are no tens in 304; so I have nothing to multiply, and nothing to write in ten's place in my answer. Two 3's are 6. Write 6. The answer is 68.

Where did Jim make his mistake?

```
 304
   2
----
  68
```

Tom thought: There are no ones in 260. Six 6's are 36. Write 6 and carry 3. Six 2's are 12, and 3 are 15. Write 15. The answer is 156.

Where did Tom make his mistake?

```
 260
   6
----
 156
```

Simon thought: Three 7's are 21. Write 1 and carry 2. 2 and 1 are 3, and three 3's are 9. Write 9. Three 2's are 6. Write 6. The answer is 691.

Where did Simon make his mistake?

```
   2
 217
   3
----
 691
```

Mary thought: Five 5's are 25. Write 5 and carry 2. Five 1's are 5. Write 5. Five 4's are 20. Write 20. The answer is 2055.

Where did Mary make her mistake?

```
   2
 415
   5
----
2055
```

Carrying Twice

1. Jack got 3 boxes of chalk from the school supply room. There were 144 pieces of chalk in each box. How many pieces of chalk did Jack get in all?

```
 11
144
 ×3
───
432
```
First, multiply the ones: Three 4's are 12. Write 2 in one's place in the answer, and carry 1 (ten) to ten's column.

Next, multiply the tens: Three 4's are 12, and 1 (carried) are 13. Write 3 in ten's place in the answer and carry 1 (hundred).

```
144
 ×3
───
432
```
Now multiply the hundreds: Three 1's are 3, and 1 (carried) are 4. Where do we write the 4? Jack got 432 pieces of chalk in all.

---

2. Tell how these numbers were multiplied:

154	126	248	237	248	144	336	219
5	4	4	6	7	9	3	8
770	504	992	1422	1736	1296	1008	1752

Copy and multiply:

	(a)	(b)	(c)	(d)	(e)	(f)	(g)	(h)
3.	293	182	865	471	590	608	346	156
	5	5	6	7	8	9	4	8
4.	434	283	255	168	575	626	119	476
	6	6	8	6	4	4	9	4
5.	425	128	345	675	183	296	233	574
	6	9	5	9	8	7	6	8
6.	367	456	522	442	336	386	125	637
	8	9	7	8	9	7	9	6

Adding by Endings

Test | **Practice**

(a)	(b)	(c)	(d)	(e)	(f)	(g)	(h)	(i)	(j)
32 3	20 2	21 5	15 4	24 3	25 2	28 3	16 7	18 3	20 4
18 2	20 3	12 2	21 4	15 3	24 2	16 2	25 3	63 6	28 2
12 3	18 4	64 6	12 4	16 3	12 5	16 4	18 5	16 6	21 6
16 5	21 2	24 4	27 7	28 6	48 4	15 2	21 3	63 4	24 1
24 5	25 4	27 2	28 4	36 7	24 6	27 4	24 7	27 3	64 7
36 5	27 5	45 8	28 5	27 6	27 8	72 8	36 3	35 7	32 7
30 2	63 8	35 2	36 4	32 4	30 3	40 2	42 2	48 5	54 3
56 3	72 7	64 3	81 3	56 6	36 8	30 4	35 8	54 5	63 7
32 2	35 5	56 7	54 6	49 3	48 6	45 5	48 2	54 4	56 5
72 5	81 4	64 4	56 4	54 7	49 5	48 8	42 3	45 7	49 4
32 6	48 7	35 6	54 2	72 3	36 6	72 6	64 5	49 6	45 4
32 5	54 8	56 2	49 2	45 2	32 8	35 4	36 2	40 4	81 6

(75)

Multiplying Dollars and Cents

$2.25
×3
───
$6.75

1. Jane and her mother went shopping for sweaters. They bought 3 sweaters that cost $2.25 each. How much did they pay for the sweaters?

$1.94
×2
───
$3.88

2. Then they bought 2 cotton dresses that cost $1.94 each. How much should they pay for the 2 cotton dresses?

$3.75
×2
───
$7.50

3. Jane needed new shoes; so they bought 2 pairs of shoes. The shoes cost $3.75 a pair. How much did the 2 pairs cost?

$1.50
4
───
$6.00

We multiply and carry dollars and cents the way we do other numbers.

Copy and multiply:

	(a)	(b)	(c)	(d)	(e)	(f)
4.	$6.94 2	$5.83 3	$6.70 2	$4.70 4	$2.80 6	$3.40 6
5.	$8.00 9	$3.09 8	$5.18 4	$3.25 3	$2.15 6	$5.05 7
6.	$2.83 6	$1.48 6	$2.36 7	$2.58 4	$7.15 5	$4.28 3
7.	$ .69 4	$ .35 9	$ .98 6	$ .45 7	$ .87 5	$ .98 8

	Test				Practice			
	(a)	(b)	(c)	(d)	(e)	(f)	(g)	(h)

Add:

	(a)	(b)	(c)	(d)	(e)	(f)	(g)	(h)
1.	429 560	318 323	146 626	348 223	454 353	479 213	547 461	393 225
2.	454 358	258 277	292 548	385 415	468 375	507 396	685 319	473 478

Subtract:

3.	900 600	966 743	877 236	854 542	487 212	968 624	1580 760	1287 805
4.	651 408	782 548	760 555	975 648	1683 726	1266 828	1240 736	1094 667

Multiply:

5.	924 2	412 4	615 9	211 9	432 4	352 3	260 5	361 8
6.	345 3	265 7	183 9	218 6	444 7	336 5	334 6	174 8

Find the answers:

	(a)	(b)	(c)	(d)
7.	4 × 2 + 2	9 × 5 + 6	8 × 5 + 5	7 × 6 + 6
8.	5 × 5 + 4	8 × 3 + 6	6 × 4 + 3	9 × 7 + 7
9.	8 × 4 + 5	7 × 5 + 4	5 × 9 + 4	5 × 3 + 4
10.	3 × 4 + 3	8 × 2 + 7	7 × 8 + 6	4 × 4 + 3
11.	8 × 9 + 6	5 × 8 + 4	9 × 9 + 8	4 × 7 + 3

Divide:

12.	8)3280	7)4270	6)1866	9)5490

An Automobile Trip

Jack and Tom went on a trip with Mr. Allen in his new car. The boys kept a record of the trip.

1. Mr. Allen stopped at the first filling station and bought 8 gallons of gasoline. It cost 23¢ a gallon. How much did the gasoline cost?

2. Mr. Allen also bought 3 quarts of oil at 35¢ a quart. How much did the oil cost?

3. How much did Mr. Allen pay for the gasoline and oil?

"This problem only asks a question," said Tom. "It does not tell us anything."

$$\begin{array}{r}\$1.84\\1.05\\\hline\$2.89\end{array}$$

"The facts that we need are the answers to problems **1** and **2**. The gasoline cost $1.84, and the oil cost $1.05. So we add to find how much the gasoline and oil cost," said Jane.

4. The first day they traveled 176 miles in the morning and 236 miles in the afternoon. How many miles did they travel that day?

5. They stayed at a tourist camp that night. The cabins were so small that Mr. Allen rented two of them. He paid $2.50 for one cabin and $3.75 for the other. How much did it cost to rent the two cabins?

6. They ate breakfast at a restaurant nearby. Mr. Allen paid $1.90 for their breakfasts and $6.25 for the two cabins. How much did Mr. Allen pay for the breakfasts and cabins?

7. This is what the meals cost the first day:

	Mr. Allen	Jack	Tom
Dinner	$1.35	$1.25	$1.25
Supper	$ .95	$ .80	$ .75

How much did each person's meals cost?
The question is really three questions in one. So we have three answers to find.

8. This is what the meals cost the second day:

	Mr. Allen	Jack	Tom
Breakfast	$ .85	$ .65	$ .60
Dinner	$1.35	$ .95	$ .95
Supper	$ .90	$ .85	$ .90

How much did each person's meals cost?

9. The first day they traveled 412 miles, and the next day 398 miles. How far did they travel in the two days?

10. About noon the second day they had a flat tire. They stopped at a filling station and had the tire fixed for $1.00. Mr. Allen paid $2.86 for gasoline and $1.08 for oil at the same station. How much was his bill?

Copy and add:

	(a)	(b)	(c)	(d)	(e)	(f)	(g)	(h)
11.	272	445	588	278	351	417	794	382
	773	329	121	903	471	895	231	448
12.	563	384	378	473	693	475	566	507
	256	452	247	594	271	336	658	306

Chapter 15
Carrying Back

Using a Ten

1. During the summer Tom Wood and his father raised 160 chickens. In the fall they sold 96 and kept the rest. How many did they keep?

2. One day they gathered 52 eggs. Mrs. Wood used 14 of them to make an angel food cake. How many of the eggs were left?

3. During one week they gathered 183 eggs. They sold 96 of the eggs that week. How many of the eggs did they have left?

Copy and subtract:

	(a)	(b)	(c)	(d)	(e)	(f)	(g)
4.	137	143	142	126	171	121	142
	39	95	49	78	85	96	86
5.	170	101	137	151	164	160	151
	95	67	48	62	75	87	95

Subtracting Hundreds

1. Jack and his father had 361 tulip bulbs. They sold 132 of them. How many tulip bulbs do they still have?

What must we do before we can subtract the ones?

How many tens will we subtract 3 from?
Subtract the hundreds.
How do we subtract hundreds?
Jack and his father still have 229 tulip bulbs.

```
Write
 361
 132
 ---
 229

Think
   5
 3 6̸ 1
 1 3 2
 -----
 2 2 9
```

2. Tell how these numbers are subtracted:

```
382    767    534    463    350    675    586    491
267    229    316    258    126    439    178    324
---    ---    ---    ---    ---    ---    ---    ---
115    538    218    205    224    236    408    167
```

Subtract and check the answers:

(a)	(b)	(c)	(d)	(e)	(f)	(g)	(h)
3. 791	693	781	493	874	786	983	691
127	466	243	157	367	377	765	559
4. 996	952	481	876	612	874	793	915
639	743	367	237	506	619	134	207

5. There are 365 days in a year. If 129 days of the year have already gone, how many more days are there left in the year?

6. There are 280 children in school. Seventy-two of them went on a picnic. How many children were left in school?

7. How many of the 280 children went on a picnic while 208 of them stayed at school?

Problems and Practice

1. Mr. James bought a car for $907. He kept the car for two years and sold it for $453. How much less did Mr. James get for the car than he paid for it?

Subtract		Think	
$907	907	$\overset{8}{\cancel{9}}{}^{1}07$	$\overset{8}{\cancel{9}}{}^{1}07$
453	453	4 53	4 53
$454	4	54	4 54

We subtract hundreds the way we subtract tens. Sometimes we have to carry back a hundred and use it with the tens.

2. Tell how these examples were worked:

```
 329    704    626    478    531    307    873
-165   -360   -186    -93   -491   -253    290
 164    344    440    385     40     54    583

 800    ⁷⁸¹00
 430    4 30
 370    3 70
```

3. The class had 800 tickets printed for their hobby show. They sold all but 430 tickets. How many tickets were sold?

4. At Camp Hardy there were 180 boys in July and 207 in August. How many more boys were at camp in August than in July?

Copy and subtract:

	(a)	(b)	(c)	(d)	(e)	(f)	(g)	(h)
5.	618	520	809	437	768	206	700	819
	174	260	373	267	172	24	510	581
6.	113	146	518	183	603	728	619	194
	98	93	163	74	283	170	456	88

Subtracting Dollars and Cents

1. The class voted to buy a picture that cost $7.50. They now have $4.15. How much more money do they need before they can pay for the picture?

We subtract money numbers the way we do any numbers. If there are dollars and cents, we put the point between the dollars and the cents.

$7.50
4.15
―――
$3.35

2. Jimmy had saved $3.15. He spent $1.25 for a pair of skates. How much money did he have left?

$3.15
1.25
―――
$1.90

3. Jack is saving his money to buy new tires for his bicycle. The tires that he wants cost $5.59 a pair. He has saved $1.75. How much does he have yet to save?

4. Jane bought 3 ties for her father. She paid $4.50 for them. She gave the clerk a 5-dollar bill. How much change should she get?

5. Jack, Jim, and Tom each bought a tie. They paid $1.55 apiece for the ties. How much altogether did the 3 ties cost them?

6. Jane got her 3 ties for $4.50. How much less did she pay for the ties than the boys paid for theirs?

Copy and subtract:

	(a)	(b)	(c)	(d)	(e)	(f)
7.	$5.18 3.75	$17.24 8.30	$10.10 6.80	$8.36 5.82	$6.47 3.84	$7.93 1.49
8.	$9.44 6.74	$11.08 5.60	$12.36 4.95	$3.15 1.08	$4.85 1.58	$8.38 2.45
9.	$4.03 1.21	$16.48 10.92	$13.75 9.80	$7.71 3.90	$5.25 1.30	$6.47 1.70

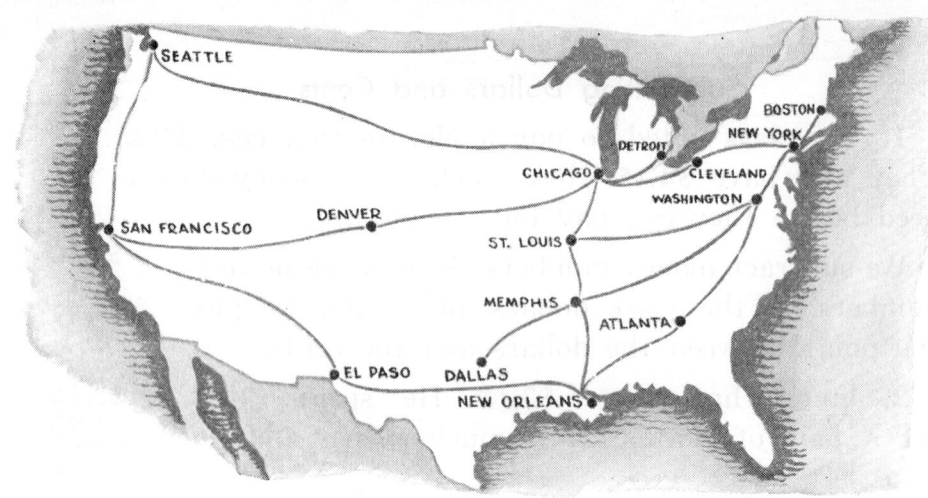

Using a Map

1. St. Louis is 874 miles from New York, and Memphis is 953 miles from New York. How much farther is it from New York to Memphis than it is from New York to St. Louis?

Often we must change 1 ten to 10 ones and 1 hundred to 10 tens before we can subtract.

Write	*Think*	
	4	8 14
953	9̸5̸¹3	9̸ 5̸¹3
874	87 4	87 4
	9	79

540
185
───
355

5̸⁴4̸¹0
1 8 5
─────
3 5 5

2. John lives 540 miles from Boston. After he has driven 185 miles toward Boston, how far is he from Boston?

3. It is 711 miles from Chicago to New York and 594 miles from Chicago to Washington, D.C. How much farther is it from Chicago to New York than it is from Chicago to Washington?

4. It is 711 miles from Chicago to New York, and it is 405 miles from New York to Cleveland. How far is it from Cleveland to Chicago?

5. It is 747 miles from Atlanta to New York, and it is 711 miles from Chicago to New York. Jack lives in Chicago, and Jim lives in Atlanta. Who lives farther from New York? How much farther?

6. From Atlanta to New York is 747 miles. From Atlanta to Chicago is 583 miles. Which is nearer to Atlanta, Chicago or New York? How much nearer?

7. It is 918 miles from Chicago to Denver, and it is 1855 miles from Chicago to San Francisco. How far is it from Denver to San Francisco? Is Denver about half way between Chicago and San Francisco?

8. Look at the map. Do you think that it is farther from Memphis to Chicago than it is from Memphis to New Orleans? How much farther is it?

Memphis to Chicago, 481 miles.
Memphis to New Orleans, 358 miles.

9. How much closer is San Francisco to Seattle than it is to Denver?

Seattle to San Francisco, 680 miles.
Denver to San Francisco, 937 miles.

10. A sign says that it is 382 miles to Cleveland and 165 miles to Detroit. How much farther away is Cleveland than Detroit?

Zeros in Subtracting

Tom said, "Subtracting isn't hard if you just remember when you use a ten or a hundred."

"Those tricky zeros mix me up," said Jim. "Don't you have trouble with them?"

"Zeros make subtracting easier," said Tom. "Let me show you how easy it is.

```
   700      6 9
            7̶0̶¹0
   467       46 7
   ---      -----
   233       23 3
```

"I have to subtract 7, and there are no ones. So I must use a ten. Do I have any tens? Yes, I have lots of them. I have 70 tens. When I use 1, I have 69 left to use. The rest is easy: 7 from 10 is 3, 6 from 9 is 3, and 4 from 6 is 2."

1. There are 800 seats in the school auditorium, and 416 people came to see the play. How many more people can be seated in the auditorium?

2. Jack had $5.00. He made a car for the soap-box derby. He spent $2.56 for boards, nails, and paint. How much money did he have then?

3. Tell how these examples were worked:

```
              4 9                 9 9                      9 9
  506        5̶0̶¹6        1000    1̶0̶0̶¹0    1004         1̶0̶0̶¹4
  288         28 8         625     62 5     738           73 8
  ---        -----        ----    -----    -----         -----
  218         21 8         375     37 5     266           26 6
```

Copy and subtract:

	(a)	(b)	(c)	(d)	(e)	(f)	(g)
4.	300	605	500	800	1000	402	900
	147	258	372	481	594	169	888
5.	600	902	806	200	1003	605	700
	487	758	498	78	764	396	654

6. The boys and girls are coloring Easter eggs for the big Easter egg hunt. The boys had 200 eggs to color. They have already colored 85 of them. How many do they have yet to color?

7. The girls also had 200 eggs to color. They worked faster than the boys. They have 156 colored. How many have they yet to color?

8. Ann's mother bought her a new pair of shoes. The price was $3.85. She paid for them with a 5-dollar bill. How much change did she get? Count her change.

9. Mrs. Allen bought a beef roast for $2.65. She paid for it with a 5-dollar bill. How much change did she get?

The clerk gave her 3 coins and 2 bills in change. What were they?

10. Jane's new dress cost $4.98. Her mother paid for it with a 10-dollar bill. How much change did she get?

11. Dick had $7.00. How much did he have left after he paid $3.98 for his new shoes?

12. Tom bought an old bicycle for $4.50. He painted it and fixed it up. Then he sold it for $12.00. How much did he make?

Copy and subtract:

	(a)	(b)	(c)	(d)	(e)	(f)	(g)	(h)
13.	402	505	807	601	303	904	706	308
	137	299	348	207	176	205	348	169
14.	801	607	304	503	206	705	408	602
	92	179	108	64	99	657	79	84
15.	202	301	703	906	805	404	602	507
	6	293	95	817	8	37	255	308

Problems

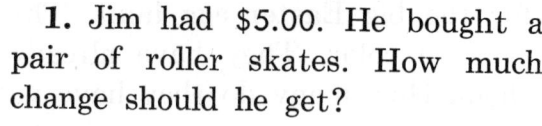

1. Jim had $5.00. He bought a pair of roller skates. How much change should he get?

2. Jane bought a book for 29¢. She gave the clerk a half dollar. How much change should she get?

Count Jane's change. Is it right?

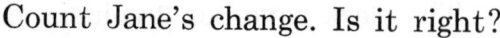

3. For weeks Tom watched at the toy store for the kind of airplane that he wanted. At last he saw one in the window. He bought it. How much should he get back if he paid for it with a five-dollar bill?

4. Mary's mother bought her a dress for $2.49. She paid for it with a five-dollar bill. How much change should she get?

Count her change.

5. Ann had 75¢. She bought a plant for her mother for 58¢. Then how much money did she have?

6. Susan counted her money. She had $2.83. She spent $1.25 for a red pocketbook. How much money did she have then?

7. How much of Bill's $2.00 will be left after he buys a knife for $1.89?

8. Mrs. West bought Jack an electric train which cost $5.98, and she bought Jim a wagon which cost $3.15. How much did she pay for both gifts?

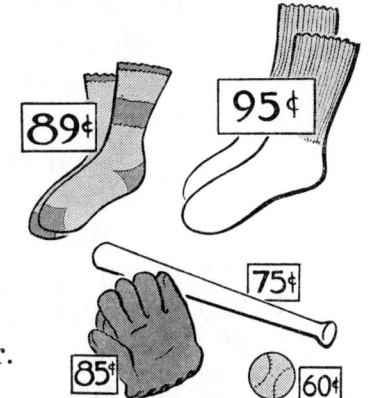

9. What is the difference in price between an 89¢ pair of stockings and a 95¢ pair of stockings?

10. Jack has a half dollar and a quarter. How much money has he?

11. Joe wants to buy a baseball bat for 75¢, a glove for 85¢, and a ball for 60¢. How much money does he need to buy them?

12. At a party Jane brought out a glass jar filled with jelly beans.

"How many beans are in the jar?" asked Jane.

There are 280 jelly beans in the jar. Jim guessed 168, and Alice guessed 200.

How close to the right number did Jim come?

How close to the right number was Alice's guess?

```
280
168
---

280
200
---
```

13. Jane has $23 in her bank at home, and Alice has $17 in her bank. How much more money has Jane in her bank than Alice has in hers?

How can you show that your answer is right?

14. Joe and Jim sold peanuts and popcorn. They got $5.35 for what they sold. They paid $3.50 for the peanuts and popcorn. How much more did they get back than they paid out?

Carrying in Dividing

1. The seats in the auditorium are arranged in rows. In each row there are 8 seats. Mr. Brown, the principal, asked Tom to reserve seats for 280 visitors. How many rows of seats did Tom reserve for the visitors?

To find the answer, Tom had to divide 280 by 8.

```
    35
8)280
   24
   ---
   40
   40
   ---
```

Think: Eights in twenty-eight, three.
Write 3 in ten's place in the answer.
Think: Three eights are twenty-four.
Write 24 under 28. Notice that 24 is less than 28.
Think: Four from eight is four.
Write 4. Notice that 4 is less than the divisor 8.
Bring down and write 0 beside the 4.
Think: Eights in forty, five.
Write 5 in one's place in the answer.
Think: Five eights are forty.
Write 40 under 40.

```
    3            3            3            3           35
8)280        8)280        8)280        8)280        8)280
              24           24           24           24
                            4           40           40
                                                     40
```

2. Notice how we divide in these examples:

```
   47           46           96           25           38
5)235        7)322        8)768        9)225        6)228
  20           28           72           18           18
  --           --           --           --           --
  35           42           48           45           48
  35           42           48           45           48
```

3. Copy and divide:

(a) 2)158   (b) 4)228   (c) 6)516   (d) 8)224   (e) 3)282   (f) 5)485   (g) 7)252   (h) 9)648

Steps in Dividing

Dividing Tens

```
    7
6)450

    7
6)450
   42

    7
6)450
   42
    3

    7
6)450
   42
   30

   75
6)450
   42
   30

   75
6)450
   42
   30
   30
```

```
    4
8)376

    4
8)376
   32

    4
8)376
   32
    5

    4
8)376
   32
   56

   47
8)376
   32
   56

   47
8)376
   32
   56
   56
```

Step 1

Divide: Write the answer in its proper place.

Step 2

Multiply: Notice that the product is **not greater** than the number divided.

Step 3

Subtract: Notice that the remainder is **less** than the divisor.

Step 4

Bring down the figure from one's place.

Dividing Ones

Step 1

Divide: Write the answer in its proper place.

Step 2

Multiply: Notice that the product is not greater than the number divided. Notice that we have no more to divide.

Find:

	(a)	(b)	(c)	(d)
1.	$\frac{1}{4}$ of 348	$\frac{1}{6}$ of 444	$\frac{1}{8}$ of 504	$\frac{1}{3}$ of 174
2.	$\frac{1}{5}$ of 285	$\frac{1}{7}$ of 273	$\frac{1}{9}$ of 666	$\frac{1}{2}$ of 156
3.	$\frac{1}{9}$ of 252	$\frac{1}{4}$ of 188	$\frac{1}{7}$ of 308	$\frac{1}{6}$ of 402

Dividing Hundreds

1. Jim, Joe, Tom, and Bill belong to the Hobby Club. They have just begun to collect stamps. Mr. Henry gave them his stamp collection. There were 948 stamps in it. The boys divided the stamps equally among themselves. How many stamps did each boy get?

Tell how we divide 948 by 4.

Remember: We divide the hundreds first. Then we divide the tens, and last we divide the ones.

Remember the steps: Divide, multiply, subtract, and bring down.

```
     237
 4)948
   8
   ──
   14
   12
   ──
    28
    28
```

2. Betty made 524 pieces of candy for the Girl Scouts' candy sale. She put the candy into 4 boxes of the same size. How many pieces should she put into each box?

3. Tell how these examples were divided:

```
     284           227           172           382           156
 3)852         4)908         5)860         2)764         6)936
   6             8             5             6             6
   ──            ──            ──            ──            ──
   25            10            36            16            33
   24             8            35            16            30
   ──            ──            ──            ──            ──
    12            28            10             4            36
    12            28            10             4            36
```

Copy and divide:

	(a)	(b)	(c)	(d)	(e)	(f)
4.	2)864	6)5304	4)2632	6)3252	7)3199	4)3072
5.	7)3969	8)4376	9)5643	6)3138	5)3795	6)4404
6.	4)3492	9)4752	2)1196	6)4386	8)5984	7)3276
7.	9)4302	4)2716	9)6777	9)3573	5)4185	9)4131

Wrong	Learning to Be Careful	Right
$\begin{array}{r}6\\2\overline{)118}\\12\end{array}$	← Jim made a mistake. He could not subtract 12 from 11. He knew there were not six twos in 11; so he started over. This time he started right. →	$\begin{array}{r}5\\2\overline{)118}\\10\\\hline1\end{array}$
	Dick did not make a mistake. He started right; so he went on to the next step. →	$\begin{array}{r}4\\3\overline{)144}\\12\\\hline2\end{array}$
$\begin{array}{r}5\\4\overline{)256}\\20\\\hline5\end{array}$	← Mary made a mistake. The remainder 5 is larger than the divisor 4. We know there is 1 more 4 in 25. There are six 4's in 25 with 1 remainder.	
	Mary had to start over, too. Did she start right this time? →	$\begin{array}{r}6\\4\overline{)256}\\24\\\hline1\end{array}$
$\begin{array}{r}6\\7\overline{)490}\\42\\\hline7\end{array}$	← Betty made a mistake. Where did she make her mistake? Did she start right the next time? →	$\begin{array}{r}7\\7\overline{)490}\\49\\\hline0\end{array}$

Look at each example below. Has it been started right?

$\begin{array}{r}2\\6\overline{)198}\\12\\\hline7\end{array}$ $\begin{array}{r}5\\5\overline{)265}\\25\\\hline1\end{array}$ $\begin{array}{r}7\\7\overline{)574}\\49\\\hline8\end{array}$ $\begin{array}{r}4\\9\overline{)324}\\36\\\hline\end{array}$ $\begin{array}{r}8\\9\overline{)738}\\72\\\hline1\end{array}$ $\begin{array}{r}6\\8\overline{)496}\\48\\\hline1\end{array}$ $\begin{array}{r}8\\6\overline{)474}\\48\\\hline\end{array}$

A Test

	(a)	(b)	(c)	(d)	(e)	(f)
1.	9)1134	8)2656	7)1771	8)2912	8)4368	6)2208
2.	6)1104	7)3808	6)3996	6)5250	5)4330	7)4802
3.	8)3672	8)3552	9)3915	5)3330	7)4662	4)3956

Using Zeros When We Divide

The fourth-grade pupils were standing in line waiting their turns to be measured and weighed. Bill had had his turn.

Jack said, "Hold my place, Bill. I want to get a drink."

"Surely," said Bill. "I'll be your zero."

Now what did Bill mean?

Study these division examples:

```
    2        20       200         3         40         400
4)8      4)80     4)800      4)12      3)120      3)1200
  8        8        8         12         12          12
  -       --       --         --         --         --
  0       00       00          0          0          00
```

Is the first quotient figure in each example written in its proper place? Is there a figure in the quotient for each figure that was brought down? What is the purpose of the zero, or zeros, in each example?

Say the quotient for each of these division examples:

3)9   3)90   3)900   6)12   6)120   6)1200   8)640   8)6400

9)8100   2)600   4)2800   7)3500   6)4200   7)6300   5)350

Zeros in Dividing

Why do we write 4 in hundred's place in our answer? How do we put 4 in hundred's place? Why do we write 00 in our answer?

When we divide hundreds, we write each part of the answer in its proper place. We divide 16 (hundreds) by 4 and write the 4 in hundred's place.

Where do we write the 2 in our answer? How do we keep the 2 in ten's place?

First, we divide the hundreds: Fours in sixteen, four. We write 4 in hundred's place in the answer.

Next, we divide the tens. When we bring down the ten's figure (0), we see that we have no tens to divide. We write 0 in ten's place in the answer to keep the 4 in hundred's place.

Then we divide the ones: Fours in eight, two. We write 2 in one's place.

Dividing Hundreds

```
     400
4)1600
   16
   ‾‾
     00
```

Dividing Hundreds and Tens

```
     420
4)1680
   16
   ‾‾
      8
      8
      ‾
      0
```

Dividing Hundreds and Ones

```
     402
4)1608
   16
   ‾‾
     08
      8
```

1. Mary and Alice took 500 Christmas seals to sell. They divided the seals so that each girl had the same number to sell. How many seals did each girl have to sell?

Copy and divide:

	(a)	(b)	(c)	(d)	(e)	(f)
2.	7)4200	5)2000	8)1608	8)4008	5)4505	6)3606
3.	2)1208	9)7209	7)6307	8)6408	8)7208	7)5607
4.	9)3609	9)5409	8)3208	6)5406	9)8109	6)1806

More about Zero

```
    250
4)1000
    8
   20
   20
    0
```

1. The Benton schools are showing a movie to raise money to buy a radio for each school. They have 1000 tickets to sell. If the tickets are divided equally among the 4 schools, how many will each school have to sell?

We cannot divide 1 by 4; so we think of 1000 as 10 hundreds. We think, "Fours in ten, two." Where do we write the 2 in our answer?

2. The boys wanted to use the vacant lot for a football field. They knew that a football field should be 100 yards long. They measured the lot and found that it was 324 feet long. Was it long enough?

```
   108
3)324
   3
  24
  24
```

First, we divide the hundreds. How do we get the 1 in our answer? In what place do we write the 1?

The first number we bring down is _____. We cannot divide 2 by 3; so we write 0 in ten's place in the answer.

We bring down the 4 and divide the 24 ones. Where do we write 8?

When we divide hundreds, we write 0 when we need it to keep a figure in its proper place.

3. About one fourth of the children at Central School come in busses. There are 416 children at Central School. About how many of them come in busses?

4. Jane's new stamp book holds 412 stamps. It is about half full now. About how many stamps are in it? About how many more stamps will the book hold?

Dividing Dollars and Cents

We divide dollars and cents the way we divide any other numbers, but we must be sure to write the dollars in dollar's place and cents in cent's place. We write the cents in the two places to the right of the point.

1. There were 8 boys at the camp. They shared the cost equally. The total expenses were $34.56. How much was each boy's share?

We divide $34.56 by 8 the way we divide 3456 by 8. We write each part of the answer in its proper place, and make the answer show dollars and cents.

```
       $ 4.32
    8)$34.56
       32
        2 5
        2 4
          16
          16
```

2. Three boys want to buy a croquet set. There are 3 sets at the store, and they cost $7.80, $8.25, and $5.07. What would each boy's share be if they bought the cheapest set? What would each boy's share be if they bought the best set?

Copy and divide:

	(a)	(b)	(c)	(d)	(e)
3.	2)$78.54	4)$37.28	6)$39.60	8)$74.56	3)$19.65
4.	5)$48.75	7)$46.55	9)$123.48	2)$375.60	4)$327.20
5.	6)$34.74	8)$72.40	3)$82.98	5)$347.25	9)$264.42
6.	8)2416	5)1535	9)7281	6)2430	7)4753
7.	8)2000	5)2100	8)3000	6)3900	4)2200

Chapter 16
Working with Thousands

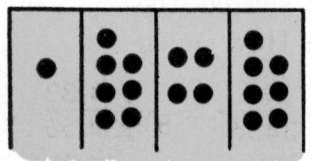

The Abacus

A simple abacus is shown at the left. Buttons or wooden discs are placed in the columns to show ones, tens, hundreds, and thousands. The abacus shows 1747. What does each abacus below show?

  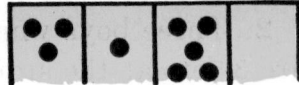

With the abacus we need no zero. Without the abacus we need zeros to hold the empty spaces.

| 1 | | 5 | 3 | | 2 | 6 | | 3 | | 3 | 1 | 5 | |

We write the numbers: 1053, 2603, and 3150. The abacus uses the same kind of counters in different positions to show different values. We use the same figures in different positions to show different values. The abacus is based on a system of counting by tens. It is called the **decimal** system. Our system of numbers is also based on the decimal system. Each column of the abacus has a value **ten times** the value of the column to its right. Each place in our number system has a value ten times the value of the place to its right.

Thousand's Place Hundred's Place Ten's Place One's Place
1 1 1 1

Reading and Writing Numbers

Write: Say:

- 5000 .... Five thousand
- 6400 .... Six thousand, four hundred
                or sixty-four hundred
- 2570 .... Two thousand, five hundred seventy
                or twenty-five hundred seventy
- 7963 .... Seven thousand, nine hundred sixty-three
                or seventy-nine hundred sixty-three
- 25,000 .... Twenty-five thousand
- 25,100 .... Twenty-five thousand, one hundred
- 12,060 .... Twelve thousand, sixty
- 25,875 .... Twenty-five thousand, eight hundred seventy-five

SAY THOUSAND NOT THOUSEN

Read these numbers:

| 28,000 | 17,305 | 67,870 | 43,760 | 3562 | 21,350 |
| 15,875 | 87,200 | 11,050 | 16,008 | 5024 | 10,001 |

Write the numbers with figures. Always use a comma (,) to mark off thousands in five-place and six-place numbers:

Ninety-seven thousand, two hundred
Fifty-four thousand, six hundred twenty
Thirty thousand, four hundred twelve
Fifty-two thousand, forty
Sixty-one thousand, ten
Twenty-two thousand, six

Read: The highest mountain in North America is Mt. McKinley in Alaska. It is 20,300 feet high.

In 1948 the building at 806 Ridge Avenue was bought for $32,500.

Reading Other Numbers

The year 1900 is read: *Nineteen hundred.*
The year 1949 is read: *Nineteen hundred forty-nine.*
It may also be read: *Nineteen forty-nine.*
Read these years:

1812   1492   1800   1906   1848   1950   1776

We read December 12, 1950, like this:

December *twelfth, nineteen fifty.*

Read these dates:
March 1, 1749   July 4, 1951   February 22, 1936

Telephone numbers are read by saying each figure in the number without saying thousand or hundred. The telephone number 4652 is read, "Four, six, five, two." Zero in a telephone number is read like the word, "Oh." The number 4450 is read, "Four, four, five, oh." A telephone number sometimes ends in 00 like 5400. We read it, "Five, four, oh, oh," or "Five, four hundred." The number 5000 is read, "Five thousand."

Read these telephone numbers:

1680   4296   4200   2004   5445   6000   3060

Can you read the numbers on automobile license plates?

We read 130-642 as "One, three, oh—six, four, two."

Read these license numbers:

Adding Thousands

1. On the Saturday after school began, Bill read in the paper that in Lake County 5052 girls and 4816 boys had started school. How many children had started school in Lake County?

> We add thousands the way we add ones, tens, and hundreds. We must be sure to write each figure in its proper place.
>
>   5052
>   4816
>   9868
>
> 9868 children started school in Lake County.

2. Five years ago 3504 girls and 3469 boys started school in Lake County. How many children were in school there five years ago?

    ¹
  3504
  3469
  6973

3. A small airplane weighs 6286 pounds. It will carry a load of 3650 pounds. How much will the loaded plane weigh?

    ¹
  6286
  3650
  9936

Copy and add:

	(a)	(b)	(c)	(d)	(e)	(f)	(g)
4.	1315 8213	3226 5143	4223 2743	3544 1240	6550 2108	2023 2636	3142 5756
5.	2426 5138	3253 4137	3465 2327	2667 6114	4334 1358	4005 5006	4226 4539
6.	4262 1585	6134 2770	6222 2096	3289 5680	4182 3797	7273 2635	3605 4288
7.	1270 2380 1160	7692 146 1050	58 125 4615	307 1572 2118	2682 4085 3262	438 59 1506	2486 7450 29

Adding Thousands

We use zeros when we need them to put each part of our answer **in its proper place**.

```
4000
5000
----
9000
```

There are no ones, no tens, and no hundreds to add. We write 000 in our answer to get ready to add the thousands. Then our thousand's **answer** will be in its proper place.

```
5207
2301
----
7508
```

There are no tens to add. We write 0 in ten's place so that our hundred's answer will be in its proper place.

Why do we write 0 in one's place? → 9410 + 6250 = 0

Why do we write 0 in hundred's place? → 2083 + 4016 = 099

Why do we write 00 in one's and ten's places? → 2500 + 3300 = 00

```
4206
5408
----
9614
```

Add the ones: 6 and 8 are 14. 14 is 1 ten and 4; so we now have 1 ten. But there are no tens to be added in the next column. We write 1 in the ten's place in the sum.

Now add the hundreds. Then add the thousands.

Copy and add:

	(a)	(b)	(c)	(d)	(e)	(f)
1.	4026 5048	7105 6308	7501 2309	7015 6038	3040 5206	2105 6308
2.	3004 5806	5008 2009	7407 1009	2053 4007	3080 5005	4066 3026

Carrying to Thousands

We carry from hundreds to thousands the way we carry from ones to tens and from tens to hundreds.

Notice how we carry in these additions:

$$\overset{1}{3}5 \atop \underline{48} \atop 83 \qquad \overset{1}{3}52 \atop \underline{480} \atop 832 \qquad \overset{1}{3}521 \atop \underline{4803} \atop 8324$$

Copy these examples and add:

	(a)	(b)	(c)	(d)	(e)	(f)	(g)
1.	3715 7784	5640 2448	1250 5844	1830 9740	1753 8520	6517 2651	2824 1554
2.	1743 2411	3714 4980	1962 1710	4540 1937	4762 2630	4731 6345	8911 1616
3.	6812 1271	5926 3530	3804 4605	2644 6433	5900 2446	2365 6800	4803 4954

4. Mary's new coat cost $24.45, and her new dress cost $6.50. How much was Mary's bill for her new clothes?

$24.45
  6.50
─────
$30.95

Copy and add:

	(a)	(b)	(c)	(d)	(e)	(f)
5.	$54.23 56.35	$19.23 45.40	$26.30 47.62	$47.50 63.30	$89.11 16.16	$68.12 12.71
6.	$19.62 32.37	$55.58 35.20	$25.40 27.20	$29.57 54.10	$39.20 42.08	$38.10 25.75

Carrying More Than Once

1. An airplane was flying 3675 feet high. Then it went up 1745 feet higher. How high was it then?

Think	Add the ones: 5 and 5 are 10. Write 0. Carry 1.
1 1 1 3675 1745 ――― 5420	Add the tens: 1 and 7 are 8, and 4 are 12. Write 2 and carry 1. Add the hundreds: 1 and 6 are 7, and 7 are 14. Write 4 and carry 1. Add the thousands: 1 and 3 are 4, and 1 are 5.

2 1 1
4532
1873
1725
―――
8130

2. In the town where Jack lives, 4532 people live in the main part of town, 1873 live on the south side, and 1725 live in the east end. How many people live in the town?

3. "That's a heavy load," said Jack.

1 1
3550
4486
―――
8036

"The truck weighs 3550 pounds, and the coal weighs 4486 pounds," answered the driver. "That is about 8000 pounds."

How much do the truck and coal weigh?

Copy and add:

	(a)	(b)	(c)	(d)	(e)	(f)	(g)
4.	3546 3693	5218 1997	1462 3608	3897 4105	4763 3237	2948 3366	3583 4427
5.	2651 1823 4548	1554 2630 4762	2411 4738 6354	4980 8917 1618	1718 6812 1937	2578 2163 3265	5839 2205 1060
6.	1865 2006 5080	5826 3765 2659	3510 2796 4067	2613 4780 3207	1768 375 4057	875 1268 3482	3030 6668 3709

The Filling Station

Jack's father has a filling station. He uses arithmetic each time he waits on a customer.

1. When Mr. James bought gasoline, the amount on the pump showed $3.68. He bought a quart of oil for $.36 and two light bulbs for $.70. How much was his bill?

2. Mr. Allen bought a new tire for $13.20 and some seat covers for $7.95. Then he got gasoline for $2.87. How much was his bill?

3. When Tom had earned enough money, he bought a new horn for the car. It cost $7.79. Later he bought a spotlight for $11.45 and some sun glasses for $1.95. How much did all of these things cost?

4. Mr. Jackson had to buy a new battery. He bought one for $12.25. Then he got some gasoline for $3.40 and four quarts of oil for $1.44. How much did Mr. Jackson spend at the filling station?

Subtracting Thousands

1. Sam read in the newspaper that 9868 children in Hill County were going to school and that 8358 children in Brown County were going to school. How many more children were going to school in Hill County than in Brown County?

```
9868
8358
1510
```

We subtract thousands the way we subtract ones and tens and hundreds. We write our thousand's answer in thousand's place.

There were 1510 more children going to school in Hill County than in Brown County.

```
    7
56 8̸10
 256 5
 311 5
```

2. One month the Gem Packing Company shipped 5680 pounds of meat to the city of York. Of this amount, 2565 pounds was beef. The rest was pork. How many pounds of pork were there?

3. In the election for mayor, Mr. Hill got 4836 votes, and Mr. Hall got 3685 votes. Who was elected? How many more votes did Mr. Hill get than Mr. Hall?

```
    7
 4 8̸ '36
  36 85
  11 51
```

4. A farmer raised 4224 bushels of corn. He sold 2075 bushels. How many bushels were left?

Subtract and check each answer:

	(a)	(b)	(c)	(d)	(e)	(f)	(g)
5.	2866	8248	2959	7869	5793	8567	7828
	1621	7115	2816	4534	4268	4248	4373
6.	9755	7736	6957	7638	9655	7942	5942
	3372	4218	3582	6493	4388	5467	3586

Subtracting Thousands

We use zeros when we need them to put each part of our answer in its proper place.

There are no ones, no tens, and no hundreds to subtract. We write 000 in our answer to get ready to subtract the thousands. Then the 4 will be in thousand's place.

8000
4000

4000

There are no ones and no tens to subtract. We write 00 in our answer before we subtract the hundreds and thousands. The 00 put the 2 in hundred's place and the 1 in thousand's place.

7600
6400

1200

9790
7380

2410

8908
6502

2406

Why do we write 0 in one's place?
Why do we write 0 in ten's place?
Why do we write 0 in hundred's place?

8675
4365

4310

7099
5038

2061

1. Tell how these examples were worked:

8904	9850	9066	8094	7001	8560	3432
7304	6650	3065	6034	5001	2554	2123
1600	3200	6001	2060	2000	6006	1309

Copy and subtract:

	(a)	(b)	(c)	(d)	(e)	(f)
2.	7736	6957	7948	9075	8137	5793
	1210	3022	5400	2045	3027	4063
3.	6724	18,930	16,790	14,081	12,904	13,096
	2104	9,700	7,390	8,021	7,100	5,036

Using a Thousand When We Subtract

1. Mr. West had 3570 bushels of apples to sell. When he sold 1850 bushels, how many bushels did he have yet to sell?

We carry back a thousand the way we carry back a ten or a hundred.

Think

```
  35      357     3570    |    ²³̸¹5     ²³̸¹57    ²³̸¹570
  18      185     1850    |    1 8      1 85     1 850
  ──      ───     ────    |    ───      ────     ─────
  17      172     1720    |    1 7      1 72     1 720
```

2. Notice how we subtract in these examples:

```
6132    8087    9396    6676    7330    9487    5754
2421    4312    2861    4842    2720    6854    2943
────    ────    ────    ────    ────    ────    ────
3711    3775    6535    1834    4610    2633    2811
```

3. Copy and subtract:

(a)	(b)	(c)	(d)	(e)	(f)	(g)	(h)
8396	9288	7195	9578	5478	6582	8686	3382
5645	5354	6380	2800	3670	4852	2856	1870

```
 $42.85
  28.75
 ──────
 $14.10
```

4. Betty Brown had $42.85 in the bank. She drew out $28.75 to buy some new clothes. How much did she have left in the bank?

Copy and subtract:

	(a)	(b)	(c)	(d)	(e)	(f)
5.	$82.90	$75.75	$90.65	$68.85	$70.86	$52.85
	57.50	58.00	45.50	49.75	54.65	37.05
6.	$70.84	$70.72	$85.59	$42.34	$98.80	$67.51
	27.13	36.21	28.49	15.00	29.30	29.41

How Many?

When we are subtracting, we often have to use a ten, or a hundred, or a thousand. Sometimes we need to look closely to tell how many tens or hundreds or thousands we have at the start.

How Many Tens?

5̲0, 5̲7, 25̲6, 135̲2, 1245̲0—each shows 5̲ tens.

5̲00, 5̲06, 15̲03, 125̲03—each shows 5̲0 tens.

5̲000, 45̲006, 5̲004—each shows 5̲00 tens.

How Many Hundreds?

2̲00, 42̲07, 362̲04—each shows 2̲ hundreds.

2̲000, 2̲004, 52̲006—each shows 2̲0 hundreds.

13̲000, 33̲050, 23̲065—each shows 3̲0 hundreds.

How Many Thousands?

6̲000, 6̲004, 86̲002—each shows 6̲ thousands.

6̲0,000, 6̲0,204—each shows 6̲0 thousands.

5̲0,826, 5̲0,806, 5̲0,006—each shows 5̲0 thousands.

Tell how many:

Tens	Hundreds	Thousands
82	804	3000
806	865	3046
6004	8042	3275
5002	80065	30852

How many tens do we have at the start? Finish each example below:

```
  2 9      7 9      3 9      4 9      8 9      5 9      6 9
 3̶0̶'2     8̶0̶'0     4̶0̶'1     5̶0̶'4     9̶0̶'5     6̶0̶'3     7̶0̶'4
 -1 5 6   -2 6 8   -1 8 3   -3 7 7   -6 4 8   -1 5 7   -2 3 9
```

Zeros in Subtracting

Miss Green put these examples on the board:

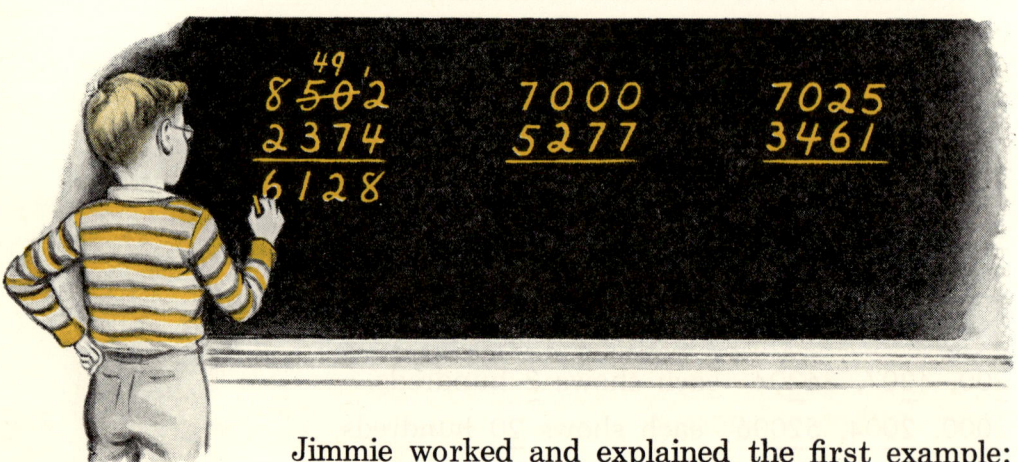

Jimmie worked and explained the first example:

"To take away 4, I have to use a ten. I notice that I have 50 tens to use. When I use 1, I have 49 tens yet to use.

"Then I subtract: 4 from 12 is 8, and 7 from 9 is 2, and 3 from 4 is 1, and 2 from 8 is 6."

Jane explained the second example:

"To take away 7, I need to use a ten. I notice that I have 700 tens to use; so when I use 1 of them, I have 699 tens yet to use."

Finish working Jane's example.

Tom explained the third example:

"I take 1 from 5. Next, I take 6 from 12. Here I have to use a hundred, but I see that I have 70 hundreds. When I use 1 of them, I have 69 hundreds yet to use. The rest is easy: 4 from 9 is 5, and 3 from 6 is 3."

Problems

1. The Electrical Supplies Store bought 10 thousand light bulbs. At the end of the month they had 7852 bulbs left. How many bulbs did they sell?

	Subtract	Think
To start we had 1000 tens. We use 1 ten and still have 999 tens to use.	10000 7852 ――― 2148	999 1000'0 785 2 ――― 214 8

2. Mr. James received $80.00 as his week's wages. He paid the grocer $16.82. How much did he have then?

	Subtract	Think
$80.00 is 800 dimes (tens). We use 1 dime (ten) and still have 799 to use.	$80.00 16.82 ――― $63.18	799 $80.0'0 16.8 2 ――― $63.1 8

3. How much change should you get:
    a. If you owe $7.50 and give the clerk $10.00?
    b. If you owe $7.50 and give the clerk $20.00?
    c. If you owe $12.75 and give the clerk $20.00?
    d. If you owe $25.64 and give the clerk $30.00?
    e. If you owe $21.43 and give the clerk $25.00?

Carrying Back More Than Once

Jane said, "I can use a ten or a hundred or a thousand when I subtract."

Alice answered, "So can I, and I can use all three in the same example. I'll show you.

```
            8 14 13
 9543     9̸ 5̸ 4̸¹3
 5784     5 7 8 4
 ────     ───────
 3759     3 7 5 9
```

"Use a ten and take 4 from 13.
Use a hundred and take 8 from 13.
Use a thousand and take 7 from 14.
Last, take 5 from 8."

"Do you write the *little figures* over your example?" asked Jane.

"Of course not," answered Alice. "I just remember when I have used a ten or a hundred or a thousand."

Tom Blake is good in arithmetic because he does his work slowly and carefully and thoughtfully. This is the way he explained some examples:

```
8703
2694
────
6009
```

"I subtracted 4 from 13 and used 1 of my 70 tens, leaving 69 yet to use. Then I subtracted 9 from 9, and 6 from 6, and 2 from 8.

```
8703
3705
────
4998
```

"I subtracted 5 from 13 and used 1 of my 70 tens, leaving 69 yet to use. There was nothing to subtract from 9. I wrote 9 in ten's place. Next I had to subtract 7 (hundreds) from 6. So I used 1 of my 8 thousands. 7 from 16 is 9, and 3 from 7 is 4.

```
8006
5009
────
2997
```

"I subtracted 9 from 16, and used 1 of my 800 tens, leaving 799 yet to use. There was nothing to subtract from 9 (tens) or from 9 (hundreds). Then I subtracted the thousands: 5 from 7 is 2."

Vacation Days

1. Last summer when the Hines family left for a trip, Mr. Hines counted the money he was taking along and found that he had $82.37. When they returned from their trip, he found that he had $15.72. How much was spent on the trip?

2. The Hines family rented a cabin by the lake. They had to pay $2.50 a day for the cabin. They stayed in the cabin 8 days. How much in all did they pay for the cabin?

Subtract and check:

	(a)	(b)	(c)	(d)	(e)	(f)
3.	$87.60 38.50	$45.75 26.05	$89.25 39.08	$45.23 12.05	$86.45 40.78	$75.68 50.49
4.	$78.50 29.75	$72.83 34.96	$86.00 58.00	$100.00 75.35	$240.00 128.76	$90.00 42.50

Multiplying Thousands

1. Mr. Smith owns the Highland Orchards. Jim read in the paper that Mr. Smith sold 1224 bushels of apples last year, and that this year he would have **twice** as many to sell. How many bushels of apples does Mr. Smith expect to sell this year?

```
 1224
  ×2
 2448
```
We multiply thousands the way we multiply ones and tens and hundreds. We write each part of our answer in its proper place.

```
 2125
    3
 6375
```
2. Mr. Hall has a filling station. He sells about 2125 gallons of gasoline in a month. Then in 3 months he will sell about _____ gallons.

```
$22.50
     2
$45.00
```
3. Our class decided to buy 2 new swings for the playground. Each swing costs $22.50. How much money do we need?

```
 1107
    9
 9963
```
Notice how we multiply 1107 by 9.

Nine sevens are sixty-three. We write 3 in its place underneath the 9. We have 6 tens to carry. Since there are no tens to multiply, we write 6 in ten's place.

Finish multiplying.

Copy and multiply:

	(a)	(b)	(c)	(d)	(e)	(f)	(g)
4.	2314 2	2330 3	1224 4	1130 6	4432 2	1107 8	3232 3
5.	$30.20 6	$40.42 4	$10.80 6	$20.15 5	$10.40 7	$11.05 8	$50.19 9

Carrying to Thousands

We **carry** from hundreds to thousands the way we carry from ones to tens and from tens to hundreds.

Notice how we carry in these multiplications:

```
   1              1              1             1 2
  75            753           7532          7582
   3              3              3             3
 ───           ────          ─────         ─────
 225           2259          22596         22746
```

Copy these examples and multiply:

	(a)	(b)	(c)	(d)	(e)	(f)
1.	2841 × 2	4510 × 9	3934 × 2	5600 × 8	6733 × 3	7622 × 4
2.	4823 × 3	7910 × 6	7842 × 2	2834 × 5	6922 × 2	9530 × 3
3.	5911 × 5	7511 × 6	7443 × 2	$16.43 × 2	$14.22 × 4	$35.22 × 3
4.	$47.10 × 7	$69.43 × 2	$18.10 × 9	$57.00 × 8	$65.00 × 7	$48.10 × 6

5. There are 5280 feet in a mile. How many feet are there in 4 miles? in 6 miles?

Copy and multiply:

	(a)	(b)	(c)	(d)	(e)	(f)
6.	293 × 5	865 × 6	471 × 7	590 × 8	608 × 9	2570 × 7
7.	1582 × 4	2479 × 3	5068 × 6	7504 × 5	3652 × 8	1075 × 4

```
 1 5 3
 1296
    6
 ────
 7776
```

Multiplying Thousands

We use zeros when we need them to keep each part of our answer in its proper place.

```
2000
   4
────
8000
```

1. Mr. Hardy bought 4 loads of coal. Each load weighed 2000 pounds. How many pounds was that?

There are no ones, no tens, and no hundreds to multiply. We write 000 in our answer to get ready to multiply the thousands. Then our thousand's answer will be in its proper place.

```
2240
   4
────
8960
```

2. Mr. Wells bought 4 loads of coal. Each load weighed 2240 pounds. How many pounds of coal did Mr. Wells buy?

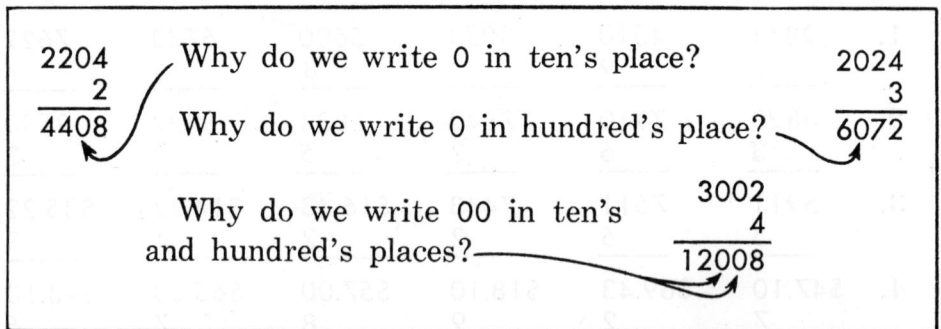

3. Tell how these examples were worked:

```
1500   1450   1175   1050   1512   1054   1306
   4      6      8      9      4      8      7
────   ────   ────   ────   ────   ────   ────
6000   8700   9400   9450   6048   8432   9142
```

4. Copy and multiply.

```
 (a)    (b)    (c)    (d)    (e)    (f)    (g)    (h)
1580   1058   1580   1058   1508   1058   1555   1166
   6      7      8      8      8      5      4      9
```

Test   Practice

Copy and subtract:

	(a)	(b)	(c)	(d)	(e)	(f)	(g)
1.	8235 3498	7000 4652	9004 1863	5947 1489	9158 3936	7093 5848	8182 4729
2.	7238 4767	9746 8845	8050 4641	5368 3742	7234 1475	5467 2978	3394 1898
3.	4567 1375	5132 2970	8465 7365	7682 4282	8407 5300	6072 1625	5225 4986
4.	$75.00 18.75	$48.50 34.78	$96.25 18.50	$58.63 29.00	$85.53 17.76	$52.34 14.92	$69.95 47.29

Copy and add:

	(a)	(b)	(c)	(d)	(e)	(f)	(g)
5.	4136 6825 4436	1356 1739 5978	1722 4914 5476	5642 6327 5031	4812 1297 9321	7506 8430 8759	1928 9071 7481
6.	$20.27 68.25 44.36	$25.65 46.30 27.20	$33.76 48.36 43.65	$35.48 12.69 21.37	$36.15 40.08 20.56	$50.05 1.68 3.45	$10.80 20.95 6.80

Copy and multiply:

	(a)	(b)	(c)	(d)	(e)	(f)	(g)
7.	263 7	195 4	451 8	247 6	594 3	785 9	670 5
8.	$2.73 4	$7.50 2	$4.65 8	$9.75 6	$17.25 7	$45.38 5	$29.60 9

Copy and divide:

	(a)	(b)	(c)	(d)	(e)	(f)	(g)
9.	9)657	2)170	8)472	7)315	4)116	3)228	9)432
10.	6)390	5)230	2)190	8)136	7)245	6)450	9)225

Dividing Hundreds and Thousands

1. Last spring Harry's father raised 8000 tomato plants. He set out ¼ of them and sold the rest. How many plants did he set out?

```
  2 thousands
4) 8 thousands

   2000
4) 8000
   8
   000
```

We are dividing thousands; so our answer will be thousands.

We think, "Fours in eight, two." We write 2 in thousand's place just above the 8. Since there are no hundreds, no tens and no ones, we write 000 in our answer to put 2 in thousand's place.

We divide hundreds and thousands the way we divide tens and ones. When we divide hundreds, we write the hundred's answer in hundred's place. When we divide thousands, we write the thousand's answer in thousand's place.

```
    5           50           500          5000
5) 25        5) 250       5) 2500      5) 25000
   25           25            25            25
                 0            00           000
```

Copy and divide:

	(a)	(b)	(c)	(d)	(e)	(f)
2.	3)900	3)9000	7)2800	7)28000	4)800	5)2000
3.	9)1800	9)18000	4)3600	4)36000	6)600	6)4200
4.	7)4200	6)42000	2)600	2)6000	8)880	8)5600
5.	8)56000	8)6400	8)4000	8)40000	3)690	9)4500
6.	9)36000	8)7200	7)4900	9)81000	4)840	6)2400

Problems

1. The football stadium at State College seats 24,000 people; so 24,000 tickets were printed for the game with Brown College. One fourth of the tickets were sent to Brown College. How many tickets were sent?

2. One third of the 24,000 tickets were sold in the city where State College is located. How many tickets were sold in the home city?

We divide thousands the way we divide hundreds, and tens, and ones. We write each part of our answer in its proper place. We must use zeros when we need them.

```
      823              8231              8230
   3)2469           3)24693           3)24690
     24               24                24
      6                6                 6
      6                6                 6
       9                9                 9
       9                9                 9
                        3                 0
                        3
```

Copy and divide:

	(a)	(b)	(c)	(d)	(e)
3.	2)6824	3)9630	9)18900	5)25550	4)12840
4.	8)56800	7)63700	4)36844	4)20840	5)35500
5.	3)24936	4)32484	7)49700	8)32888	9)36900

Carrying in Dividing

1. "I worked 8 weeks this summer and made $98.80. That was $12.35 a week," said Jack.

Was Jack right? Did he make $12.35 a week?

```
      $12.35
   8)$98.80
      8
      ──
      18
      16
      ──
       2 8
       2 4
       ───
         40
         40
```

2. "My brother worked 3 weeks this summer in the drug store and made $101.25. That was $33.75 a week," said Tom.

Was Tom right?

3. "My brother worked in a garage this summer for 6 weeks. He made $136.50. How much was that a week?" asked James.

Copy and divide:

	(a)	(b)	(c)	(d)	(e)
4.	3)14277	6)48906	6)47058	8)26008	6)49908
5.	5)$43735	7)$188.23	7)$306.11	9)$195.57	4)$261.36
6.	7)58975	4)$170.20	8)77824	9)$408.06	7)38101

Zeros in Dividing

1. A large dairy company sold 4248 quarts of milk last week. How many quarts did they sell in one day if they sold the same number each day?

Since the 4 in thousand's place is less than 6, we use it with the 2 hundreds and divide 42 hundreds by 6.

```
    70
6)4248
  42
   4
```

We write 7 in hundred's place, multiply and compare, and bring down the 4. We see that the 4 is less than 6. So we write 0 in ten's place in our answer, and bring down 8.

Now we divide 48 by 6.

```
   708
6)4248
  42
   48
   48
```

2. Notice how we divide in these examples:

```
    507         8380         3050         1005         1339
5)2535      4)33520      7)21350      5)5025       6)8034
  25           32           21           5            6
   35           15           35          025          20
   35           12           35           25          18
                32            0                       23
                32                                    18
                 0                                    54
                                                      54
```

Each time we bring down a number we must write a figure in the quotient. If the number to be divided is smaller than the divisor, we write 0 in the quotient.

Copy and divide:

	(a)	(b)	(c)	(d)	(e)
3.	4)24408	4)36200	5)25450	5)45350	6)36300
4.	9)36549	8)56320	8)32640	9)81549	6)18636
5.	7)30863	6)36216	9)63981	8)94400	7)21602
6.	8)46240	7)47404	5)10750	9)54783	4)37208

Chapter 17
Multiplying by Tens

At the Railroad Station

Tom and Henry watched a long train of cars thunder past the station. They counted 126 cars in the train.

"Do many long trains like that go by?" asked Henry.

"Yes," said the station agent. "Yesterday 5 trains like that went through here, and last week 50 such trains went through here."

How many cars are there in 5 trains of 126 cars?

How many cars are there in 50 trains of 126 cars?

Before we can answer the last question, we must know how to **multiply by tens**.

About Tens

We add tens the way we add ones, but we must write the ten's answer in ten's place. When we need to, we use 0 to help us write the ten's answer in ten's place.

1. Copy and add:

(a)	(b)	(c)	(d)	(e)	(f)	(g)	(h)
40	30	90	36	75	57	89	72
50	62	50	84	80	36	56	28

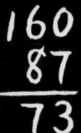

We subtract tens the way we subtract ones, but we must write the ten's answer in ten's place. When we need to, we use 0 to put the ten's answer in ten's place.

2. Copy and subtract:

80	100	140	97	165	80	120	150
30	60	80	57	85	32	76	87

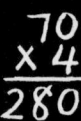

We multiply tens the way we multiply ones, but we must write the ten's answer in ten's place. When we need to, we use 0 to put the ten's answer in ten's place.

3. Copy and multiply:

40	61	73	80	52	50	75	65
2	5	9	7	8	5	4	8

We divide tens the way we divide ones, but we must write the ten's answer in ten's place. When we need to, we use 0 to put the ten's answer in ten's place.

4. Copy and divide:

(a) 2)80   (b) 4)160   (c) 3)69   (d) 4)368   (e) 6)456   (f) 8)760   (g) 6)408

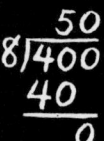

How do we **multiply by tens**? Perhaps you know.

Multiplying by Tens

1. Jack has 5 rows of pennies. In each row there are ten pennies. His pennies show 5 tens. How many pennies has he? Five 10's are how many?

2. Jim has 10 rows of pennies with 5 pennies in each row. His pennies show 10 fives. How many pennies has he? Ten 5's are how many?

Are 5 tens the same as 10 fives?

How much are 3 tens?   Then how much are 10 threes?
How much are 9 tens?   Then how much are 10 nines?
How much are 12 tens? Then how much are 10 twelves?

Say the products:

10 × 4	10 × 7	10 × 16	10 × 27	10 × 45
10 × 62	10 × 85	10 × 33	10 × 56	10 × 78

Multiplying by Tens

1. Saturday Jim rode in the truck with the man who delivers bread to the stores.

"Today we leave 48 loaves of bread at each of the 30 stores," said the man as he stopped at the first store.

"That's a lot of bread," said Jim. "Exactly how many loaves is that altogether?"

We must multiply 48 by 30.

We multiply by tens the way we multiply by ones, but we start writing our answer in ten's place.

First, we write 0 in one's place in the answer.

Then we start multiplying. We must remember we are multiplying 48 by 3 (tens). Three 8's are 24. We write 4 in ten's place directly under the 3 (tens) we multiplied by, and we carry 2. Three 4's are 12, and 2 are 14. We write 14.

There were 1440 loaves of bread to deliver.

```
  48
   3
 ---
 144

  48
  30
 ----
 1440
```

2. There are 24 paper plates in a package. How many plates are in 20 packages?

3. Tom saw 28 sacks of flour. Each sack weighed 50 pounds. Find the total weight of the flour.

```
   28
  ×50
 ----
 1400
```

4. Study these multiplications:

```
  26     26     18     18     67     67     52     52
  10     20     10     40     10     50     10     70
 ---    ---    ---    ---    ---    ---    ---    ---
 260    520    180    720    670   3350    520   3640
```

5. Write the products:

(a)	(b)	(c)	(d)	(e)	(f)	(g)	(h)	(i)
35	22	64	72	38	82	46	98	57
×30	×50	×40	×60	×70	×80	×90	×20	×30

Multiplying by Tens

1. Tom counted 126 cars in a train. The station agent told him that at least 50 such trains went by last week. How many cars went by last week?

```
 126
   5
-----
 630
```

```
 126
  50
-----
6300
```

We multiply by 5 tens the way we multiply by 5 ones, but we must start writing our answer in ten's place.

First, we write 0 in one's place.

Then we start multiplying: Five 6's are 30. Write 0 and carry 3. Five 2's are 10, and 3 are 13. Write 3 and carry 1. Five 1's are 5, and 1 are 6. Write 6.

6300 cars went by the station last week.

2. Notice how we multiply in these examples. Cover the answers, multiply, and see if you get the same answers.

136	269	573	365	427	359	233
20	30	40	50	60	80	70
2720	8070	22,920	18,250	25,620	28,720	16,310

Copy and multiply:

	(a)	(b)	(c)	(d)	(e)	(f)	(g)	(h)
3.	74	59	38	615	716	27	183	275
	20	30	40	50	60	90	80	30
4.	75	96	84	276	347	85	446	389
	70	10	80	80	60	90	70	50

Something New in Multiplying

Let us see how the children worked this problem without the help of their books or teacher:

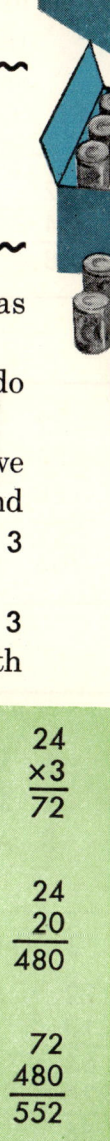

Mr. James, the grocer, has 23 boxes of canned tomatoes in his store. In each box there are 24 cans. How many cans of tomatoes are there?

Jim said, "The way to find out how many cans he has is to multiply 24 by 23."

"That's easy to see," said Jane. "But just how do we multiply by 23?"

Alice said, "Let's not look in our books. Maybe we can figure it out. We know how to multiply by ones, and we know how to multiply by tens. 23 is the same as 3 ones and 2 tens."

"That's right," said George. "Then the grocer has 3 boxes with 24 cans in each box, and he has 20 boxes with 24 cans in each box."

Jane suggested, "Let's multiply and see what we get. In the 3 boxes the grocer has 3 times 24, or 72 cans. In the 20 boxes he has 20 times 24, or 480 cans. In the 23 boxes he has 72 cans and 480 cans, or 552 cans."

"We have found the answer," said George. "First, we multiplied by the ones and next by the tens, and then we added."

"But isn't there a way to do it all at once?" asked Jim. "How do we multiply by ones and by tens, and then add, all in the same example?"

```
  24
  ×3
  ──
  72

  24
  20
  ───
  480

  72
  480
  ───
  552
```

Multiplying by Ones and Tens

1. The children want to know how many tickets to make for their play. The auditorium has 24 rows of seats, and there are 32 seats in a row. If they make as many tickets as there are seats, how many tickets will they make?

To find the number of seats, we multiply 32 by 24.

```
  32        32        128
  ×4        ×20      +640
 ---       ----      ----
 128       640        768
```

24 means 4 ones and 2 tens; so we multiply 32 first by 4 ones and then by 2 tens, and we add the answers.

First, we multiply 32 by 4 ones, and write the answer 128. Next, we multiply 32 by 2 tens. We start writing our answer in ten's place; so we write 0 under 8 in one's place. Notice that 640 shows 64 tens.

```
  32
 ×24
 ---
 128
 640
 ---
 768
```

The 128 is one part of the answer, and 640 is another part. To get the whole answer, we add both parts.

The children should make 768 tickets.

---

1. Multiply by the ones.
2. Multiply by the tens.
3. Add the partial products.

```
    83
    27
  ----
   581  ⎫
  1660  ⎬ partial products
  ----  ⎭
  2241
```

---

2. Tell how each of these products was found:

```
  22     34     58     35     67     46     95
  13     12     43     24     45     52     68
 ---    ---   ----    ---    ---    ---    ---
  66     68    174    140    335     92    760
 220    340   2320    700   2680   2300   5700
 ---    ---   ----    ---   ----   ----   ----
 286    408   2494    840   3015   2392   6460
```

Problems and Practice

1. Betty heard Mrs. Adams say that 24 dozen eggs would be colored for the Easter egg hunt. How many eggs did they plan to color?

2. The fruit man took 16 loads of peaches to market. There were 34 bushels in each load. How many bushels of peaches did he take to market?

3. If there are 18 dozen oranges in a basket, how many oranges are in the basket?

4. Mr. East has 24 rows of tomato plants with 22 plants in each row. How many tomato plants does he have?

5. Thirty-one fourth-grade pupils take milk at school. How many bottles of milk do they take in a month that has 19 school days in it?

6. The drugstore buys 24 cases of soda pop each week. There are 24 bottles in a case. How many bottles of pop are bought each week?

Copy and multiply:

	(a)	(b)	(c)	(d)	(e)	(f)	(g)	(h)
7.	31 25	42 41	17 19	63 26	35 37	96 49	73 54	81 76
8.	64 53	26 67	61 41	42 28	87 93	39 81	58 54	79 27
9.	52 29	68 18	59 35	34 91	45 76	86 52	20 37	97 68
10.	91 27	37 14	54 46	45 64	78 27	93 59	46 24	89 64
11.	58 18	36 45	64 82	28 63	47 95	21 49	23 76	19 91

Problems and Practice

```
144 —multiplicand
 15 —multiplier
 720 ⎫
1440 ⎬ partial products
2160 —product
```

1. There are 144 pieces of chalk in a box. How many pieces are there in 15 boxes?

2. There are 158 blocks in Jack's building set. How many blocks will there be in 36 sets like Jack's?

Copy and multiply:

	(a)	(b)	(c)	(d)	(e)	(f)	(g)
3.	131 13	241 12	111 17	125 36	159 26	237 14	168 25
4.	216 46	118 79	124 68	345 29	243 37	326 25	514 16
5.	426 22	162 34	416 15	321 28	526 13	329 30	217 40

6. Study these examples:

```
  40      140      150      400      404      120
  17       17       30       17       17       60
 ───      ───     ────     ────     ────     ────
 280      980     4500     2800     2828     7200
 400     1400              4000     4040
 ───     ────              ────     ────
 680     2380              6800     6868
```

Copy and multiply:

	(a)	(b)	(c)	(d)	(e)	(f)	(g)
7.	60 32	500 18	302 24	109 89	402 72	80 92	800 92
8.	90 40	200 40	200 45	201 45	407 18	90 42	300 30
9.	50 60	210 45	600 15	308 30	240 34	70 52	802 68
10.	71 80	606 42	930 25	440 50	708 80	50 17	810 10

Multiplying Dollars and Cents

1. Each member of the Bird Club wanted a pin. Each of the 30 members brought a quarter. Miss Green gave Jack the 30 quarters and asked him to go to the store after the pins. Jack gave the clerk $7.50. Did Jack give him the right amount?

```
$ .25
   30
$7.50
```

2. Mr. Dan bought 24 cases of canned tomatoes. He paid $2.36 a case for them. How much did he pay for the canned tomatoes?

Each case cost $2.36.
So 24 cases cost 24 times $2.36.

We multiply dollars and cents the way we multiply any other numbers. But we must be sure to write the sign to show dollars and the point to show cents. We put the point before the last 2 figures of the answer.

```
$2.36
   24
 9 44
47 20
$56.64
```

Mr. Dan paid $56.64 for the canned tomatoes.

3. Notice how these examples are worked:

```
 $1.98      $7.50      $3.25       $4.50       $1.67
    40         20         17          25          15
 $79.20    $150.00     22 75       22 50        8 35
                       32 50       90 00       16 70
                      $55.25     $112.50      $25.05
```

Copy and multiply:

	(a)	(b)	(c)	(d)	(e)	(f)	(g)
4.	$1.65 25	$1.75 40	$2.09 16	$1.10 75	$ .89 38	$ .32 89	$3.04 24
5.	$5.00 16	$3.45 24	$ .75 69	$2.50 38	$1.08 75	$ .08 75	$4.85 12

In Place

Always keep each part of the partial product in its proper place. Start writing each partial product directly below the multiplier.

83 27 --- 581 1660 ---- 2241	83 27 --- 581 166 ---- 2241	When we multiply by the tens to get a partial product, we need not write 0 in one's place. But we must start writing our answer in ten's place.

Tell how the multiplications below are worked:

```
   83        58        67        95        69
   27        43        54        68        44
  ---       ---       ---       ---       ---
  581       174       268       760       276
  166       232       335       570       276
 ----      ----      ----      ----      ----
 2241      2494      3618      6460      3036
```

Copy the examples, and see if you can work them without using 0 to fill the empty space.

The children who worked the examples on the board made mistakes. There is a mistake in each example. Find the mistakes and tell how to correct them.

```
  Mary        Joe         Jim        Alice
   25         70          36          43
   66         38          94          82
  ---        ---         ---         ---
  150        560         144          86
  150        210         324         344
  ---        ---         ---         ---
  300        770         468         430
```

Checking Multiplication

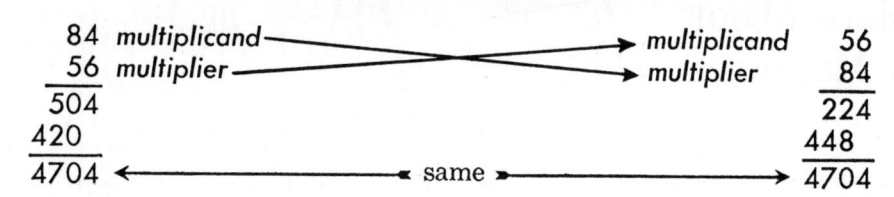

Are the products the same?

To check multiplication, we change the places of the numbers we have multiplied and multiply again. If the answers are the same, we can be quite sure that our work is correct.

Multiply and check:

	(a)	(b)	(c)	(d)	(e)	(f)	(g)	(h)	(i)
1.	21	15	31	12	27	46	32	10	13
	35	18	46	59	18	12	24	98	27
2.	23	27	16	35	21	28	15	13	82
	19	34	25	23	47	14	44	76	12
3.	17	34	19	18	24	24	13	26	19
	24	23	39	16	37	38	51	36	16
4.	56	16	74	37	68	25	15	14	52
	17	54	13	27	12	39	42	23	36

5. The fourth grade went to visit the museum. There were 24 children who went on the trip. They each paid 75¢. How much did they pay altogether?

6. The King family went to a park on their vacation. They rented a cabin for $4.50 a day. They stayed there 15 days. How much rent did they pay for the cabin?

Chapter 18
More about Measures

The Ton

As Tom and his father drove up to the bridge, Tom saw a sign. It read: LIMIT 5 TONS.

"What does the sign mean?" asked Tom.

"It means the bridge might break down if a load heavier than 5 tons were taken onto it."

A **ton** is the measure we use to weigh very heavy things, as coal and iron. The weight of railroad cars is given in tons. **A ton is 2000 pounds.**

---

1. How many pounds are there in 3 tons? 4 tons?

2. How many pounds are there in $\frac{1}{2}$ ton? $\frac{1}{4}$ ton?

3. Do you multiply or divide to change 4000 pounds to tons? Do you multiply or divide to change 8 tons to pounds?

4. How much will 13 tons of coal cost at $24 a ton?

5. Mr. Fields ordered about 4 tons of hay. He got 3 loads. The first load weighed 1980 pounds. The second load weighed 2520 pounds, and the third load weighed 3300 pounds. How many pounds of hay did Mr. Fields get? Did he get more or less than 4 tons?

Problems about Coal

1. Mr. Woods, the coal dealer in town, bought a new truck. He drove it onto the scales and found that it weighed 5780 pounds. When he had the coal loaded, he drove the truck onto the scales again. The total weight of the truck and coal was 12,543 pounds. How much did the coal weigh?

2. Find the weight of the coal on each of these loads:
    a. Total weight of truck and coal... 12,097 pounds
    b. Total weight of truck and coal... 11,783 pounds
    c. Total weight of truck and coal... 13,076 pounds
    d. Total weight of truck and coal... 12,840 pounds
    e. Total weight of truck and coal... 11,918 pounds
    f. Total weight of truck and coal... 12,562 pounds
    g. Total weight of truck and coal... 12,209 pounds

3. The bill that Jack's father got showed "3870 pounds of coal." Was that more or less than 2 tons?

4. Mr. Hall and Mr. High each ordered 2 tons of coal. Mr. Hall's load weighed 3960 pounds, and Mr. High's load weighed 4040 pounds. Which load came nearer to weighing exactly 2 tons?

Pounds and Ounces

1. Name some things that we buy by the pound at the grocery store; at the meat market; at the hardware store.

2. How can you find how heavy you are or how much you weigh?

3. If a pound of butter were cut into 16 pieces of the same weight, each piece would weigh 1 ounce. How many ounces are in 1 pound?

4. Margaret bought $\frac{1}{2}$ pound of candy. Look at the scales. How many ounces of candy did she buy?

5. How many ounces are in $\frac{1}{4}$ pound?

6. How many ounces are in $\frac{3}{4}$ pound?

7. Bring to school a list of things that your mother buys by the ounce.

8. If butter costs 60¢ a pound, what will $\frac{1}{2}$ pound cost? What will $\frac{1}{4}$ pound cost?

9. How much will a 5-pound roast cost at 79¢ a pound?

10. If it costs 3 cents to mail a letter that weighs one ounce, how much will it cost to mail a letter that weighs 6 ounces?

11. Three pounds of coffee cost $1.65. How much does one pound cost?

Dozen and Dozens

Jerry's mother sent him to the store to buy a dozen eggs. The grocer put them in a little cardboard box to keep them from being broken. How many eggs did Jerry buy?

The grocer asked Jerry a "catch" question. He asked, "Which is more, 6 dozen dozen, or one half dozen dozen?"

Right off Jerry said, "They are both the same."

Then he thought about it and said, "No, they are not the same. Six dozen dozen are 72 dozen, but one half dozen dozen are only 6 dozen."

1. A case of eggs holds 30 dozen. How many eggs are in a case?

2. A poultry man went to market with 90 dozen eggs in his truck. How many eggs did he have altogether?

---

12 things = 1 dozen   12 dozen = 1 gross
144 things = 1 gross

---

3. There are 12 things in a dozen. How many things are there in 12 dozen? What is 12 dozen called?

4. There are 8 boxes of chalk on a shelf in the supply room at school. In each box there is a gross of chalk. How many pieces of chalk are there altogether?

5. A shopkeeper ordered 6 gross of clothespins. How many clothespins did he order?

6. Last year we ordered and sold 12 gross of pencils for our school store. How many pencils did we sell?

This year we will probably sell 15 gross, or ____ pencils.

How to Estimate Answers

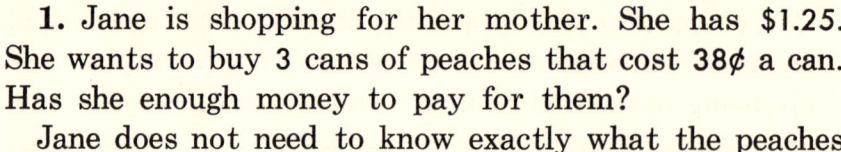

1. Jane is shopping for her mother. She has $1.25. She wants to buy 3 cans of peaches that cost 38¢ a can. Has she enough money to pay for them?

Jane does not need to know exactly what the peaches will cost. If she knows about how much they will cost, she will know whether or not she has enough money.

Jane thinks, "38¢ is almost 40¢. Three 40's are 120. The peaches will cost a little less than $1.20. So I have enough money to buy them."

When we find **about** what an answer is, we **estimate** the answer.

2. Bill has $1.50. He wants to buy a film for 28¢ and a collar for his puppy that costs 98¢. Bill needs to know whether he has enough money to buy them both.

Bill **estimates** the amount of money he needs. He thinks, "98¢ is almost a dollar, and 28¢ is almost 30¢. I need about a dollar and thirty cents."

Can he buy both of the things that he wants?

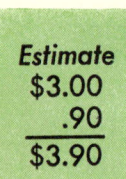

Estimate
$3.00
  .90
$3.90

3. Ann wants a purse that costs $2.98 and a scarf that costs $.89. About how much money does she need?

4. Estimate the cost of 3 books at 48¢ each.

5. Miss Able wants to buy 3 pairs of hose that cost $1.29 a pair. Will they cost more or less than $4.00?

6. Jack bought 2 dozen oranges at 59¢ a dozen. Estimate the cost of the oranges.

7. Jack wants a bicycle that costs $27.50. He has saved $7.15 for it. Has he saved about ¼ or ⅓ of the money he needs to buy the bicycle?

Problems

Let us estimate the answers to these problems and then work them.

1. A bag of flour weighs 24 pounds. Jack said, "Four bags of flour will weigh almost one hundred pounds."
How much will 4 bags weigh?
Was Jack's estimate about right?

2. "How many books are in the bookcase?" asked Helen.
Jim said, "I can find out in a hurry. There are 48 books on the top shelf, and there are 4 shelves. So there are about ____ books on the 4 shelves."
What did Jim **suppose**? Did he suppose there were the same number of books on each shelf?

3. The Bell family use 125 pounds of ice a day. How many pounds will they use in 7 days?

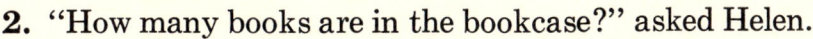

4. The Good Citizens' Club made trash cans for the playground. They bought barrels for $3.45 and paint for $1.65. How much did they spend?

5. Tom came to our house to play at 15 minutes after 2 o'clock. His mother said that she would come for him in about 40 minutes. About what time did she come for him?

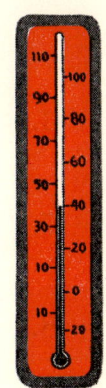

6. Dan sold his bicycle for $7.80 which was $6.50 less than he paid for it. How much did the bicycle cost?

7. The 4 girls in the Good Citizens' Club promised to sell Christmas seals. If each girl sells 250 seals, how many will they sell altogether?

8. Jim looked at the thermometer and said, "It is now 40°. If it gets much colder, our flowers will freeze."
How much above freezing (32°) was the temperature?

Estimating Answers

We can estimate to tell whether or not our answers are sensible.

1. Mary sold 8 tickets to the play. Each ticket sold for 30¢. She collected $2.40. Was that about right? Exactly how much money should Mary turn in?

We estimate to see if our answers are about right. Then we check to see if they are exactly right.

Estimate
$ .35
 10
─────
$3.50

2. Joe sold 9 pints of red raspberries at 35¢ a pint. Estimate how much Joe would get for the berries. Then find the exact answer.

3. Betty wants to buy 3 yards of material for a dress. The material costs 48¢ a yard. How much money will she need?

4. Estimate the cost of 4 books at 98¢ each.

5. Bob bought tickets to the ice show for three friends and himself. The tickets cost 88¢ apiece. Estimate how much money Bob needed. Then find the exact amount that the tickets cost.

These are multiplication examples. First, estimate the answers. Then find the exact answers.

	(a)	(b)	(c)	(d)	(e)	(f)	(g)	(h)
6.	98 7	31 9	49 5	107 8	199 6	42 5	98 4	219 4
7.	58 6	79 5	18 9	72 8	69 7	24 6	82 3	51 5
8.	$ .29 5	$ .98 4	$1.25 6	$6.98 7	$5.10 9	$2.05 8	$1.98 3	$1.49 2

Dry Measures

People used to use pint, quart, peck, and bushel to measure such things as fruit, vegetables, and grains. These measures are not used much today. Buying and selling by the pound is easier and more exact.

> 2 pints (pt.) = 1 quart (qt.)
> 8 qt. = 1 peck (pk.)
> 4 pk. = 1 bushel (bu.)

One basket of apples may weigh 52 pounds and another basket 48 pounds. We cannot be sure that a basket has exactly a bushel in it unless we weigh it. We still use the bushel measure because the basket is an easy way to carry such things as fruit and vegetables. We sometimes buy small fruits and berries in pint and quart boxes.

Some things are heavier than others. All states do not use the same weight for a bushel. Here are various weights of bushels:

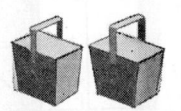

Apples......48 pounds   *Oats*......32 pounds
Grapes......48 pounds   *Wheat*......60 pounds
Potatoes.....60 pounds   *Shelled corn*..60 pounds

1. How much would 25 bushels of potatoes weigh?

2. How much would $\frac{1}{2}$ bushel of apples weigh?

3. What will 40 bushels of oats weigh?

4. How much will 60 bushels of shelled corn weigh?

5. A peck of apples weighs 12 pounds. What is the weight of a bushel of apples?

6. A quart of cherries weighs 2 pounds. What is the weight of a peck of cherries?

A Mile

Walter and his father walked down the road from their house. After a while they came to a creek, where they sat down to rest.

"How far have we walked?" asked Walter.

"It is just a mile from this creek to our front gate," answered his father. "We walked it in about 20 minutes."

"So that's how far a mile is," said Walter.

"Let's look around and find some other things that are about a mile away," suggested Walter's father.

"How long is a mile?" asked Walter's father.

"I remember reading that there are 5280 feet in a mile," answered Walter. "A man can step about 1 yard, or 3 feet, so he will take 1760 steps in walking a mile. That means there are 1760 yards in a mile."

"How far is 10 miles?" asked Walter's father.

"It is 10 miles from our house to Springfield," said Walter. "And it is about 100 miles from Springfield to St. Louis."

1. In some cities 10 blocks equal 1 mile. If you live in the city, find out how many blocks there are in 1 mile.

2. Find some place that is about 1 mile from your school.

3. Find some place that is about 1 mile from the post office.

4. What town is about 10 miles away?

5. What city is about 100 miles away?

1 mile = 5280 feet
1 mile = 1760 yards

Changing Measures

1. At the picnic several boys had a jumping contest. Jack and Sam measured how far each boy jumped. Find how many inches each boy jumped:

    a. Henry jumped 4 ft. 2 in. or _____ in.
    b. George jumped 4 ft. 6 in. or _____ in.
    c. John jumped 3 ft. 11 in. or _____ in.
    d. Jack jumped 4 ft. 3 in. or _____ in.
    e. Bill jumped 3 ft. 9 in. or _____ in.
    f. Tom jumped 4 ft. 4 in. or _____ in.

To change 5 feet 3 inches to inches, first change 5 feet to inches.
    Think: There are 12 inches in 1 foot. In 5 feet there will be 5 times 12 inches, or 60 inches.
    Now add the 3 inches.
    5 feet 3 inches = 63 inches.

$$\begin{array}{r} 12 \text{ in.} \\ \times 5 \\ \hline 60 \text{ in.} \end{array}$$

$$\begin{array}{r} 60 \text{ in.} \\ +3 \text{ in.} \\ \hline 63 \text{ in.} \end{array}$$

Problems Using Time

1. The farmer looked at the sky and said, "It will probably rain within the next 48 hours." In how many days does he mean?

2. Ray wanted to know how long he could play until supper time. Did he look at the calendar?

3. The newsboy brings the *Herald* newspaper each day in the week. During a period of 9 weeks, how many papers does he bring?

4. Ruth wants to know how many days there are until vacation begins. Does she look at the clock or the calendar?

5. 1948 was leap year. What is leap year?

6. Which of these years was leap year?

    1492   1865   1912   1920   1936

7. What year will be the next leap year?

```
       487
    4)1948
      16
      ——
       34
       32
       ——
        28
        28
```

290

Traveling Long Distances

1. Harold King's brother drives a freight truck from Baltimore to Hagerstown. The distance between the two cities is 73 miles. How many miles does he drive in making a **round trip**?

2. Last month Harold's brother made 23 round trips between Baltimore and Hagerstown. The distance traveled on each round trip was 146 miles. How many miles did he drive last month?

3. The distance between Cincinnati and Chicago is 297 miles. During the summer and fall months last year a truck driver drove his freight truck between the two cities 18 times. How many miles did he travel?

4. How many miles is the round trip distance between Cincinnati and Chicago?

5. How many miles would a person travel in making 27 round trips between Cincinnati and Chicago?

6. The distance between New York and Liverpool, England, is 3,707 miles. How many miles would we travel in making a round trip?

7. A captain on one of the ocean liners made 8 round trips between New York and Liverpool last year. How many miles did the captain travel?

8. From San Francisco to New York by air is 2568 miles. One of the automobile roads from San Francisco to New York is 3180 miles. How much shorter is the distance by air than the distance by car?

9. Walter and his father walked a mile in 20 minutes. How long will it take them to walk $\frac{1}{2}$ mile? How long will it take them to walk $\frac{1}{4}$ mile?

Chapter 19
Two-Step Problems

Getting Ready

Alice, Jerry, Billy, and Betty went to the dairy to order milk for the picnic.

"We shall need 160 pints of milk," said Alice. "How much will that cost?"

"Since the milk is for the school picnic," said the milkman, "I will make a special price of 40 cents a gallon."

"Thank you," said Alice. "Please deliver the milk to the school Saturday morning between 8:30 and 9:00. We will have the money for you then."

At School

When the children got back to school, Betty told the class that the milk would cost 40¢ a gallon.

"How many gallons are in 160 pints?" asked Jerry.

Billy said, "There are 2 pints in a quart. So we divide 160 by 2 to find how many quarts there are in 160 pints. There are 4 quarts in a gallon. So we divide 80 quarts by 4 to find the number of gallons. There are 80 quarts in 160 pints, and there are 20 gallons in 80 quarts."

Are Billy's answers right?
How many gallons are there in 160 pints?

Then Alice asked, "If the milk costs 40 cents a gallon, how much will that be a pint?"

Jerry answered, "At 40 cents a gallon, a quart would cost $\frac{1}{4}$ of 40¢, or 10¢. A pint would cost $\frac{1}{2}$ of 10¢, or 5¢."

How much will 160 pints of milk cost at 5¢ a pint?
How much will 20 gallons of milk cost at 40¢ a gallon?

2 pt. = 1 qt.   4 qt. = 1 gallon (gal.)   8 pt. = 1 gal.

One-Step Problems

Read each problem carefully. Tell whether you must add, subtract, multiply, or divide to answer the question.

1. Ann bought 3 books. One cost 48¢, another cost 98¢, and the third one cost 75¢. How much did the 3 books cost?

2. May bought 3 books. Each book cost 89¢. How much did all of May's books cost?

3. Sam wants to buy a hook-and-ladder jeep that costs $21.50. He has saved $15.85. How much more must he save before he has enough to pay for the jeep?

4. Mary had $5.00. She bought a pair of pajamas for $1.49. How much money did she have left after she paid for them?

5. Five boys bought a football that cost $4.95. They shared the cost equally. What did each boy pay?

6. West School received a large picture to hang in their auditorium. Each of the eight classes paid an equal share of the cost of framing the picture. The cost of framing was $9.60. How much did each class pay?

7. "Our class should pay $1.20," said Mary. "There are 20 of us. Then each of us should pay 6¢."

Was Mary right?

8. Some of the children gave a dime as their share. Mary counted the money. There was $1.50. How much too much money did they have?

These problems are called **one-step** problems because we find the answer by doing one thing only. We add, subtract, multiply, or divide.

Two Questions

Betty, Ann, Jane, and Sue have bought the prizes for a May party. Each of them had a dollar to spend.

1. Betty bought a flower bowl for 15¢ and a little plant for 15¢. How much did her prizes cost? How much change did she get from her dollar?

```
 $.15      $1.00
  .15        .30
 ----      -----
 $.30      $ .70
```

We use the answer to the first question to find the answer to the second question.

2. Ann bought a box of crayons for 25¢ and a box of paints for 40¢. How much did Ann pay for prizes? How much of her dollar did she have left?

3. Jane got 2 hair ribbons that cost 25¢ each. How much did the two hair ribbons cost? How much change should she get from a dollar?

4. Sue got a bird book for 25¢, a poem book for 20¢, and a puzzle book for 10¢. How much did Sue pay for the books? How much did Sue have left from one dollar?

5. For the grand prize the girls picked out a beautiful book that cost $1.50. They counted their money. They had 70¢, 35¢, 50¢, and 45¢. How much money did the girls have altogether? How much did they have left after they paid for the book?

One Question

You have been working problems that ask two questions. Often a problem that needs two questions will ask only one question. Then you must ask and answer the other question before you can answer the question that the problem asks.

Joe had a movie in his garage. He showed a cowboy picture. He charged 8¢ to see the show.

1. Bill bought a ticket for Mary and himself. How much change did he get from a half dollar?

Before you can find how much change Bill got, you will need to know how much money he spent altogether. The question you must ask and answer is: *How much did he spend in all?*

2. Jack bought 4 tickets that cost 8¢ each. How much change did he get from one dollar?

3. Sixteen children came to see the show the first day, 22 came the second day, and 18 came the third day. How much money did Joe take in at the 3 shows?

4. Tom had one dollar. He spent 35¢ for a knife, 10¢ for a ball of string, and 20¢ for a battery for his flashlight. How much money did Tom have after he paid for these things? Could he see the show?

MEAT SANDWICH	12¢	SALAD	8¢	APPLE SAUCE	4¢
CHEESE SANDWICH	9¢	CORN	5¢	ICE CREAM	7¢
SOUP	8¢	BEANS	5¢	COOKIE	3¢
2 CRACKERS	1¢	MILK	4¢	FRUIT JELLO	5¢

Two-Step Problems

1. Jane got a bowl of soup, a meat sandwich, a glass of milk, and a dish of applesauce. How much change did she get from a half dollar?

What question must you ask?

Do you add, subtract, multiply, or divide to answer it?

What must you do to find the answer to the question that the problem asks?

In the problems below, first find the "hidden" question. Say the question that you must ask. Then tell what you must do to find the answer to each of the two questions.

2. Betty got a bowl of soup, 2 crackers, a glass of milk, and 4 cookies. How much should she pay for lunch?

3. Bill had 50¢ to buy his lunch. He decided to save half of his money. Select a good lunch for Bill that will cost about half of his lunch money.

4. How much should Dick pay for his lunch if he has a meat sandwich, a salad, a glass of milk, and 2 dishes of ice cream?

These problems are **two-step** problems because you must find the answer to two questions. One question is hidden. The problem asks the other question.

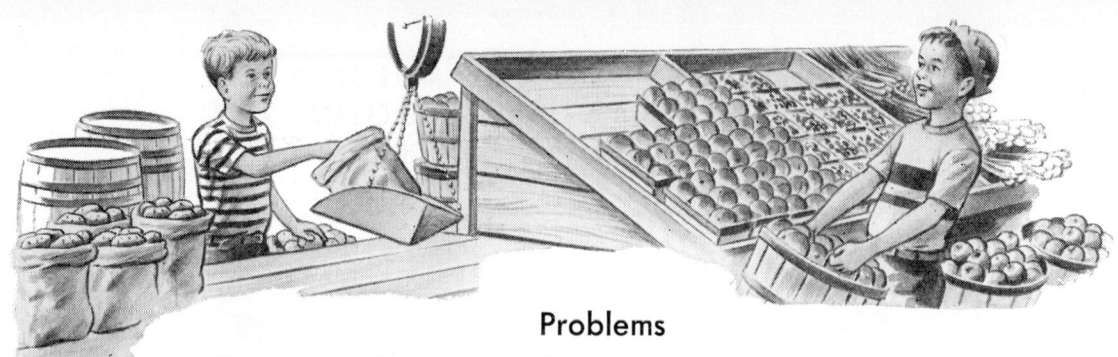

Problems

In some of these problems you must first answer a question that is hidden in the problem. You will need to answer this "hidden" question before you can answer the question the problem asks.

Jim and Joe helped Mr. Adams at his vegetable stand on Saturdays. They started early in the morning to get ready before the people came to buy.

1. Jim's first job was to put the potatoes from two 60-pound bags into small bags to be ready for sale. He had to weigh out 5 pounds of potatoes for each bag. How many 5-pound bags did he need?

2. Joe sorted 65 bushels of peaches. He packed the good ones into baskets ready to sell, and the bad ones in baskets to throw away. Joe had to throw away 17 bushels of peaches. Mr. Adams sold the good ones at $2.59 a bushel. How much did he get for the good peaches?

3. Next Jim checked the cider. Four of the barrels were full, and one was half full. Each barrel held 32 gallons. How many gallons of cider were there?

4. Joe opened 4 big bunches of onions and made small bunches of 8 onions each. There were 96 onions in each of the big bunches. How many small bunches did Joe make?

5. Jim put 16 gallons of blueberries into quart boxes. How many quart boxes did he fill?

6. Joe weighed squash and marked the prices on them. The squash was to be sold at 4¢ a pound. What price should he put on a squash that weighed 6 pounds?

7. To one lady, Jim sold 4 pounds of apples at 12¢ a pound and a gallon of cider for 75¢. What was the amount of her bill?

8. To a man, he sold a squash marked 16¢ and 3 quarts of blueberries at 29¢ a quart. How much should this man pay?

9. Joe sold a gallon of cider for 75¢, a dozen eggs for 45¢, a box of blueberries for 29¢, and a bushel of peaches for $3.50. How much change should Joe give the customer from a five-dollar bill?

10. Mrs. West bought 3 bunches of green onions at 8¢ a bunch and a gallon of cider for 75¢. How much was her bill?

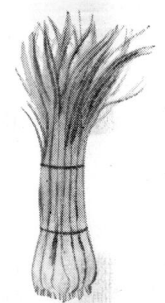

11. Mr. North bought a bushel of peaches for $3.50, a bushel of tomatoes for $1.50, a watermelon for 69¢, and a dozen eggs for 45¢. What change should he get from a ten-dollar bill? Count it.

12. Jack had a dollar. He bought a watermelon for 59¢ and a pound of apples for 12¢. Did he have enough money to buy a 29¢ box of blueberries also?

13. Jim worked 8 hours and made 45¢ an hour. He bought a watermelon. Mr. Adams let him have it for 29¢. How much did he have left from his day's pay?

Finding the Average

Aunt Mary is making Helen a quilt. She has only 20 more blocks to make.

"If I can make 4 blocks each day, I can finish the quilt in 5 days," she said. "Today is Monday. It will be finished when you come home from school Friday."

Aunt Mary did not always have as much time to sew as she planned. She made only 2 blocks on Monday. On Tuesday she made 3 blocks, and on Wednesday she made 3 blocks. But on Thursday she made 6 blocks, and on Friday she made 6 more blocks.

```
  2
  3
  3
  6
  6
 ——
 20

    4
5)20
  20
```

Did she finish the blocks in 5 days?

Did she make exactly 4 blocks each day?

How many blocks did she make in the 5 days?

How many blocks would she have made if she had made exactly 4 blocks each day?

Although Aunt Mary did not make exactly 4 blocks each day, she did make the 20 blocks in 5 days. We say that 4 blocks are the **average** number she made each day.

Jane, Bill, and Sue are standing behind the wire that Jane's father put up for the sweet peas to climb on. The top of Jane's head is **even** with the top of the wire, and Bill's head is a little **above** the wire. Sue's head is a little **below** the wire.

Sue said, "If I stand on a brick and Bill bends down a little, we will all be the same height."

Sue was thinking about the **average** height.

1. Jane is 48 inches tall, and Bill is 51 inches tall. Sue is only 45 inches tall.

Let us find the average of their heights.
We must suppose their heights are the same.
We add the heights of the 3 children.
Then we divide the sum of their heights by the number of heights. The answer will be the height if all 3 children measured the same.

The **average height** of the 3 children is 48 inches.

```
 48
 51
 45
---
144
```

```
    48
3)144
   12
   --
   24
   24
```

2. Find the average of these heights: Jack is 49 inches, Mary is 46 inches, Ann is 47 inches, and Joe is 50 inches.

To find the average, we **suppose** the same for all.

To find the average, we divide the total amount by the number of things.

Finding the Average

1. The distance from Dick's house to the city is 105 miles. His father made the trip to the city in 3 hours. Find the average distance he traveled each hour.

Suppose he went the same distance each hour. How far would he have gone each hour?

Here we know the total number of miles. We need only to divide the total by the number of hours to find the average distance for each hour.

2. Mr. Johnson used 7 gallons of gasoline to make the trip of 105 miles. Find the average number of miles he went on each gallon of gasoline.

3. The White family went on a 6-day camping trip. Their expenses for the trip were $51.42. What was their average expense each day?

4. During one school week Jack spent $1.15 for his lunches. What was the average cost of each lunch?

5. One week Mrs. Brown bought 28 quarts of milk. Find the average number of quarts she bought each day.

6. Jack earned $3.00 working 4 Saturdays. What was the average amount he earned each Saturday?

7. Betty spent $6.75 for 5 presents. What was the average cost of each present?

8. The total weight of 3 girls is 243 pounds. What is the average weight?

9. What does "Average 88" mean?

10. Mr. Farmer sold 3 pigs. The total weight of the pigs was 750 pounds. What was the average weight of each pig?

Grade Card Earl Sims				
Reading	90			
Arithmetic	95			
Language	85			
Geography	88			
History	82			
Average	88			

Finding the Average

1. Mrs. James was getting ready to can peaches.

"I guess 50 quarts will be enough," she said. "That is about my **average** for the last four years."

She canned 48 quarts four years ago, the next year she canned 52 quarts, the next year 47 quarts, and last year 53 quarts.

Suppose she canned the same number of quarts each year. How many quarts would that be a year?

2. The Allen family went for a three-day automobile trip. The first day they went 254 miles, the second day they went 197 miles, and the third day they went 224 miles. What was their average number of miles a day?

3. Four families live in the same block with Jane. The number of people in the families are 4, 6, 2, and 4. What is the average number of people in a family?

4. Jack weighs 77 pounds, Mary weighs 64 pounds, Ann weighs 65 pounds, and Joe weighs 70 pounds. What is the average weight of the children?

5. There are 26 pupils in the third grade, 23 in the fourth grade, 19 in the fifth grade, and 24 in the sixth grade. What is the average number of pupils in a grade?

6. What is the average weight of these boys: Tom, 82 lb.; Dick, 91 lb.; Jim, 78 lb.; Sam, 77 lb.?

7. Find the average weight of the 3 bushel baskets of potatoes.

8. Jack jumped 3 times. He jumped 48 inches, 52 inches, and 50 inches. What was the average distance he jumped?

Problems

Read your problems carefully. Some of them are two-step problems. Find the answers. Check your work.

1. On each of 6 days Mrs. Olds put 78 eggs into her egg box. On Saturday she put in 84 eggs. That evening she took all of these eggs to the store. How many eggs did she take?

2. Mrs. Olds sold 8 dozen eggs one day. How many eggs did she sell that day?

3. Mrs. Olds bought 96 baby chickens at 5¢ each and a bag of feed for $2.98. How much did she pay for the chickens and the feed?

4. Joe Olds shells and grinds 36 ears of corn for the chickens each day. How many ears will he shell and grind in 4 weeks?

5. A bushel of corn weighs 70 pounds. Find the weight of 44 bushels of corn on the cob.

6. At $1.48 a bushel, how much will 44 bushels of corn cost?

Travel Problems

1. When Mr. West started on his trip, the speedometer of his car showed 8465. When he got home, it showed 9103. How many miles had he gone?

speedometer

2. The gasoline tank on Mr. West's car holds 15 gallons. The car averages 17 miles on a gallon of gasoline. How many miles will the car go on a full tank?

3. The Jones family went on a trip. On Friday they drove 176 miles. On Saturday they drove 205 miles, and on Sunday they drove 180 miles. What was their average distance a day?

4. The speedometer on Mr. Hill's car shows 18,643. How many more miles must Mr. Hill drive his car to make 40,000 miles in all?

5. Mr. Hill's car has gone 18,643 miles. Mr. Jones's car has gone 32,970 miles. How many miles farther has Mr. Jones's car gone than Mr. Hill's car?

Should you measure the **distance** to the next town in feet? Why? Should you measure the **length** of your room in miles? Why?

The inch, foot, and yard are measures of **length**.

The mile is a measure of **distance**.

Do you understand the difference between a length and a distance?

Chapter 20
Getting Ready for Next Year

Getting Ready for Spring

"The cold weather is over until next winter," said Mr. Wallace. "We can take down the storm windows and put them away. Jim, if you will wash the windows, I will pay you 15¢ for each window, 25¢ for each big picture window, and 8¢ for each door."

Jim said, "I'll take the job."

1. Mr. Wallace took down the storm windows for Jim. Jim washed the 16 storm windows and the 3 large storm windows for the picture windows. How much was he paid for washing the storm windows?

2. Then Jim washed the 16 windows, the 3 large picture windows, and the glass in the 3 doors. How much did he earn washing these windows?

3. How much did Jim earn in all?

306

Practice

Subtract and check:

	(a)	(b)	(c)	(d)	(e)	(f)
1.	283 149	908 675	812 568	700 428	1068 580	1005 879
2.	500 267	860 187	742 396	801 198	1600 873	1705 897
3.	$5.04 1.86	$7.60 5.85	$6.00 4.86	$5.62 3.80	$10.00 8.24	$15.50 8.95

Add and check:

	(a)	(b)	(c)	(d)	(e)	(f)
4.	24 82 96 75	190 864 578 607	960 808 779 687	5667 4896 6874 3806	6705 982 1077 869	7758 1009 998 85
5.	$3.65 4.77 2.86 .75	$4.40 1.86 5.92 6.38	$ .15 .86 1.94 4.83	$12.85 10.60 8.70 4.56	$80.20 92.50 48.75 10.50	$25.00 2.80 16.90 .75

6. Find the sum: $7.84, $.96, $3.75, $.07, $12.80.
7. Find the difference between 1050 and 786.
8. $20.80 − $8.95 = ? 9. $15.06 − $4.78 = ?
10. Write with figures:
    a. Six thousand, three hundred
    b. Two thousand, four
    c. Eight hundred ten
    d. Four hundred one
11. What time does Clock A show?
12. What time does Clock B show?

A.

B.

How Far?

The swimming pool is 50 feet long and 24 feet wide. The boys are seeing how far they can swim.

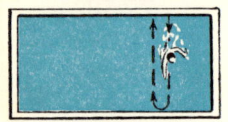

1. Jim swam the length of the pool and back to the starting point. How far did he swim?

2. Joe swam across the pool twice. How far did he swim?

3. Fred swam all the way around the pool. How far did he swim?

Add these columns:

	(a)	(b)	(c)	(d)	(e)	(f)	(g)	(h)	(i)
4.	74	75	40	34	20	10	15	44	19
	12	26	40	44	50	70	40	39	12
	68	80	79	57	30	80	88	95	90
5.	65	65	43	87	81	98	34	43	28
	43	56	76	21	33	17	80	62	86
	70	43	66	35	46	26	55	93	87
6.	75	55	78	67	74	83	98	77	97
	60	64	56	78	74	59	37	89	68
	76	90	89	67	79	78	86	54	66

The Party

1. The fourth-grade pupils are having a party for their mothers. They have bought 12 yards of ribbon to make bookmarks for favors. Each bookmark takes 9 inches of ribbon. They want to make 50 bookmarks. Have they enough ribbon?

How many inches are there in 1 yard?
Then how many inches are there in 12 yards?
How will you find how many bookmarks can be made from the 12 yards of ribbon that they have?

2. The boys are figuring how much ice cream and cookies they should buy. One quart of ice cream will serve 6 people. Will 2 gallons of ice cream be enough for 50 people?

How many quarts are in a gallon?
How many people can be served from 1 gallon?
How many people can be served from 2 gallons?

3. Ice cream costs 65¢ a quart, or $2.40 a gallon. The children decided to buy 2 gallons and 1 quart of ice cream. How much will the ice cream cost?

4. They decided to get 4 pounds of cookies that cost 75¢ a pound. How much will the cookies cost?

5. The children decided to begin the party at half past two in the afternoon and to be ready to go home at a quarter to five.

Find the clock that shows when the party began.
Find the clock that shows when the party was over.

6. How long did the party last?
Did it last 2 hours and 15 minutes?

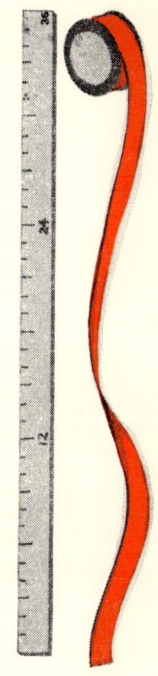

```
4:45
2:30
────
2:15
```

Problems with Hidden Facts

In each of these problems there is a fact that is not given. You must know it before you can work the problem.

1. Ann bought 2 dozen roses at 15¢ a rose. How much did the roses cost?

What must you know before you can find the number of roses that Ann bought? If you did not know there are 12 things in a dozen, you could not work the problem.

2. Jane must practice her music lesson 4 hours each week. She practices on 5 days of the week. She wants to practice the same number of minutes each day. How many minutes should she practice each day?

3. Jack and Bill made 9 gallons of grape juice. They sold it at 15¢ a quart. How much did they get for the grape juice?

4. Susan wants to make new curtains for the window in her room. She needs two pieces of material 54 inches long. Her mother has 3 yards of some pretty red and white material that Susan may have if there is enough to make the curtains. Is there enough?

5. Mrs. Young has 2 quarts of lemonade. Has she enough to give each of 8 children a glass of lemonade?

6. Mrs. Bell bought 3 pounds of bacon. She sold $\frac{1}{6}$ of it to Mrs. West, who had forgotten to buy bacon. How many ounces of bacon did Mrs. West get?

A Test

Multiply:

	(a)	(b)	(c)	(d)	(e)	(f)	
1.	376	560	848	976	439	208	(215)
	8	7	9	6	5	4	(218)
							(220)
2.	128	406	560	156	900	947	(273)
	32	45	18	97	64	51	(274)

Divide:

3. 4)380   8)2048   7)4963   6)492   9)306   5)605

4. 6)390   7)6650   8)7040   9)819   4)392   8)752

(179-82)
(202-05)

5. Find:

(a) $\frac{1}{3}$ of $2.49   (b) $\frac{1}{2}$ of $2.10   (c) $\frac{1}{6}$ of $5.52   (d) $\frac{1}{8}$ of $10.80

6. 15 × $6.87 = ?   7. $43.74 ÷ 6 = ?

8. How many inches are 6 yards, 2 feet, and 10 inches?

9. How many quarts are 14 gallons and 3 quarts?

10. Is the jar about $\frac{1}{3}$ or about $\frac{1}{2}$ full?

11. What fractional part of the stars are white?

12. What temperature does the thermometer show?

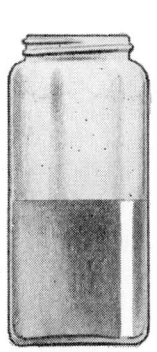

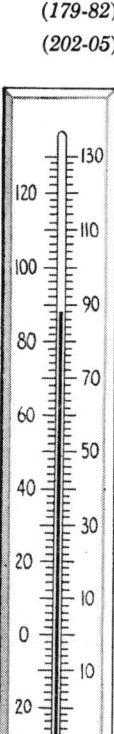

People of Other Lands

Some of the fourth-grade girls saw an exhibit of dolls dressed as people of other lands.

Mary said, "It would be nice if we could buy the dolls for our school. There are over 90 dolls. I am sure we cannot buy all of them, but maybe we can buy a few."

1. At $1.25 each, how much would 90 dolls cost?

2. At $1.25 each, how much would 20 dolls cost?

3. The girls thought it would be cheaper to buy dolls and make dresses for them. They found that they could buy 20 dolls at 35¢ each. How much would the 20 dolls cost?

4. To dress the dolls, the girls estimated they would need:

$\frac{1}{2}$ yard of green silk cloth at 90¢ a yard
2 yards of white cotton cloth at 37¢ a yard
$\frac{1}{4}$ yard of black silk cloth at 96¢ a yard
3 spools of thread at 6¢ each

How much would this material cost?

5. How much would the dolls and material cost?

6. How much could the girls save by buying the 20 dolls and materials for dressing them instead of buying the dolls already dressed?

Two Problems in One

1. Bill had $2.00 in his pocket. He bought a set of Chinese Checkers and a box of dominos. How much money did he have left?

2. Tom had $5.00. He bought the target game and a set of horseshoes. How much did he have left?

3. Jane said, "I want to buy the donkey game and the Chinese Checkers, but I have only $1.50."
How much more money does she need to buy them?

4. Sam bought the target game, the set of dominos, and the horseshoes. How much change should he get from a 5-dollar bill?

5. Dick has $1.50. What two games can he buy? How much money will he have left if he buys them?

Ordering from a Menu

MENU

Meat
   Roast beef   60¢
   Lamb stew   50¢
   Fried chicken   75¢

Vegetables
   Potatoes   10¢
   Green beans   8¢
   Corn on cob   15¢
   Turnips   7¢

Salad
   Fruit salad   17¢
   Green salad   14¢
   Lettuce   12¢

Dessert
   Ice cream   12¢
   Apple pie   15¢

Drink
   Coffee   6¢
   Milk   10¢

Mr. West took Mrs. West, Peggy, and Billy to the cafe for dinner.

1. Mrs. West ordered first. She had fried chicken, potatoes, lettuce, ice cream, and milk. How much did her dinner cost?

2. Peggy ordered next. She chose lamb stew, potatoes, fruit salad, ice cream, and milk. What was the cost of her dinner?

3. For his dinner Billy took roast beef, corn on cob, lettuce, ice cream, and milk. How much did his meal cost?

4. Mr. West had lamb stew, green beans, fruit salad, apple pie, and coffee. What was the cost of his food?

First, we add the ones: 8 and 7 are 15, and 5 are 20, and 6 are 26. We write 6 in one's place and carry 2 (tens).

Next, we add the tens: 2 (carried) and 5 are 7, and 1 are 8, and 1 are 9.

Mr. West's dinner cost 96¢.

   50¢
     8¢
   17¢
   15¢
     6¢
   ―――
   96¢

Extra Numbers in Problems

Some of the problems tell things that you do not use when you solve the problem.

Read each problem carefully. Make a list of the things that the problem tells. Cross out any that you will not use to work the problem. Now read the important things that the problem tells. Then solve the problem.

1. There are 23 boys and 17 girls in the fourth grade at South School. Each of the girls brought 5¢ for Camp Fire dues. How much money did the girls pay in dues?
    a. ~~There are 23 boys in the fourth grade.~~
    b. There are 17 girls in the fourth grade.
    c. Each of the girls brought 5¢ for dues.

2. Jane has 25 books. She let Mary take 4 books home, and she let Jim take 4 books home. How many of her books has she loaned?

3. Jack picked 24 quarts of strawberries. He sold some of them at 15¢ a quart. Mrs. East bought 7 quarts; Mrs. West bought 8 quarts; and Mrs. North bought 4 quarts. Jack's mother canned the berries that he did not sell. How many quarts of berries did she can?

4. The girls in the Bird Club sold lemonade for 5¢ a glass, cake for 8¢ a slice, and cookies for 2¢ each. Bill bought a glass of lemonade and 3 cookies. How much did he pay for them?

5. Mrs. James bought 150 little chickens at 8¢ each and a bag of feed for $1.98. How much did she pay for the chickens?

6. Betty got 6 pencils at 5¢ each. How much change should she get from one dollar?

TABLES OF MEASURES

Liquid Measure
2 cups = 1 pint (pt.)
2 pints = 1 quart (qt.)
4 quarts = 1 gallon (gal.)

Dry Measure
2 pints = 1 quart (qt.)
8 quarts = 1 peck (pk.)
4 pecks = 1 bushel (bu.)

Measures of Weight
16 ounces (oz.) = 1 pound (lb.)
2000 pounds = 1 ton (T.)

Measures of Length
12 inches (in.) = 1 foot (ft.)
3 feet = 1 yard (yd.)
36 inches = 1 yard
1760 yards = 1 mile (mi.)
5280 feet = 1 mile

Measures in Counting
12 things = 1 dozen (doz.)
12 dozen = 1 gross
144 things = 1 gross

Measures of Time
60 minutes (min.) = 1 hour (hr.)
24 hours = 1 day
7 days = 1 week
12 months = 1 year (yr.)
365 days = 1 year
366 days = 1 leap year

Months with 31 days:
January, March, May, July,
August, October, December

Months with 30 days:
April, June, September, November
February has 28 or 29 days.

Measures of Money
5 cents = 1 nickel
10 cents = 1 dime
25 cents = 1 quarter
50 cents = 1 half dollar
100 cents = 1 dollar
5 nickels = 1 quarter
20 nickels = 1 dollar
10 dimes = 1 dollar
4 quarters = 1 dollar
2 half dollars = 1 dollar

INDEX

Abacus, 43, 244

Addition
  carrying in, 73–81, 86, 189–90, 208–11, 213–14, 225, 247–50, 263, 314
  checking, 46
  column, 16–19, 45, 48–49, 65–67, 78–81
  dollars and cents, 48–49, 65–67, 74, 76, 81, 86, 188, 213, 225, 249, 314
  eighty-one facts, 8
  by endings, 75, 221
  hundreds, 194–95, 209–11, 213–14, 225
  practice (oral), 8–9, 46, 75–76, 195, 213, 221
  practice (written), 16, 19, 46, 49, 66–67, 77, 80, 86, 189, 209–10, 213–14, 225, 247–50, 308
  problems, 14, 47–49, 66, 76–81, 86, 194–95, 208–11, 213–14, 224–25, 247, 249–51
  tens, 46, 48–49, 59, 65–66, 95, 189–90, 221, 269
  thousands, 247–50, 263
  zero in, 19, 46, 48–49, 66–67, 194–95, 248–50

Averages, 300–03, 305

Borrowing; *see* **Carrying:** in subtraction

Calendar, 129

Carrying
  in addition, 73–81, 86, 189–90, 208–11, 213–14, 225, 247–50, 263
  in division, 178–88, 190–91, 236–43, 263–67
  in multiplication, 82–85, 87, 119, 140, 143, 153, 190–91, 215–20, 222, 260–63, 269–79
  in subtraction, 88–93, 189–90, 226–35, 252–59, 263

Change, counting, 61, 206, 234–35, 257

Dividing
  by 2, 28, 170; by 3, 29, 170; by 4, 30, 171; by 5, 31, 172; by 6, 111, 114, 174, 186; by 7, 118, 175, 186; by 8, 138–40, 176, 186; by 9, 142–43, 177, 186
  by ones, 24–25, 28–34, 59, 95, 111, 114, 117–19, 138–40, 142–43, 150,

Dividing by ones—*continued*
  152–53, 157–59, 168–87, 190–91, 202–05, 236–43, 263–67

Division
  carrying in, 178–88, 190–91, 236–43, 263–67
  checking, 57, 183–84, 239
  dollars and cents, 24, 71, 157-59, 184–85, 191, 203, 243, 266, 286
  hundreds, 202–05, 238–43, 264–67
  practice (oral), 24–25, 114, 170, 174, 182, 184, 205, 236, 238–40, 264–65
  practice (written), 56, 71, 117, 119, 140, 143, 152, 171–72, 175–77, 181–83, 185–87, 191, 203, 205, 236–39, 241, 243, 264–67
  problems, 27, 36, 56–57, 71, 157–59, 168–69, 173, 178, 184–85, 202–05, 238, 241–43, 265–66
  remainders in, 168–77
  sixty-five facts, 24
  steps in, 57, 180–82, 237–38
  tables, 111, 114, 118, 140, 143
  tens and ones, 56–57, 59, 71, 95, 111, 114, 117–19, 138–40, 142–43, 150, 152–53, 157–59, 170–87, 190–91, 236–37, 263
  thousands, 264–67
  zero in, 56, 71, 202–05, 240–42, 264–67

Dollars and cents
  adding, 48–49, 65–67, 74, 76, 81, 86, 188, 213, 225, 249, 314
  making change, 61, 206, 234–35, 257
  dividing, 24, 71, 157–59, 184–85, 191, 203, 243, 266, 286
  multiplying, 22, 55, 69, 87, 155–56, 222, 260–61, 277
  practice (oral), 55, 60–61, 64, 76, 184, 200, 212–13, 277
  practice (written), 49, 55, 63, 65–69, 71, 86–87, 92–93, 185, 188–89, 205, 213, 222, 225, 229, 243, 254, 259–61, 263, 266, 277, 286, 307, 311
  problems, 17, 32, 48–49, 65–68, 70–71, 76, 81, 86–87, 92, 96–97, 115–16, 120–23, 131–33, 135–36, 148–49, 155–63, 178, 184–85, 187, 189–90, 203, 206–07, 213–14, 222, 224–25, 229, 232-35, 243, 251, 254, 257, 259, 266, 277, 296–97, 314

317

Dollars and cents—*continued*
reading and writing, 62–65, 212
subtracting, 67–68, 92–93, 189, 229, 254, 257, 259

Estimating answers, 135–36, 284–88

Finding and correcting mistakes, 63, 86, 183, 219, 239, 278

Fractional parts
equal, 38–39, 144–45, 188
of a group, 40–41
of a number, 40–41, 144–45
problems, 38–41, 144–45, 188
of a whole, 38–39

Fractions
halves, 38, 40–41, 144, 188
thirds, 38, 40–41, 188
fourths, 38–41, 144, 188
fifths, 39, 41, 145, 188
sixths, 39, 41, 145, 188
eighths, 144–45, 188
meaning of, 38–41, 144–45
writing, 38–39, 144–45

Hundreds
adding, 194–95, 209–11, 213–14, 225
carrying to, 211, 213–14, 218–20, 222
dividing, 202–05, 238–43, 264–67
multiplying, 199–201, 215–20, 222
reading and writing, 42–44, 53, 193
subtracting, 196–98, 226–35

Measures
changing, 289
dozen, 41, 82, 128, 283
dry, 133, 287
length, 130, 288–89
liquid, 131, 293
temperature, 137
time, 51–52, 58, 124–28, 290
weight, 132, 280–82

Money (*see also* **Dollars and cents**)
coin value, 60
of historical interest, 155

Multiplication
carrying in, 82–85, 87, 119, 140, 143, 153, 190–91, 215–20, 222, 260–63, 269–79
checking, 279
dollars and cents, 22, 55, 69, 87, 155–56, 222, 260–61, 277
hundreds, 199–201, 215–20, 222

Multiplication—*continued*
practice (oral), 22–23, 32, 55, 82–83, 113–14, 171–72, 200, 220, 261–62, 270–72, 274, 276–78
practice (written), 55, 69, 82–83, 85, 87, 119, 140, 143, 151, 191, 199–201, 215, 218, 220, 222, 260–62, 271–72, 275–77, 279, 286
problems, 26, 35, 54–55, 84–85, 87, 120, 147, 155–56, 200–01, 215–16, 218, 220, 222, 260–62, 270–72, 275, 277, 279
sixty-five facts, 22
tables, 110, 114, 118, 140, 143
tens and ones, 54–55, 59, 84–85, 87, 95, 140, 143, 153, 190–91, 270–79
thousands, 260–63
zero in, 54–55, 69, 199–201, 260–62, 270–72

Multiplying
by 1's, 109; by 2's, 28; by 3's, 29; by 4's, 30, 171; by 5's, 31, 172; by 6's, 110, 112–14; by 7's, 118–19; by 8's, 138–40, 176; by 9's, 142–43, 177
by ones, 22–23, 28–34, 59, 69, 84–85, 87, 95, 109–10, 112–14, 117–19, 138–40, 142–43, 150–51, 153, 155, 190–91, 199–201, 215–20, 222, 260–63
by tens and ones, 270–79

Number cards, 13, 23, 25

Number games, 8, 10, 19, 22, 24, 147

Number system, 6–7, 21, 53, 244

Numbers
meaning of, 6–7, 21, 42, 192, 244
reading and writing, 6–7, 21, 43–44, 53, 62–65, 193, 245–46

Ones
adding, 8–9, 12–13, 16, 19, 34
dividing by, 24–25, 28–34, 59, 95, 111, 114, 117–19, 138–40, 142–43, 150, 152–53, 157–59, 168–87, 190–91, 202–05, 236–43, 263–67
multiplying, 22–23, 28–34, 109–10, 112–14, 117–19, 138–40, 150–51, 153
multiplying by, 22–23, 28–34, 59, 69, 84–85, 87, 95, 109–10, 112–14, 117–19, 138–40, 142–43, 150–51, 153, 155, 190–91, 199–201, 215–20, 222, 260–63
subtracting, 10–13, 34

Practice, oral
  addition, 8–9, 46, 75–76, 195, 213, 221
  division, 24–25, 114, 170, 174, 182, 184, 205, 236, 238–40, 264–65
  dollars and cents, 55, 60–61, 64, 76, 184, 200, 212–13, 277
  fractional parts, 39, 41, 145, 188
  mixed, 12–13, 28–33, 94, 117, 138–40, 143, 147, 150, 171–72
  multiplication, 22–23, 32, 55, 82–83, 113–14, 171–72, 200, 220, 261–62, 270–72, 274, 276–78
  numbers, 21, 44, 53, 64, 193, 212, 245–46, 255, 257
  subtraction, 10–11, 50, 197, 227–28, 253–54

Practice, written
  addition, 16, 19, 46, 49, 66–67, 77, 80, 86, 189, 195, 209–10, 213–14, 225, 247–50, 308
  division, 56, 71, 117, 119, 140, 143, 152, 171–72, 175–77, 181–83, 185–87, 191, 203, 205, 236–39, 241, 243, 264–67
  dollars and cents, 49, 55, 63, 65–69, 71, 86–87, 92–93, 185, 188–91, 205, 213, 222, 225, 229, 243, 254, 259–61, 263, 266, 277, 286, 307, 311
  fractional parts, 59, 188, 190, 205, 237, 311
  mixed, 34, 59, 94–95, 117, 153, 190, 223, 263, 269, 307, 311
  multiplication, 55, 69, 82–83, 85, 87, 119, 140, 143, 151, 191, 199–201, 215, 218, 220, 222, 260–62, 271–72, 275–77, 279, 286
  subtraction, 50, 67–68, 89–93, 189, 197–98, 226–29, 232–33, 252–54, 259
  numbers, 44, 53, 63, 65, 125, 127, 245

Problem-solving
  deciding on a process, 37, 45, 52, 70, 101, 115–16, 120–23, 141, 146, 148–49, 160–63, 173, 187, 189, 206–07, 280, 294, 296, 304–05, 309, 312
  estimating answers, 135–36, 284–86
  extra numbers, 106
  finding hidden question, 298–99, 310
  hidden facts in words, 128–34, 280–88, 290
  important facts in, 47, 51, 96–100, 103, 106–07, 154
  making problems, 167

Problem-solving—*continued*
  missing fact, 166
  picture as aid, 66, 76, 78, 164
  reading carefully, 14–15, 26–27, 35–37, 47, 51–52, 97, 99, 102, 104–05, 154
  telling the story, 47, 51, 97, 102
  without question, 165

Problems
  addition, 14, 47–49, 66, 76–81, 86, 194–95, 208–11, 213–14, 224–25, 247, 249–51, 308, 314
  averages, 300–03
  division, 27, 36, 56–57, 71, 157–59, 168–69, 173, 178, 184–85, 202–05, 238, 241–43, 265–66
  dollars and cents, 17, 32, 48–49, 65–68, 70–71, 76, 81, 86–87, 92, 96–97, 115–16, 120–23, 131–33, 135–36, 148–49, 155–63, 178, 184–85, 187, 189–90, 203, 206–07, 213–14, 222, 224–25, 229, 232–35, 243, 251, 254, 257, 259, 266, 277, 296–97, 314
  fractional parts, 38–41, 144–45
  measures, 124–37, 280–91, 293, 298–99
  mixed, 17, 32, 35, 37, 45, 51–52, 58, 70, 96–97, 115–16, 121–23, 128, 130–36, 141, 146, 148–49, 160–67, 187, 189, 191, 206–07, 224–25, 234–35, 280, 282, 284–85, 287, 289, 291, 294, 296
  multiplication, 26, 35, 54–55, 84–85, 87, 120, 147, 155–56, 200–01, 215–16, 218, 220, 222, 260–62, 270–72, 275, 277, 279
  subtraction, 15, 51, 67–68, 89–92, 196, 226–33, 252, 257, 259, 281
  two-step, 295–306, 309–10, 312–13, 315

Reading; *see* **Vocabulary**
Remainders, 168–77
Roman numerals, 127

Signs, 62, 82, 117, 137, 163
Situations, studying
  auto licenses, dates, telephone numbers, 246
  buying and selling, 17, 68, 70–71, 81, 86–87, 92, 115, 122, 187, 189, 213, 222, 251, 297
  camping, 84, 214, 259

319

Situations, studying—*continued*
  earning money, 66, 70, 87, 105, 136, 157–58, 163, 191, 206, 235, 266, 298
  making change, 61, 161, 163, 206, 229, 234–35, 257
  making things, 36, 189, 312
  ordering from a menu, 314
  picnics, 5, 45, 101, 217, 292–93
  reading a calendar, 129
  reading a clock, 125–27
  savings and thrift, 35, 49, 66, 97–98, 149, 158, 163, 229
  scorekeeping, 18–19
  sharing expenses, 185, 189
  travel, 78–79, 215–16, 224–25, 230, 268, 291, 305
  using a map, 76, 78–79, 164, 230–31
  using a timetable, 124

Subtraction
  carrying in, 88–93, 189–90, 226–35, 252–59, 263
  checking, 50, 93, 198
  dollars and cents, 67–68, 92–93, 189, 229, 254, 257, 259
  eighty-one facts, 10
  hundreds, 196–98, 226–35
  practice (oral), 10–11, 50, 197, 227–28, 253–54
  practice (written), 50, 67–68, 89–93, 189, 197–98, 226–29, 232–33, 252–54, 259
  problems, 15, 51, 67–68, 89–92, 196, 226–33, 252, 257, 259, 281
  tens, 50, 59, 67–68, 95, 189–90, 269
  thousands, 252–59, 263
  zero in, 50, 67–68, 196–98, 232–33, 252–59

Tens
  adding, 46, 48–49, 59, 65–66, 95, 189–90, 221, 269
  dividing, 56–57, 59, 71, 95, 111, 114, 117–19, 138–40, 142–43, 150, 152–53, 157–59, 170–87, 190–91, 236–37, 263
  multiplying, 54–55, 59, 84–85, 87, 95, 140, 143, 153, 155, 190–91, 270–79
  multiplying by, 270–79
  reading and writing, 7, 21, 42–44, 53, 193
  subtracting, 50, 59, 67–68, 95, 189–90, 269

Tests
  addition, 59, 95, 190, 223, 263
  comprehensive, 94–95, 311
  diagnostic, 59, 153, 190, 263
  division, 59, 95, 153, 190, 223, 239, 263, 311
  multiplication, 59, 85, 95, 153, 190, 223, 263, 311
  problem, 52, 207
  self-test, 8, 10, 22, 24, 151–52, 221
  subtraction, 59, 95, 190, 223, 263

Thermometer, 137, 161, 164, 285

Thousands
  adding, 247–50, 263
  dividing, 264–67
  multiplying, 260–63
  reading and writing, 192–93, 244–46
  subtracting, 252–59, 263

Ton, 262, 280–81

Vocabulary
  addition, 14, 46, 49
  division, 57, 117, 169–71, 174, 180–83, 204, 237, 241
  dollars and cents, 60, 64, 155, 212
  fractional parts, 38–39, 144–45
  measures, 125–26, 128–33, 137, 262, 280, 282–83, 287–88, 291, 293, 305
  multiplication, 82, 91, 110–11, 268–69, 274, 276, 279
  number system, 6–7, 18–19, 21, 42–44, 53, 74, 127, 192–93, 245–46, 255
  reading, 15, 27, 35, 37, 52, 58, 66, 68, 79, 88, 90, 98, 100, 102, 157, 159, 193, 225, 245, 305
  subtraction, 15

Zero
  in addition, 19, 46, 48–49, 66–67, 194–95, 248–50
  in division, 56, 71, 202–05, 240–42, 264–67
  in dollars and cents, 62–65
  in multiplication, 54–55, 69, 199–201, 260–62, 270–72
  as placeholder, 6, 18–19, 42–44, 53, 62, 244–46, 269
  reading and writing, 42–44, 53, 62–65, 193
  in subtraction, 50, 67–68, 196–98, 232–33, 252–59
  used in temperature, 137